AMERICAN INSTITUTE FOR ECONOMIC RESEARCH

THE ECONOMICS AND POLITICS OF BREXIT

THE REALIGNMENT OF BRITISH PUBLIC LIFE

STEPHEN DAVIES

The Economics and Politics of Brexit:
The Realignment of British Public Life
By Stephen Davies

Copyright © 2020 by The American Institute for Economic Research, Creative Commons Attribution International 4.0.

ISBN: 9781630692025

Cover art: Vanessa Mendozzi

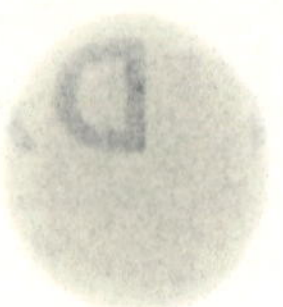

THE ECONOMICS AND POLITICS OF BREXIT

THE REALIGNMENT OF BRITISH PUBLIC LIFE

STEPHEN DAVIES

AIER | AMERICAN INSTITUTE *for* ECONOMIC RESEARCH

CONTENTS

INTRODUCTION

Britain has now left the European Union (EU), although the form and details of the future relationship between the United Kingdom and the EU remain to be worked out. The most vocal responses to this have typically combined anger and sometimes despair with shock, bewilderment and confusion. "How on earth did this happen?" is the common shared sentiment or question. In all of this the feelings of satisfaction and vindication felt by the other side of the debate are less expressed and much less examined, not least because that would cut against the answers to the questions just set out that are widely held and believed by many of those expressing the confusion and outrage. What is striking is the way so much of the media class and commentariat, as well as most of academia and much of conventional politics, has been left dumbfounded by the events of the last three years. The result of the referendum, the subsequent political developments, and the denouement of the 2019 Election have all come as a massive and unexpected shock – a bolt from the blue one might say. The extent of the confusion and cognitive dissonance on display is remarkable.

This confusion on the part of people who are, to put it mildly, seldom short of an explanation for why things have gone the way they did is itself something that needs explaining. Simply put, it reflects a series of misunderstandings: about why the referendum was called in the first place; why the referendum campaign and result worked out the way they did; why Parliament after 2017 was unable to come to a collective decision over how to move the process forward; and what ultimately produced a decisive victory for the Conservative Party on a platform of 'Get Brexit Done.' This set of misunderstandings in turn derives from a more profound lack of comprehension. Many people in positions of power and influence in Britain today do not yet understand or grasp the real nature of the social, cultural and political changes taking place in British society. This incomprehension is all the more inexcusable because these changes are also taking place in other societies across the world, not least in many of the member states of the EU. The lack of understanding also means that people opposed to Brexit and upset by the outcome of the election have misguided and inaccurate ideas about what is likely to happen in the next five to ten years. Consequently, they will take longer than they should to put together an effective politics to respond to these events.

The insight that helps to make sense of what has happened is straightforward, although the detail is complex. The United Kingdom, in common with most other developed democracies and quite a few less-developed countries, is undergoing a political realignment. People are now starting to recognise this as the increasing use of this terminology makes clear. However, there is still too much of a focus on the immediate and short term, and obvious, and not enough on the often-hidden fundamental change. Much current comment argues that the referendum and Brexit has brought about a realignment of voting and politics. This however gets things back to front. Rather, it was a social and political realignment that led to the referendum being called, that led to that referendum having the outcome that it did, and has finally led to the Election result and the consummation of Brexit. Brexit, in other words, is a consequence of the realignment, not its cause. What it has done is accelerate and catalyse that realignment, so that it has happened more swiftly and dramatically than it would have otherwise. The popular vote in 2016, and the reaction to it of many of the elite, crystallised something that was already appearing but in a relatively inchoate form. This process of realignment will now drive and shape the way Brexit is applied and the detailed form it takes, and the future pattern of UK politics.

What though is a realignment? It is easy to think of political realignment as being about the outcome of particular decisive elections, as reflected in the share of seats in Parliament. That though is rather the symptom or outcome of the realignment rather than its actual content. A realignment is, essentially, a change in the nature and content of the fundamental political divides in a political community, which breaks up old alliances and voting patterns and creates new ones as friends become foes and enemies become allies. This in turn is produced by the exhaustion of old divides and, most importantly, shifts in the structure and balance of class divisions and power. These make older arguments obsolete or less important and raise the salience of new ones, which come to define political conflicts and identities in new ways. The outcome is a change in voting patterns that happens over a longer period than a single Parliament. Under the British electoral system of First Past The Post (FPTP) this finally reaches a level where it brings about a massive shift of seats at an election. At this point a new political alignment has become established. (In political systems with Proportional Representation the process takes the same amount of time but is more visible while it is happening, because it is reflected in changes in the composition of the legislature on a continuing basis). In British political history realignments have happened at roughly regular intervals, which we can trace right back to the emergence of party politics in the Exclusion Crisis of the 1670s. This realignment is thus not the first, and looking at previous ones, such as the one that happened in the 1920s, can give us a better understanding of the one that is currently near completion, and which Brexit has come to symbolise while being caused by it. In the simplest terms the present realignment is one where the main division in society has switched from being primarily about economics to being about culture and identity (although economics remains important as a secondary division). Another way of thinking about the new division is to see it as being about a divide between cosmopolitanism and nationalism, or novelty and security – hence the importance of questions such as Brexit.

It is this framework that makes sense of the events that have baffled and wrongfooted the mainstream media and political class. Take firstly the result of the 2015 election and David Cameron's decision to honour his manifesto promise to hold a referendum on the UK's membership of the EU. This is commonly presented as an act of insouciant, even rash, opportunism on his part. According to this account he made the initial pledge in the manifesto and then acted on that pledge for reasons of short-term and short-sighted party expediency. There was no deeper reason, and so he bears much of the blame for the consequences of what was a personal and expedient decision. Naturally, like all politicians he was concerned with turning matters to his own and his party's advantage and in a way that would head off difficulties and challenges (he hoped). However, when we look through the prism of realignment at the position he and his party were in we have a better understanding of his decisions. The referendum was not in fact a short-term and frivolous expedient. It was something that had by 2015 become politically necessary, because of gradual structural changes in political divisions and loyalties, which had already begun to manifest themselves in votes at that point.

Similarly, the result of the referendum and the way the campaign worked out and developed over its course makes sense from this perspective, rather than being an inexplicable act of collective self-harm. The emerging pattern of political divisions told informed observers that the vote was going to be at the very least much tighter than most official opinion anticipated, even before the campaign happened. During the campaign one side (Leave) showed that it understood what the new dividing issues in British politics were, and that this referendum was being fought on them rather than the old ones. Consequently, its campaign was effective and mobilised the voters on one side of that new divide, including, crucially, many who had given up voting over the previous decade. The other side (Remain) fought a campaign based on the old alignment of politics and lost, because their arguments did not engage with the concerns and disagreements that now motivated the key groups of voters.

From the understanding that the referendum and the politics around it were the product of a realignment, a reordering of priorities among large numbers of voters as a new fundamental division appeared and older ones became less significant, we can also make sense of the aftermath of the referendum and the events of the last three years. The referendum accelerated the appearance of new divisions in British political debate, which cut across older ones (although those still remained as a powerful but now secondary force) and crystallised them into new political identities, which then led many people to vote in new ways. A key part of this process was the way the losing side came to react to its defeat. This showed both a realisation (but too late) of what the issues were and what was at stake, and also a refusal to accept the legitimacy of not only the result but also the concerns and motives of the voters who had supported this outcome. There was also a quite striking level of self-deception and delusion on display, which led many commentators and politicians to pursue a strategy that was self-defeating.

This in turn produced both the inconclusive result of the 2017 General Election, and the Parliamentary deadlock that followed it. A deadlock in Parliament was entirely predictable and was predicted by several (including myself). The fundamental reason was that the party division in Parliament did not reflect the new division in the country that had led to and been revealed by the referendum result. The division that was present in Parliament was a three-way one, which gave a real-life demonstration of a mathematical paradox known for over two hundred years to mathematicians, political scientists, and economists but which was apparently unknown to most MPs and political commentators. This stable but destructive dynamic was made worse by Theresa May's failed effort to bring about a resolution by calling an early election in 2017. The decision to do this, and the platform on which she ran, both showed that she, and many of the leadership of the Conservative Party, had grasped the essentials of the new alignment. However, the execution was maladroit and incompetent while the Labour Party managed to straddle the new aligning division and keep both sides of it happy – for this one election. That meant they could focus on the still relevant but now secondary division over economics, in a way that made the best of their relatively weak starting point.

What that 2017 election did, on closer examination, was to show that the realignment of politics that the referendum had accelerated was advancing rapidly. However, it had not reached a tipping point, where it would show up clearly in the results in individual seats, given the nature of the British electoral system. The practical result was for the paralysis in Parliament to actually intensify, making the situation the election was meant to have resolved become even worse. By the Spring of 2019 this had reached a point where a fundamental reordering of the party system within Parliament was a real possibility. Had this happened the realignment would have followed the pattern previous ones had, in the nineteenth century, with a realignment at the level of high politics in Parliament being followed by a change in the party system outside Westminster. There would also have been a resolution of the national division over Brexit, around some kind of softer exit with continuing closer connections to the EU. This however did not happen, for a number of reasons. One was the persistence and strength of party-based tribalism and loyalty. The two major ones were that the Remain side in Parliament systematically overestimated their strength and overplayed their hand, and that the main opposition party had a leader who was simply unacceptable to most MPs as Prime Minister.

This in turn led to a crisis of the party system over the Summer of 2019. At one point it appeared that both of the main parties were in danger of being swept away by a wrenching realignment of voting patterns that would see both of them substantially challenged or even replaced by challenger parties that were more in tune with the new alignment. Faced with this both parties reacted. The response of the Conservative Party was decisive and effective (the history of the party means this should not have been a surprise to anyone). They changed their leader and moved to align themselves clearly and unmistakably with one side of the new alignment. The Labour Party's response by contrast was half-hearted and hesitant. This reflected however a brutal reality, that there were at that point no good options for the party or its leadership. As with other social democratic parties all over the developed world, the new alignment confronted them with an existential choice as to which half of their electoral coalition they would give priority to, given it was being pulled apart by the new aligning division. In the event they fudged that decision and were undone: unfortunately for them, they were in trouble no matter what they did.

The election, and its dramatic results, has resolved the question of the UK's EU membership decisively and brutally. Thanks to the earlier intransigence and incomprehension of the Remainer side, this will likely be a much sharper and more clear-cut separation than seemed probable even six months ago. What it has also done is to bring the realignment of British politics much closer to its final resolution. The realignment process, which started to stir and become visible around 2013 and 2014, has now become clear and obvious. It is almost complete, in the sense that one side of the new alignment is already clear, dominated by the reinvigorated and transformed Conservative Party. The form and nature of the other side is still emerging but will become firm during the next five years. Thereafter politics will have its daily ups and downs and turns of fortune but the broad pattern, loyalties and enmities will be stable for several decades to come.

This book tells that story, of how British politics is undergoing a realignment and how this led to the calling of a referendum, produced a vote to leave the EU, led a large part of the political and media class to lose their reason, and has finally been resolved in a way that determines important features of the new alignment that is now clearly with us. It is organised in the following way. The first chapter contains the political science theory and sets out what political alignments are in stable modern political systems and how these periodically reset as old divisions become exhausted and new ones emerge. It explains, in very simple terms, how this is ultimately driven by changes in the economic and class structure of society brought about by innovation and the investment cycle. There are also historical illustrations of how this works from British history. The essential features of the current realignment are identified and set out. Readers who want to skip the theory and go straight to the narrative can go directly to the next chapter. The following six chapters deal with the events of the last six or seven years, from the emergence of new political alignments through the calling of the referendum and its outcome, to its aftermath and finally the Election of 2019 and its result. The final chapter of the six sets out simply what has happened and how it should be understood, given the theory presented in the first chapter and the narrative inspired by that theory that is set out in the subsequent chapters. It then looks at what is still yet to happen in terms of the realignment and speculates about what may happen in the next few years. The short conclusion tries to put these British events into a wider context and explain how they are one part of a wider story of the realignment of politics in most (though not yet all) developed countries and quite a few middle-income countries.

CHAPTER 1

ALIGNMENT AND REALIGNMENT

What Political Alignments Are, and How They Work

For those who follow politics on a day-to-day basis, which includes most of those active in it, it is hard to see patterns or structure in it. Instead there is a rush of constantly changing particulars, events, personalities, votes, and elections. From this perspective ideas and beliefs matter because they provide ways of understanding the world and the motivation for action but it is the combination of people, individual men and women, and contingent and random events that drives the story. This is certainly true in part and no account of politics can ignore the personal and contingent. The longer-term perspective of the historian and the more detached viewpoint of the political scientist and sociologist both reveal patterns and structures that shape and limit what is possible in politics in a given place and time, the framework within which the individual politicians act. These patterns in turn are not fixed. Over time they change, and those changes are not usually a steady, constant process; rather they happen relatively swiftly and for those caught up in them, unexpectedly. One of the most fundamental of the ordering structures of politics is the political alignment (or dispensation as some call it). The change in this, the realignment of politics, is thus one of the most profound and consequential shifts in the deep structure of politics.

What though is a political alignment? It is not the same as a constitutional settlement, or a legal and political order (both of which are often included under the rubric of the term 'political dispensation'). It is rather the way political argument and discussion is structured, during a period of time, in a political community with stable politics and rule-bound competition between factions or parties. It is the basis on which people who are politically active, and even those whose only political participation consists of voting at (some) elections identify themselves with a particular side in politics. Political alignments are the way people decide if they are on the blue or red team, left or right broadly defined. The poi

nt is that these divides are binary. The category of 'centre' is ultimately defined by reference to the two primary sides (usually for convenience and by tradition called 'left' and 'right'). Thus, it is not a meaningful category in its own right and politicians and voters who try to define themselves in this way find themselves constantly having to clarify which of the two primary sides they lean towards, given that centrism is not a synonym for simple indifference or apathy. There is typically one issue or set of related issues that people use to decide which side they stand on. This is the aligning issue; it is their position on that question that determines which of the two 'sides' they are on and how far out on that side they are (to be centrist means to hold a moderate or heavily qualified position on that aligning issue).

Why and how does this happen? If you think about it, organising or thinking of politics in that way is strange. Why reduce the complexity of disagreement and debate to a binary division? And how does this happen? In a contemporary political community people disagree about many things. A minority of these points of disagreement are settled through the collective decision-making process of politics. This is still a large number of issues however. For example, people will disagree about such questions as criminal justice policy, whether the death penalty should be part of the legal system, what kind of tax policy should be followed, the foreign policy orientation of their country, and its immigration and citizenship policy. These are just a few of the questions at stake in political discussion. Mathematically, there are more ways of combining positions on the individual questions than there are people in the population. Thus, one person might favour higher taxes, support the death penalty, be in favour of strict immigration controls, and be a dove on foreign policy. Someone else might support lower taxes, be opposed to the death penalty, while also being a supporter of strict immigration controls and a dovish foreign policy. Yet other people would have different combinations of views again. In reality we do not find such a random and individualised assortment of positions (although there is more of that than you might imagine). What you do find on examination is that certain combinations of views on particular questions are common and others are rare. However, there is no obvious or logical reason why certain kinds of views on different issues should go together. There is no logical reason for example why environmental pessimism should typically go along with support for an interventionist economic policy – one can make a perfectly good case that taking a gloomy view of our environmental prospects combines well with scepticism about the capacity for government intervention in economic matters. Moreover, combinations of this kind are not stable, but change over time. At one time for example, support for eugenics was strongly associated with socialist or 'progressive' views on economic policy whereas now that is not true. This would not happen if the positions on different questions were naturally associated with each other (which would be the case if they were logically connected, or associated with psychological proclivities for instance). So, the reality, that people who take a certain position on one issue are disproportionately likely to share a certain position on another, logically unrelated issue, is something that requires explanation.

Furthermore, the actual organisation of politics always has a binary quality in any political order with some kind of representational element or party system. We do not elect individual members of the legislature who then form shifting and ad hoc coalitions on an issue by issue basis. In reality there are always two broad sides. This is true regardless of the electoral system, which only determines the form that division into two sides takes. In a system that uses First Past The Post (FPTP) there will be two large portmanteau parties that contain a range of broadly allied factions. In one that employs some form of Proportional Representation (PR) there will be many parties but these will be organised into two broad camps or alliances and everyone will be well aware of this. This binary division partly reflects political necessity. Effective government and administration require a stable majority with a composition that does not shift randomly and constantly. This means that people will compromise or qualify their opinions in order to be sure of getting their way on the question that they care most about. Moreover, there is one key feature of politics that is always binary and either/or. You are either in power or you are not. You cannot be a little bit in power any more than you can be a little bit pregnant or almost unique – it's either one thing or another.

This all suggests an explanation for the binary nature of political argument and the clustering of views and opinions. In any given time or place there are some issues from the wide range that exist that have a particular salience. That is, they matter to a large number of people, more than the other things that people disagree about. That means in turn that people will ally with those who share their views on a salient issue even if they disagree about other less salient ones. At any particular time, there is usually one issue that is particularly salient to a very large part of the population. This is the aligning issue. It is that issue that divides the public up into two broad confederations or tribes, and politics and political argument comes to be organised around it. One consequence is that the people who agree on the aligning issue and are on the same side with regard to it will come over time to share similar views on other, objectively unrelated questions. (There are sociological and psychological reasons for this).

This though poses two further questions. Firstly, what makes an issue strongly salient to a large part of the population? Secondly, is it simply a matter of numbers that determines which issue becomes the aligning one? There are several ways of answering the first question. One approach would emphasise the role of ideas and arguments, which are seen as autonomous, and independent of things such as economic and social relations. In this view the salience of certain divisions reflects the arguments that are dominant in intellectual discussion at a given time. This makes intellectuals and artists the people who ultimately determine what politics is about and what the big divisions are. Not surprisingly this argument is popular with those who make their living by writing and teaching. The alternative (which I personally support) is a materialist explanation. In this view the divisions of opinion that exist in society are not only or primarily a matter of intellectual judgment: they reflect and derive from real conflicts of interest, and material circumstance and everyday lived experience. The way material life and in particular economic life (production and consumption) is structured will produce genuine conflicts of interest and also different actual experience, which will lead large numbers of people to have particular views of what the answer to major political questions should be and those different answers, deriving from different interests, will produce political divisions and disagreements. The particularly salient issues are ones that are relevant to and reflect the material circumstances of large numbers of people. To put it another way, the main salient issue will come from a significant conflict of interest in society. This in turn will reflect the way the life of society is structured and that comes from a complex combination of innovation, technology, and earlier economic and political history (legacy effects). This means that ideas should be seen as both attempts to understand and make sense of the world and also as being frequently instrumental; that is, intended not so much to discover truth as to rationalise interests and help bring about a desired end. This does not mean that ideas do not matter; quite the contrary. To the extent that they help accurate understanding or work to motivate people towards action they can have massive effects. Conversely if the intellectual understanding that people have is incomplete or inaccurate then they will act in ways that are harmful to their own interests as well as those of others.

As far as the second question is concerned the answer is that it is not simply a matter of numbers. An issue that is of importance to a relatively small number of people will not be salient enough to become the one that politics is organised around, the aligning issue. Raw numbers though are a necessary condition not a sufficient one. The other element that makes an issue highly salient is that in addition to mattering to a large number of people (because of its reflecting a significant social and economic division) it matters to the critical class of political investors. These are people or organised groups of people who stand to gain or lose directly from political argument going one way rather than another and who also have significant means at their disposal. They may be wealthy individuals, or institutions and organisations that dispose of large amounts of resources, such as corporations, trade unions, and campaigning organisations (churches and organised religious groups were also historically important). Because they have resources and stand to gain or lose significantly from the outcomes of the political process they invest in politics. These are the people and organisations that fund politicians and political parties, donate to think tanks and campaigns, buy advertising, and control or use media outlets (Ferguson, 1995). An issue that matters to political investors will be prominent and gain a lot of attention even if it has low salience for the great majority. However, it will not be the aligning issue unless it matters to both political investors and large numbers of ordinary people and, very importantly, is a question that divides the political investor class as well as the wider population.

At any given time, there will be one issue that is the primary aligning question in a political community, the issue that all other debates tend to align around and which divides the community into two broad camps. However, there is usually at least one secondary aligning issue, a question that is also highly salient but not quite as salient as the primary one. This will also be an issue that will lead to divisions but these will often be within the two main camps as well as between them. That is because the combination of the two aligning issues, primary and secondary, will divide the electorate as a whole into four loosely defined groups or quadrants (they will almost certainly not be equal in size as parts of the electorate so you should not imagine the division being into four quarters). Typically, two of the quadrants will be the dominant combinations of views on the two aligning issues, those being the combinations shared by the largest numbers of people and enough political investors. A great deal of actual day-to-day politics will be about competition between the two dominant quadrants and the parties and political investors associated with them for the support of the two subordinate ones. Sometimes there are as many as three salient issues (producing, in theory, eight blocs of voter) but this is unusual. People who have the combination of views that places them in one of the subordinate quadrants may find that there is no party or political force that fully represents their combination of views – this is particularly likely in a FPTP political system. One possible result is that they will be ignored and their opinions and interests disregarded by the political process. Alternatively, they may find that they are the swing voters who are courted by the two dominant blocs. In that case, over time, the political centre of gravity will tend to move towards them. As we shall see this is precisely the two processes that we can see happening with two groups of voters in UK politics over the last couple of decades, and this explains the course of recent events.

Why Realignments Happen

Political alignments of the kind just described do not last forever. Eventually an alignment will break down and will be replaced by another. A new aligning issue will appear so that old divisions become less important or even disappear completely while now ones arise. As part of this process people who were on the same side of the old aligning issue (and so in the same broad political 'tribe') may find that they are on opposite sides of the new one: conversely, those who were once opposed over the old question can discover they agree about the new one. Allies become foes and enemies become friends. A political shuffling happens and there is a radical shift of voting patterns. Sometimes new parties appear and old ones split and recombine, on other occasions the existing parties persist – or at least something with the same name and many of the same personnel does – but their ideology and voting base are significantly altered. This is the process of realignment, the replacement of the old aligning issue by a new one and the working out of this in electoral and party politics. Realignments of this kind can retrospectively be seen to have taken place slowly and gradually but the visible and practical changes usually happen swiftly, in a matter of a decade or so. Once the realignment is complete a new alignment has taken shape and this then persists for some time. There are two important additional points to make: sometimes it is the secondary aligning issue that changes in which case you have a minor realignment whereas if the primary issue changes there is a more fundamental and radical one; the visible form that realignment takes is different in PR and FPTP systems but the underlying reality is the same.

How and why does this realignment happen? Why does an alignment not simply persist? There are two main reasons why political alignments eventually come to an end. The first is that after some time the aligning issue becomes exhausted because a broad consensus has come into being. This is actually the political process at work. One of the central functions of politics is to work out and discover, through debate and compromise, what kind of position there may be with regard to a particular issue that a large majority of an initially divided public can accept. In other words, the political process takes an issue that initially provokes deep and passionate division and with time (several decades in most cases) produces a modus vivendi, something that the great majority can live with. The process of debate and compromise that produces this may seem sordid to the purist but it should actually be regarded as noble and honourable, given that the alternatives are deep social conflict or actual violence. In some cases, you get more than a modus vivendi, and actual near consensus emerges. Here one side has won the argument insofar as it has persuaded the great majority of the population of the rightness of its position. In both cases, consensus and modus vivendi, the range of debate over the once-aligning issue diminishes to mere adjustment or emphasis or even stops entirely. Clearly at that point the question or issue no longer divides the public into two broad camps, because there is broad agreement.

The second way an aligning issue can lose its importance is for its salience with the public to decline or even disappear. In simple terms you could say that it does not matter to people as much as it did or even stops mattering at all. This comes from changes in the material circumstances of large numbers of people which mean that things that once mattered centrally to them because of their everyday circumstances no longer do so in the same way. This is a change in the class interests and divisions that exist in society. This in turn means that old established conflicts that led to one set of issues being relevant and hence the aligning issue in politics either decline in importance or even disappear outright while new conflicts appear. They in turn produce a new aligning issue. History suggests that in the UK and several other countries shifts of this kind take place every forty years or so. There is clearly a generational aspect to this but it also reflects a pattern of cyclical change in the economic structure of society, produced by the long wave investment cycle (the Kondratiev Cycle as it is commonly called).

When an alignment has become exhausted and played out for either of these reasons (or a combination of both) politics becomes highly technical. Ideology becomes less important and perceived competence more so. Much public debate comes to be dominated by policy experts or 'wonks' as they are called. The categories of left and right still exist, there are still two sides in politics but there is a growing feeling that the two sides are increasingly alike and indeed there is some truth in this. At the same time new divisions are appearing and gathering force but a large and growing number of voters feel that their concerns about this question are ignored or treated lightly by the political process. Eventually however this new division finds expression in politics and the public increasingly divides along this new line of disagreement rather than the old, now exhausted one. This is of course the realignment process. As said, there is a reshuffling of political loyalties and enmities. New, often surprising alliances form and old loyalties suddenly fracture. The realignment happens at the popular level among voters, rather than being led from above, because it reflects societal shifts in class interests and conflicts. To think that it is caused by politicians or the media is to confuse cause and effect. What does happen however is that ambitious and astute political operators (political entrepreneurs we might call them) spot the emerging new division and take advantage of it. Moreover, the new division or alignment typically divides the political investors as well and some of them see their interests as being at stake in the new division: as a result they start to fund and support new political figures and movements or support the articulation of new fresh perspectives and arguments by public intellectuals, journals, and think tanks.

This process can take different forms, depending on the nature of the electoral system and other features of the political culture. In a system with proportional representation the realignment is apparent and visible while it is happening, because it shows up in changes in the pattern of voting that are immediately translated into seats in the legislature. It also usually involves the emergence of new parties and splits or combinations among old ones – this reflects the reality that it is easier to set up a new party and get into the legislature under such a system. In a FPTP system such as the British one it is much more difficult to create a new party with any chance of success or to successfully break away from an existing one, because the electoral bar for success is higher. In addition, there can be significant changes in the vote share of parties or in the distribution of votes without this being initially reflected in actual results in seats. This means that in systems of that kind the realignment will be invisible to all but dedicated psephologists and political scientists for quite a while, even though it is going on. Eventually however a tipping point is reached when the shift in votes is both large enough and sufficiently geographically concentrated to flip large numbers of seats and determine the outcome of a national election and at that point there is an apparently sudden and dramatic change. Because of the greater difficulty of setting up a new party, what often happens instead is that an existing party is transformed. It retains the same name and many of the same personnel as before but its voting base, regional strength and weakness, and ideology and policy orientation all change, often dramatically. After one party in a FPTP system has transformed in this way the other eventually follows suit, driven to do so by electoral pressures. Interestingly, in the British case it is the Conservative Party that has undergone this kind of transformation several times in its history, which is one of the reasons for its electoral success and longevity when compared to comparable parties in other countries.

While it is happening, the realignment process is often perceived to be a collapse or crisis of the political centre. Sometimes this is an accurate perception but often such a view misses the point. It is not that the centre ground of politics is weakened or vacated but rather that it is transformed and its content radically redefined. As has already been pointed out, the category of the centre has no inherent meaning; it is defined by the opposing poles of left and right. Those in turn are defined by whatever the aligning issue is at a given time. If the aligning issue changes then left and right change their commonly understood meaning because they now come to refer to positions with regard to the new issue rather than the old one. As a result, what it means to be in the middle has a new content as well. The reason why the narrative of a 'decline of the centre' seems plausible is because in the final stages of an alignment the centre is indeed dominant, due to the process of convergence described earlier. As the new alignment takes hold the new, fresh conflicts and disagreements that come to dominate political debate are still sharp and intense so political debate comes to have a more passionate quality for a while and the stakes seem higher – and in many cases they are, as the terms and location of the new centre have yet to be defined. One often amusing aspect of this redefinition of left, right and centre is the way in which people can discover that, without their own views having changed one iota, they apparently moved from left to right or vice versa. One example of this was the Victorian agitator, secularist, and co-operator George Jacob Holyoake who remarked towards the end of his life that having spent most of his career being described as an extreme radical he was now labelled an extreme reactionary, without his own views having shifted. The reason was that he was indeed far left under the political alignment of mid-Victorian Britain, in which one of the main aligning issues was the status and position of the Church (Holyoake's thoroughgoing secularism and atheism making him an extremist radical with regard to that issue) but was seen as far right on the newly emerging aligning question of the extent of government intervention in the economy (where his support for complete free trade and minimal government, albeit combined with support for cooperativism, made him a right winger).

The History of Realignment in the United Kingdom

All of this is rather abstract. What though is the concrete form it has taken in history, particularly the history of the United Kingdom? There are reasons why the story of regular realignments can be traced more clearly in the UK than in many other countries, particularly those of Continental Europe (Canada, Australia, the United States and Scandinavia are similar to the UK in this respect). There are two main reasons for this, which reflect the United Kingdom's long and comparatively fortunate political history. The first is that the United Kingdom has avoided major disruptive political events such as revolutions, civil wars, or conquest as the result of being on the losing side of a major war. This gives its political history a degree of continuity not found in some other countries. Secondly, the United Kingdom was the first modern political community (apart perhaps from the Dutch Republic and Sweden) to create a system of regular competition between identifiable and persistent political parties, with a recognisable government and opposition. This was one of the great political innovations, not least because it gave the political order as a whole much greater stability and made it less dependent on the vagaries of individual personality, and because it replaced the very high stakes and often violent factional politics of medieval and renaissance monarchies. The party system can be traced back as far as its first emergence during the Exclusion Crisis of the 1670s and has persisted since then, apart from an episode of purely factional politics during the eighteenth century (from roughly 1763 to 1783). The parties have come over time to appeal to a larger electorate and there have been obvious and significant changes such as the development of mass party organisation in the later nineteenth century and the impact of modern electronic media in the later twentieth century but the system has continued. This means that we can observe over time the kinds of questions that were the basis for party divisions and competition and the interests that the competing parties represented and appealed to, and more importantly, how all of these changed. If we do this it becomes apparent that since as far back as 1671 there have been a succession of stable alignments, in which the basis for political competition and the issues at stake were stable and recognised. In between these are what we can identify as relatively shorter episodes of realignment, in which the basis for division alters to some degree and the patterns of support for parties shift, often dramatically. The historical pattern we can identify is captured in Table 1.

Table 1. British Political Eras and Realignments

PERIOD OF ALIGNMENT	REALIGNMENT EPISODE
1671 - 1715	1715 - 1725
1725 - 1756	1756 - 1763
1763 – 1783 (Period of Faction Politics)	1783 - 1792
1792 - 1832	1832 - 1846
1846 - 1886	1886 - 1893
1893 - 1922	1922 - 1931
1931 - 1975	1975 - 1983
1983 - 2015	2015 - ?

The details of this political history would take a large book and need not detain us here. Several points should be noted however. There is a regular quality to the political cycle we can observe here but it is not mechanical. The periods of stable alignment vary in length, from forty-four years to as little as twenty-nine. Similarly, the episodes of realignment generally last for about ten years but one lasted for fourteen years, from 1832 to 1846 while at the other extreme the one triggered by Gladstone's conversion to Irish Home Rule in 1885 only lasted seven (and some would argue was even shorter). During the episodes of realignment, we can observe dramatic party splits and the sudden formation of alliances that would have struck most observers as fantastical only a few years earlier. For example, few would have believed in 1881 that within a few years the arch-Radical Joseph Chamberlain would be allied with the most hardline of Tories, Lord Salisbury or would have credited in 1715 that William Pulteney would be allied a few years later with his arch-foe Bolingbroke against his sometime ally but now inveterate enemy Walpole. These dramatic reversals go along with major changes in the bases of party support and, above all, the basis of party competition.

This can be seen if we look swiftly at two of the realignments, those of 1886 – 1893 and 1922 – 1931. The latter is particularly significant because it brought about a change in the major aligning issue and inaugurated a politics that is now drawing to a close (with a major amendment or minor realignment taking place during the 1975 – 1983 period). In the first, the issues that had dominated mid-Victorian politics such as the status and role of the Church, and reform of the constitution and form of government, became much less important. Instead a new aligning issue appeared in the shape of Irish Home Rule and associated with that, a debate over imperialism as the central element of not just foreign and defence policy but also increasingly economic and fiscal policy and the very nature of the British State. At the same time economic and social questions, which had been largely a settled matter since the great divisions of the 1840s, began to revive. This all reflected changes in Britain's economic position and the way its business and commerce were organised and, related to that, the decline of one social conflict and the start of another. The competition between the landed and financial classes on the one hand and the manufacturing and commercial on the other, which had found expression in the competition between the Gladstonian Liberal Party and the Tory party of Disraeli, faded, with the two once antagonistic groups becoming increasingly allied against continuing middle-class radicalism and the emergence of organised labour as a social and political interest. (This also found expression in many Dissenting businessmen switching to Anglicanism.) There was of course a huge split in the once-dominant Gladstonian coalition, with Joseph Chamberlain and the Liberal Unionists, plus the remaining Whigs, forming a new Unionist alliance with the Conservatives, which went on to dominate politics. This in turn led to a significant switch in voting behaviour and the distribution of support within the country (a major increase in support for the Conservatives in Scotland for example).

In the 1920s, several things happened as part of the realignment of 1922 – 1931. The most visible sign of this was the collapse of the old Liberal Party and the emergence of the Labour Party as one of the two main parties. This reflected the definitive emergence of an organised working class as a major force in politics and social life, and of the conflict between that and business as the principal social divide. (The aristocracy and the question of their position and interests stopped being a major issue at this time.) This meant that questions such as Irish Home Rule or constitutional reform disappeared completely as defining questions in politics and were replaced by the question of the economic role of government versus private enterprise, which having been a secondary aligning issue now became the dominant one. This new alignment tore apart the old Liberal electoral coalition, which also lost much of its social and organisational base with the sudden demise of the culture of Nonconformity. The two parts of the Liberal coalition migrated to the two new poles, of the new Labour Party, and a transformed Conservative Party, now very much the party of business, the middle class, and the professions. Many politicians switched parties, some more than once and quite a few promising political careers were cut short by the ruthless workings of the electoral system. In 1931 the United Kingdom finally abandoned the trade and fiscal policy of Free Trade, which had guided it since 1846, and moved decisively to a new kind of political economy, one that was more British nationalist and in which the state had a much larger role. (The 1945 election was not so much a turning point as a decisive victory for one side of the new alignment with its division between socialism and capitalism, both defined in national terms and a redefining of what that nation was) (Edgerton, 2018).

The Alignment that is Passed – How It Came About and What It Was

Ever since the 1920s British politics has been dominated by the question that emerged as the main aligning issue in that decade. This is the question of the economic role of government, the division, if you will, between socialism and capitalism as alternative models of how a modern economy should be organised. This has been the main aligning issue throughout that near hundred-year period. However, there was a realignment that qualified that debate between the middle of the 1970s and the mid-1980s and it was that still-significant secondary realignment that produced the politics of the generation and time that is now ending. What happened was that the main issue was recast in a dramatic and decisive way, while a new secondary aligning issue appeared, replacing an older set of issues that had become exhausted by the end of the 1960s. Between the late 1920s and the 1960s the secondary aligning question in politics had been a multi-sided argument over how to define the UK's position in the world, and in particular over the connection between British nationalism and the global connections of the British Empire. By the late 1960s and early 1970s this had become exhausted, with the effective dismantling of the Empire and the cementing of the UK's place in the NATO alliance. A firm consensus began to emerge around the belief that Britain's geopolitical future and to a great extent its identity were now defined by membership in the EEC (later to become the EU) along with a close relationship with the United States.

The new secondary aligning issue, which took shape in the 1960s but came to play a significant part in politics by the 1980s, was over the question of social liberalism. In other words, the question of how far government and the political and public policy process should be used to uphold a set of traditional (or supposedly traditional) moral norms and rules. One side argued the case for government not being involved in matters of expression or sexuality, adopting a broadly libertarian position, while the other maintained the view that government had both a right and a responsibility to act in these areas. At the same time there was a renewed and also new debate over the still-dominant aligning issue of free markets versus government intervention. This was not simply a reassertion of an older argument for free markets and economic liberalism, of the kind that had been made in the 1930s and 1940s, even though many of the participants saw it that way. Although there are striking similarities between the economic rhetoric and thinking of Margaret Thatcher on the one hand and Neville Chamberlain on the other there were also profound differences. The kind of market advocacy that came to play a leading part in political discussion from the 1980s onwards had important new elements. Above all, it was much more internationalist and globalist in orientation and it had a strongly American flavour. There was a much greater focus on deregulation and the idea of a self-governing market than had been the case with the more managed and institutionalised model of business and capitalism put forward by British Conservatives from the 1920s onwards. In policy terms there was now a strong emphasis on radical reform and deregulation of the labour market and of industrial relations, and of a movement from manufacturing to services, above all financial services. The City of London, rather than the industrial Midlands, became the promised land.

These developments derived from and were driven by changes in the UK's economic structure and class relations. By the 1970s the modus vivendi that had emerged between labour and business was under severe strain. The long-term problems of the British economy meant that it was increasingly difficult to reconcile the demands and claims of the organised working class, the middle classes, and investors at the same time. This led to political stalemate and ineffectuality and increasingly severe conflict between organised labour and the owners and managers of business. At the same time two significant changes were taking place within British capitalism. The first was a growth in the importance of services as sources of both wealth and employment. The most visible aspect of this was the steady rise in the importance of the financial services sector, the City as it is usually known, but there was also a growth in the importance of commercial leisure and entertainment with industries such as popular music and production of it and related kinds of entertainment becoming increasingly important (they are now as important for the UK economy as financial services are). The second was the steady rise in the social position and social power of the managerial and supervisory class, at the expense of both the owners of enterprises and organised labour. Both of these trends can be traced back for decades, even as far as the 1930s, but both reached a critical tipping point in the early 1970s.

The Conservative Party, apparently in crisis after a crushing defeat in 1966 and a period in office that was generally seen as a failure after its surprise win in 1970, reinvented itself and came to embody a new position on the dominant economic issue while espousing a strong reaction to the emergence of the new secondary alignment. Under Margaret Thatcher the party espoused the new form of radical free market thinking and made itself the vehicle for the newly ascendant social and economic forces. The Thatcher government is well known for its reform of labour relations and attack on the position of the trade unions and organised labour. What is less recognised is its equally strong attack on the traditional establishment and professions, as gentlemanly capitalism was swept away by reforms such as the Big Bang that transformed the City. The party came to advocate the interests of a meritocratic entrepreneurial class while older commercial and business elites were sidelined. Large manufacturing concerns, represented by the CBI, were given second place to the newly energised financial services sector.

The Labour Party's initial response (or at least that of a great part of it) was the Alternative Economic Strategy. Just as the Conservatives transformed and reinvigorated one side of the still dominant issue of economics, the left of the Labour movement sought to develop a radical socialist alternative that would also depart from and critique the national capitalist consensus of the 1930s to 1970s. This however was much less electorally successful, partly because it came to be associated with an equally radical reorientation of the UK's geopolitical position, through leaving the EEC and NATO and adopting both a position of neutrality in the Cold War and an economic policy of autarky that went against the general thrust of global trade policy since Bretton Woods. Quite simply this was too much for voters to take. However, starting with the reforms brought in by Roy Jenkins as Home Secretary during the 1960s the Labour Party took the initiative with regard to the new secondary aligning issue of social liberalism versus moral conservatism, over specific questions such as the legalisation and social tolerance of homosexuality, abortion, the 'sexual revolution,' liberalisation of speech and pornography laws, and a move towards liberalism in criminal justice policy. We should realise what a significant shift this was. As recently as the late 1950s or early 1960s the Labour Party was in many respects as socially and culturally conservative as the Tory Party, if not more so. As the Labour Party clearly adopted one side of the new division the Conservative Party responded by opposing the moves in a liberal direction and becoming the defender of moral traditionalism and 'family values.' Significantly though, for most Conservative politicians (and many of their voters) this was always a less important issue than the economic one. Interestingly, as time passed, the reverse came to be true for many Labour politicians.

The result of this realignment in the 1970s and early 1980s is captured in the diagram of Table 2. This portrays a political alignment familiar to any person who was of voting age in the 1980s or 1990s. The bottom axis is the dominant one of markets versus state intervention. If you were at the left end of that axis then you favoured a radical socialist alternative to capitalism, at the right end you were an advocate of laissez faire. The vertical axis measures social liberalism versus social authoritarianism. If you were at the top of that axis you were a radical libertarian (someone like Peter Tatchell for example) while if you were at the bottom of it you were an unrepentant moral traditionalist (Peter Hitchens or Mary Whitehouse would be the representative figure here). As the diagram shows this combination of primary and secondary aligning issues divided the electorate into four broad blocs or tendencies. The two dominant quadrants, with the largest numbers of voters and, more importantly, significant numbers of political investors, were the upper left and lower right ones. The upper left, here labelled as 'social democrats,' were those who combined social liberalism with economic interventionism and egalitarianism. The lower right, here labelled as 'free market conservatives' combined support for free market economics with moral traditionalism and authoritarianism.

(It is worth pointing out that intellectually both of these positions are incoherent: capitalist individualism and consumerism undermines moral traditionalism while there is a serious tension or even incompatibility between cultural individualism and economic and social collectivism. This however did not matter in terms of the politics - since when were political views philosophically consistent?

These two quadrants were clearly and obviously represented by the Labour and Conservative Parties respectively throughout the 1980s and most of the 1990s. (The same is obviously true until recently for the Democratic and Republican Parties in the US, where a similar alignment can be observed). That still left two sets of voters not explicitly represented, however. The first, in the upper right quadrant, were consistent libertarians who favoured both free market economics and social liberalism. The second were in the lower left quadrant, voters who were consistent collectivists, supporting both collectivist economics and government intervention on the one hand and also moral and social collectivism with government action to uphold social norms. These were the two groups of voters competed for by the two parties. All four quadrants are more than just combinations of opinions. The specific combinations of views on the two axes tended to correlate with a number of other variables, above all age, education, occupation, and geographical location. The key element here is the increasingly dominant role played by one particular social group. This was the technocratic and increasingly meritocratic (and hence university educated) managerial class. People with that kind of background were increasingly found in certain parts of the country, above all London: they shared a support for a broadly free market approach to economics while being divided over how much redistribution there should be, and they were strongly socially liberal. This was the group whose emergence had driven much of the initial realignment in the 1970s. Their antithesis were the older, less educated voters both working-class and middle- class, found in rural and coastal areas and small towns and older manufacturing and mining areas, who you could well describe as Old Labour and Old Conservative.

The Conservative Party, like their Republican counterparts in the US, were able to appeal to predominantly working-class voters in the lower left quadrant on cultural issues. However, they always had the challenge that those voters strongly rejected their economic policy positions. The Labour Party had the opposite problem. They could assume many of the votes in the lower left quadrant would be theirs because of hostility to the Tories' economic thinking and traditional loyalty to the party those voters' parents and grandparents had created and supported in the earlier twentieth century. They had trouble however appealing to the largely middle class and professional voters in the upper right quadrant because those voters were deeply sceptical of the Party's economic policy, particularly on taxes. The solution for both parties, initially Labour, latterly the Tories, was to compete for the votes of the libertarians (actually libertarians lite) in the upper right quadrant.

Table 2. The Alignment of Politics 1970s to 2010s

SOCIAL DEMOCRATS	LIBERTARIANS
Economics – interventionist Welfare – redistributionist Social Politics – liberal Cultural politics – individualist	Economics – free market Welfare – welfare sceptics Social politics – liberal Cultural politics – individualist
TRADITIONAL COLLECTIVISTS	**FREE MARKET CONSERVATIVES**
Economics – collectivist Welfare – egalitarian & contributory Social politics – conservative Cultural politics – traditionalist	Economics – free market Welfare – moderately sceptical Social politics – conservative Cultural politics – traditionalist

The Breakdown of the Alignment and the Nature of the (Emergent) New One

Consequently, a very important feature of this alignment as it developed was that it came to be dominated by liberalism, even though the Liberal Party (latterly the Liberal Democrats) remained only a third force and minor party. As time went on the Conservative Party came to be defined by economic liberalism. The Labour Party came for many of its members (if not its voters initially) to be defined by social liberalism. Both parties in other words became more liberal: the Tory Party became less and less conservative and the Labour Party less and less socialist. Both also became ever more markedly middle-class, and middle-class in a very specific way. They came to be dominated by the meritocratic, university educated, technocratic managerial class that had driven the politics of both economic and social liberalism (Lind,

2020). What this meant in terms of the four quadrants was that the consistent libertarians in the upper right quadrant increasingly became the key swing voters that both parties were competing for and so the two parties' positions converged on that quadrant (without ever fully landing inside it - it was rather that both parties came to lean towards the preferences of the voters in that quadrant). Meanwhile the voters in the lower left quadrant were simply ignored or taken for granted and this became increasingly true of voters in the lower right quadrant as well.

All of this came to fruition after 1997. Under Tony Blair and New Labour, the Labour Party moved a long way to the right on the economic axis and took on board a lot of economic liberalism (while remaining egalitarian). The Conservative Party abandoned much of its social conservatism and traditionalism, slowly at first but rapidly after David Cameron became leader. The shift towards social liberalism in the Conservative Party was as dramatic as the Labour Party's earlier move to economic liberalism, the two movements symbolised by the legalisation of gay marriage and the abandoning of Clause 4 respectively. This of course left a significant number of voters who rejected both kinds of liberalism almost completely unrepresented, as well as others who had problems with at least one half of the new consensus. By the late 2000s the alignment that had come into being with the political debates of Benn and Thatcher had reached the state of exhaustion and domination by techniques described earlier - similar to the position that politics had reached at the end of the previous alignment in the 1960s. The social argument, the secondary one, had been completely exhausted, mainly because a true near-consensus had been reached on many of the specific questions that were part of it, such as social acceptability for homosexuality. What we will do in the next chapter is to look in more detail at the real but temporary triumph of liberalism and the technocratic class that had driven it and the way it began to break down following (but not simply due to) the financial crisis of 2008.

This slow breakdown and the emergence of a new kind of politics and a new division has finally fed through into another realignment. This has seen the replacement of social liberalism as an aligning issue by a related but distinct division over identity and place. We may describe this as a division between cosmopolitanism and globalism both cultural and economic on the one side and cultural and (increasingly) economic nationalism on the other. It is also simultaneously a division between a notion of identity that sees it as rooted and attached to both place and a historical inheritance and a different way of thinking about identity that emphasises choice and individuality (Goodhart, 2017). A final way of thinking about this new aligning issue is to think of it as being around an opposition between novelty and innovation on one side and familiarity and security on the other. This realignment however is more significant than the one that took place in the 1970s; it is in fact the most profound change to our politics since the previous major realignment in the 1920s. That is because the new issue has not only replaced the old one over social liberalism: it has also become the primary aligning issue, with the continuing division over economics relegated to secondary status. This produces the new world of politics captured in the diagram here.

Table 3. The Emergent New Alignment

RADICAL COSMOPOLITANS	COSMOPOLITAN LIBERALS
Economics – green socialism Welfare – strongly egalitarian Identity – cosmopolitan Culture – radical subjectivism	Economics – free market Welfare – egalitarian redistribution Identity – cosmopolitan Culture – individualist
NATIONAL COLLECTIVISTS	**NATIONAL LIBERALS**
Economics – interventionist Welfare – national contributory Identity – nationalist Culture – traditionalism	Economics – moderately free market Welfare – national based Identity – nationalist Culture – Traditionalism

The bottom axis, which is now the secondary one, remains the division over the relative role of markets and politics in economic life. The vertical axis, which is now primary, measures the new division over identity and cosmopolitanism versus nationalism. The four quadrants this kind of alignment produces are these. In the lower left quadrant are voters who combine traditional left-wing economics with cultural traditionalism and nationalism - we may call them national collectivists. Their neighbours in the lower right quadrant share their views on the now main aligning issue of identity and nationalism but are more sympathetic to markets - we may call them national economic liberals (or advocates of 'capitalism in one country'). In the upper right quadrant are what we may call 'liberal cosmopolitans. They are broadly free market (but typically somewhat egalitarian), strongly socially liberal and cosmopolitan and internationalist. The upper left quadrant are voters who are strongly left on economics (but often in a rather fuzzy and inchoate way at the moment) and also very much on the cosmopolitan and internationalist end of the new division. They are also strongly committed to a certain kind of identity politics that emphasises personally chosen identity and radical subjectivism and which derives intellectually from post-modernism.

The four groups are also divided geographically, socially, and by economic status (though not so much by income). The voters in the two upper quadrants are typically younger and live in major metropolitan centres that are globally connected. This obviously means London but also includes significant globally connected provincial metropoles such as Manchester, Bristol, Leeds, and Birmingham. The voters in the two lower quadrants are typically older and live in the countryside and coastal areas plus smaller towns in the ex-industrial regions. These Old Labour and Old Conservative voters were once deeply divided on economics and still are to some degree. They are however very much on the same side when it comes to the new issue of nationalism versus cosmopolitanism. Increasingly the economic question does not divide them as much as it once did, mainly because the lower right quadrant voters (Old Conservatives or National Liberals) are becoming less attached than they were to free market economics (while still sceptical of traditional socialism). Something to note from the table, which is a reflection of electoral reality, is that the two lower quadrants are closer to each other in their views and attitudes than the upper two are to each other. This means it is easier for a politician in the lower right quadrant to appeal to voters in the lower left than it is for one in the opposite upper left quadrant to appeal to voters in the upper right one. It is that disparity that explains much of the most recent electoral results, as we shall see later.

The big division however between the two upper and two lower quadrants is education, which correlates strongly with age. People in the upper half are usually graduates, while those in the lower half typically have not been to university. This correlates increasingly with age because of the massive expansion of the universities under New Labour. This is in many ways the key or central division of the new alignment, because it unites economics and culture. The connecting element is the meritocratic labour market, in which formal academic attainment is used to regulate and control access to high paid and (more importantly) high status jobs and occupations. Graduates mostly work in the dynamic parts of the UK economy, which are part of the city region and network-based world economy. They also have a set of shared cultural outlooks and beliefs, which emphasise novelty, pluralism and cultural individualism. This partly comes from the university experience but also reflects their experience in the world of work. In fact, their set of beliefs can be fairly described as an ideology in the strict original meaning of that word, as used by Friedrich Engels, a theory about the nature of the world and one's place in it that appears to be neutral but justifies and explains their privileged position. Meritocracy produces both an economic conflict of interest and a clash of cultural perceptions and self-perceptions.

The new four-way division in the electorate clearly emerged by the middle of the 2010s, as we shall see in the next chapter. However, until the election of 2019 it was not clearly reflected in the official party system and in particular in Parliament. The story we will now move on to tell is that of how the new division led to the referendum being called and then produced a narrow Leave majority. Since then, disruptions in Parliament and decisive action by one of the two parties have brought the party system into line with the new alignment of voters, at least on the right. One feature of this story is that the realignment has happened more rapidly on the right (the lower half of Table 3) than on the left (the upper half of that table). In the event right-wing and centre-right politicians have shown a better understanding of what is happening and have responded to it more swiftly and effectively than their left-wing and centre-left counterparts. This lack of understanding on the part of the liberal left in particular was most notable in the aftermath of the 2016 referendum, and led to a series of strategic misjudgements, which culminated in the 2019 election.

Two Points – Scotland and Global Comparisons

There are two additional points that need to be made here. The first is the question that clearly has to be addressed – what about Scotland? The story told so far, and the analysis presented, is very much an English (or more properly English and Welsh) one. Scotland it seems is a different story but not, however, completely different. A realignment also took place in Scottish politics at the same time as the one in England and Wales and is also almost complete. As with the one we have described, the main element of the realignment was a movement away from economics to identity as the main aligning issue. However, in Scotland this took the form of a division over Scotland's historically distinct identity and its relations with the rest of the UK. This made Scottish separatism and the question of continued Union or Independence the principal aligning issue. Moreover, in this case the left, or rather that part of the Scottish left that was in favour of independence, was able to adapt most swiftly to the new division (as well as helping to create it of course) and so the form that the new politics has taken is different from the one that has emerged in England and Wales. The Conservative Party has also adapted already to the new alignment in

Scotland, positioning itself as the main Unionist party. The problem it faces is that a significant number of Unionist voters will not support it because of the continued salience of economics. The Scottish National Party meanwhile has established a hegemonic position for the moment, partly because of astute leadership but also because it has succeeded in subordinating economic disagreement to the independence issue for many voters. This means that it can appeal to voters who disagree about economic matters, in a way its rivals have not been able to do. The present situation is set out in Table 4.

Table 4. The New Scottish Alignment

LEFT NATIONALISTS	RIGHT NATIONALISTS
(Most) SNP Green Party (Some) Labour	(Some) SNP
LEFT UNIONISTS	**RIGHT UNIONISTS**
(Most) Labour Lib	Scottish Conservatives Dems

We will look in more detail at how the realignment took place in Scotland after 2010, and its effects there, in the next chapter. The final chapter will look at how the dynamics of the situation will likely play out in the next few years (one point to bear in mind is that the Scottish Parliament and local elections are conducted by PR so the form the realignment takes there will be different to what we observe in the UK as a whole, although the underlying political forces are the same). Northern Ireland meanwhile has also seen the early phase of a change in its politics, which may herald the end of a kind of politics that we can trace back to 1922 or even 1912.

The pattern of realignment set out earlier does not apply only to the UK. A very similar set of developments can be observed in the United States, most of the EU countries and many middle-income countries such as Turkey and India. In fact, it is easier to list the developed countries where this kind of realignment of politics has not happened, or not yet happened anyway (Japan and most of the Far East, New Zealand, Ireland, and Portugal). This adds emphasis to the point made earlier, that Brexit did not cause a realignment of British politics but was rather a consequence of that realignment – since Brexit only affects UK politics, why do we observe similar processes and events at work elsewhere? The global nature of this realignment (usually described as a rise of 'national populism') tells us firstly that it is in part a localised response to a global set of trends and developments, and secondly that the economies and political systems of the world are much more aligned and integrated than was once the case, so their political cycles and evolution are much more synchronised. (Eatwell and Goodwin, 2018) This means that we should think of Brexit not as a uniquely British phenomenon but as the distinctive form that a widespread process took in the particular context of British politics. As such it is of interest not only to people concerned with and interested in Britain and its politics but to anyone with an interest in the course of politics worldwide. The social shifts and changes that produced a change in political divides and alignments and then led to Brexit in the British case are also happening in other countries. The political result (the rise of national collectivism and the slow appearance of a liberal response to that) can also be seen elsewhere. Brexit therefore speaks to and casts light on wider questions such as whether we are moving into a post-liberal political era, and what forms the rise of national collectivism may take (in the British case it seems to have taken a milder form than elsewhere although the jury is still out on that).

CHAPTER 2

WHY THE REFERENDUM HAPPENED – THE RISE OF NATIONAL POPULISM AND THE START OF REALIGNMENT

The Climax of Technocratic Liberalism

In 2001 politics in most of the Western world was dominated by a kind of technocratic liberalism. This was notably the case in the UK, where Tony Blair led the Labour Party to a second decisive victory over a Conservative Party that had still not recovered from its fearful beating in 1997. The politics of New Labour had the following elements, which it shared with left-of-centre parties in countries such as France, Germany, and the United States. The first was a generally free market economic policy, significantly further in that direction than had historically been the case for centre-left parties. It was not simply free market however. Rather it was a vision of a market-directed but regulated economy with politics limiting and directing the scope of market forces through regulations designed and administered by an elite. The second was an active redistributive role for government: taxes levied on the products of market driven growth were then used to fund transfers to those on lower incomes. In the British case these took the form of means-tested income supplements for those in employment but on low pay, plus a housing benefit to deal with the costs of the UK's increasingly dysfunctional housing market. The third part was social liberalism, with support for things such as gay rights and cultural progressivism. The final element was supra-nationalism. This was the belief that certain issues and challenges should be dealt with by bodies such as the United Nations or European Union, at a level above that of the sovereign state (the states in question would surrender some of that sovereign power to the supranational bodies by the mechanism of Treaties). This is different from internationalism, in which sovereign states cooperate without surrendering their sovereignty.

The Conservative Party at this point had no real alternative position to any of this, so the argument was mainly about details. The final feature of the dominant kind of politics was technocratic elitism. In this way of thinking and practice politics was about an enlightened and qualified elite, that did things for and to people and provided them with government actions that gave them benefits such as prosperity, equality, and security. The role of voters here was largely passive. This style of politics both reflected and led to a hollowing out of traditional party politics, in a self-reinforcing positive feedback loop. As Peter Oborne described it in *The Triumph of the Political Class*, politics became the preserve of an increasingly uniform (and literally interbred) social group that had typically gone to fee-paying schools, studied PPE at Oxford (not so much Cambridge, interestingly), and came from a professional and upper middle-class background (Oborne, 2008). Even though they might support and be active in different parties the members of this class shared a common worldview, which Oborne accurately captures. Both major parties shed members and as the decade went on became largely shell parties, with little existence outside Westminster. There had been a 'strange death' of both Labour and Tory England, as Gregory Elliott and Geoffrey Wheatcroft described in two books published in 1993 and 2005 (Elliott, 1993; Wheatcroft, 2005). One prominent aspect of this decay of grassroots politics was the ever more central role of the national media in politics, above all the medium of television. Political activity was increasingly focused on controlling and driving the narrative of the by now 24-hour news cycle, and the political and media classes were interconnected (and often literally interrelated and married) in a way that had not been true previously.

This professionalisation of politics and increasing convergence of policy was the result of being in the closing phase of an alignment, with the often-bitter arguments and conflicts of the 1980s and early 1990s having produced a modus vivendi or consensus. It was shaped by social and other trends that had ruptured the consensus that had come about at the close of the alignment before that; specifically the steady growth of a qualified middle class, the decline of traditional industry, and the rise of a service economy in which finance and the media (including entertainment) were key sectors. There were, though, significant sections of the population who felt increasingly that they were not represented and who had concerns that the dominant narrative either ignored or misrepresented. One group, which did attract some attention but not that much, were the economic losers of the economic trends of the previous thirty to forty years. These were people who had once worked in manufacturing or other traditional industries such as mining. They lived mainly in the ex-industrial regions and smaller towns. These were parts of the country, such as South Yorkshire, where staple industries that provided stable and long-term employment had largely disappeared. (In some cases, the industry was still there but it no longer provided as much employment). The main problem facing their communities was the way that the world economy had undergone a particular pattern of globalisation after the late 1980s. One aspect of this, which was noticed, was increasing economic integration across national borders through things such as transnational supply chains and branding. The other, less noticed, was the way the world economy stopped being built up of national economies that largely coincided with national states and became rather a network of interconnected city regions (Bershidsky, 2019). This was wonderful news if you lived in a globally connected city region such as London but not so much if you lived in one that had poor connections, such as Sheffield.

This structural change meant that much of the political response to the challenge of the 'left behind' missed the point. The challenge for the people who lived in the old industrial regions (and also the coastal areas and much of the countryside) was not so much poverty and low income, which is why generous income transfers, while welcome, did not address the underlying problem. The real problem was (and is) lack of economic security and predictability. The difficulty was not just that the employment that increasingly did come to these places was low productivity and hence low paid, but that it was insecure and casualised and often associated with working conditions that were unpleasant and oppressive. A significant number of people welcomed the greater flexibility of zero hours contracts and portfolio employment but for many this was very stressful. The idea pushed by the Blair and Brown governments in particular was that the solution was 'education, education, education' in Tony Blair's well-known slogan. The problem though was that the jobs that were available to people who acquired the educational qualifications were not located in places like Wakefield or Rotherham – they were rather in London and the M4 corridor so getting them meant leaving the place you were born in and migrating to one of the metropolitan areas.

This was related to the second issue that the politics of the noughties was unable to address, and it was this second one that eventually blew up the consensus that was so dominant in 2001. This was the question of cultural insecurity. This was a growing feeling among the same group of voters affected by the economic problems described that their identity was disparaged and under threat. This feeling was shared however by a second group of voters. These were generally older voters, who had not been to university but were more economically successful than the first group and tended to live more in the South of England as well as the countryside and older suburbs. The sentiment shared by both groups was that the nature of both the national community as a whole and the specific local community in which they lived had changed in ways that they found unsettling and uncomfortable. For many this feeling came to focus on the single issue of immigration, particularly after the expansion of the EU in 2004. This was followed by large scale migration from Eastern Europe into the United Kingdom, which was unable to apply the same kinds of controls as other EU countries because of its not having a system of identity cards and recording of residence. In addition the Blair government chose not to enforce a delay on full freedom of movement between the UK and the new member states, unlike most other countries. The feeling of a major decision having been made without consultation was intensified by an important aspect of the then dominant politics, which was the stress upon supranationalism and innovation at the expense of the traditional and national. The rise of concerns about identity can be tracked by looking at the percentage of voters who spontaneously mentioned immigration as a concern in the national surveys undertaken for British Social Trends which showed that it was always above 15% of those sampled for the cohort with at least one of the three qualities of being traditionally working-class, over 55 and having left education at sixteen throughout the 2000s. The proportion of respondents of that type raising it as a concern reached a peak of around 30% in 2007 before falling back thereafter and then rising sharply again after 2010 (Ford and Goodwin, 2014).

Alongside such findings was another one that revealed the emerging disaffection of many voters from the increasingly uniform political class. This was the proportion of voters strongly agreeing with the statement 'People like me have no say in government.' Voters who were working-class and without academic qualifications were twice as likely to strongly agree as voters who were both middle-class and university-educated. This was connected to another emergent belief among working-class and poorer voters in general, which was that the Labour Party in particular and the political establishment in general tried to help ethnic minorities and the rich more than working-class voters or all voters in general (Ford and Goodwin, 2014). This reflected another important and seldom noticed divide between the professional middle class and the rest of society, above all the declining but still substantial working class. The latter strongly supported a welfare state founded on the two principles of contribution and universality within a nation state (seen as a mutually supportive welfare community), whereas the former supported one based on the idea of directing assistance to disadvantaged groups in accordance with principles of need. This made welfare a form of charitable assistance from the successful to the losers. Successful and losers though in what?

The answer to that question reveals the key division, which united the problems of economic insecurity and cultural anxiety, and increasingly alienated a significant bloc of voters from the political status quo. This was the workings of the meritocratic labour market and what we may call the consolidation of meritocracy (given its rise had been pointed out by Michael Young in 1961) (Young, 1961). From the 1980s onwards more and more occupations and jobs required a degree-level qualification. These jobs were typically located in the successful parts of the British economy, both geographically and sectorally. This meant that formal academic success and attending university became essential for economic flourishing for an ever-larger part of the working population. For those unwilling or unable to go to university it meant a constrained and insecure economic position. This meritocratic labour market also produced and intensified cultural divisions. One of the central problems with meritocracy, which Michael Young identified, is that it divides society into a class of smug and self-satisfied winners (who feel that they are successful because of merit), and resentful and despondent losers. From that it is a short step to identifying success with virtue and lack of it with moral failing, such as being insufficiently open-minded. One response by the successful is to feel sorry for the less successful and to try and help or compensate them, but this is seen (rightly) as patronising and condescending and is deeply resented.

The division in attitudes between graduates and non-graduates that polls and surveys identify also has its origins in actual experience.

(Despite the fantasies of some Conservatives and Republicans it is not the product of indoctrination at university by post-modernist dons – they might like to be so influential but they are not). Graduates work mainly in the parts of the economy that are most internationally oriented and have regular contact with customers and fellow employees from very different parts of the world and backgrounds. They live in large metropolitan cities that are very much multi-ethnic and multi-cultural and are therefore relaxed about immigration and demographic change. They have a weaker attachment to place (which is common for the young anyway) and are more likely to see themselves as having connections and identities that go beyond the national – partly because that is their actual experience. This is the division that David Goodhart identifies between 'anywheres' (usually graduates) and 'somewheres' (predominantly non-graduates) (Goodhart, 2017). This is both an economic and a cultural or attitudinal division with the two aspects of the divide connected by the economic role of education since the 1960s. Since the 1980s and particularly since 1997 policy and public discussion came to be dominated by the concerns and sentiments of the 'anywheres' with the 'somewheres' simply ignored or when noticed, denigrated as racially prejudiced and narrow-minded. This divide grew steadily in the decade after 2001.

Challenges to the Party System

The growth of this disaffection among many voters was a problem for both major parties but particularly for the Labour Party. On an international level this trend (which was happening in almost all developed economies) was a particular problem for social democratic parties of the centre-left. It came to tear their electoral coalition apart, dividing it into two mutually uncomprehending and hostile camps. On the one side were younger, educated, and mainly metropolitan voters who were increasingly exercised by political issues such as environmentalism and climate change, social equality for ethnic minorities and marginalised sexual identities, and (on the radical end) aggressive anti-Westernism. These voters were hostile to attempts to limit or control immigration, sceptical towards traditional national identity, and strongly in favour of supranational governance. They were also, increasingly, left-wing on economics and hostile to the 'neoliberal' (i.e. free-market) consensus in economic policy. On the other side were older, traditionally working-class voters who shared the hostility to free-market economics but were viscerally opposed to the first group on all of the other issues. Trying to keep both groups of voters in the same coalition was increasingly difficult to near-impossible and the result was and has been a decline in support for social democratic parties throughout Europe (Portugal and possibly Spain are the only real exceptions). In Britain as elsewhere in Europe, it was one-time Labour voters who began to drift away into non-voting and then to rally behind an alternative party. This of course was the United Kingdom Independence Party (UKIP). However, because of the vagaries of the UK's electoral system and the nature of the group of voters and political activists who rallied behind UKIP it was actually the Conservative Party that felt the pressure first.

Why though was the EU the issue that brought together the 'somewheres' and came to embody one side of the new cultural division over such questions as immigration, national identity, and cultural politics? Firstly, all of the evidence suggests that the great majority of the UK electorate always viewed the EU in a way that was not widely shared on the Continent or even in Ireland. Although, as events after 2016 were to show, there was a significant minority who identified with the EU as a political project and supported it on that basis, that was not how the great majority of UK voters and politicians saw it. Instead, they saw membership of the EU as essentially an economic arrangement, entered into for reasons of practical convenience, rather than as a political project. This meant that historically the passion was all on the side of the people, initially a small group, who thought the EU *was* a political project and vehemently rejected it on the grounds that it was incompatible with national identity and self-determination. This obviously put them on the same side as those who were on the national identity side of the new division, and they became the (often obsessive) nucleus around which a larger movement cohered. Secondly, the EU as an entity embodied and was based upon the principles that the emergent 'somewhere' coalition disliked, in particular supranationalism and the principle of free movement across national borders. It thus came in the eyes of many voters to symbolise and embody trends that they did not like and rejected in British social and political life.

Among the politically active there were some who disliked the EU because it restricted the range of political opportunities open to UK politicians and voters, and made radical departures that they favoured impossible. On the one side were radical free marketeers and libertarians who saw it as the essential barrier to sweeping free market reforms that would turn the UK into a larger version of Singapore or Hong Kong. On the other, less well known but still active, were radical socialists who thought the EU was a capitalist plot, with rules and institutions that prevented any departure from financial orthodoxy and 'neoliberalism.' These two groups were actually small in number but intellectually active and crucially included a number of significant political investors. However, it would be a huge mistake to see the Referendum and its aftermath as the product of a conspiracy by such people: in particular it is wrong to think that it was driven by 'dark money' coming from evangelical free marketeers. That was not the basis on which the Leave side fought and won the Referendum campaign, as we shall see, and those who anticipate a sweeping free market revolution once Britain finally leaves the EU, either in hope or trepidation, will be surprised and discomfited.

From Fringe Group to Populist Insurgency

Following the referendum on UK membership of the EEC in 1975, the question of Britain's being in Europe was as settled as any argument could be. Only a small number of hardy eccentrics and obsessives still carried a flame for the cause. The issue simply dropped off the scale of political salience as being a matter that voters cared about. This began to change in the early 1990s, under John Major. For many Conservative MPs and activists, who were fully on board with membership of the EEC, the kinds of extension of power and capacity contained in the Maastricht Treaty, which turned the EEC into the EU, were simply a step too far. They objected both to the association of the EU with the market friendly version of social democracy described earlier and to the significant transfer of national powers to the EU but it was the latter that was the real sticking point for many of them. The result was a bitter division within the Party, which crippled Major's government and contributed in no small part to the Party's disastrous election performance in 1997, their worst defeat since 1906. Following that the issue once again dropped off the political radar for most voters, as the Blair government followed a strongly pro-EU line, and scrapped some of the exemptions from European rules that the Major government had negotiated. However, Euroscepticism (as hostility to the direction of the EU's evolution was now called) remained a powerful presence in the Conservative Party, both in and out of Parliament, making it impossible for any figure identified with the EU cause to become leader, no matter how well-qualified and impressive in other ways. This, however, was widely seen as an internal Conservative problem, the once-vibrant tradition of left-Labour hostility to the EEC having almost vanished. Consequently, hostility to the EU came to be seen as the distinctive mark of a kind of hopelessly reactionary Conservative sensibility that was holding the party back and preventing it from mounting an effective challenge to New Labour.

It was at this point, with anti-EU sentiment seen as a single issue of interest only to cranks, most of them reactionary Tories, that UKIP began to slowly emerge, though not yet as a serious political force. The party had been founded in 1991 at the start of the Conservative Party's ructions over Maastricht, by Alan Sked, adopting the name UKIP in 1993. Initially therefore it grew out of Conservative politics and most of its activists and leading figures came from that party. After the collapse of the Referendum Party in 1997 (following the death of its leader and funder, Sir James Goldsmith) it was the only party available to unreconciled opponents of EU membership who could not vote bring themselves to vote Conservative. At first its electoral performance was typical of a fringe party – it got 6.5% of the vote in the 1999 European Parliament elections but fell back to 1.5% in the 2001 UK General Election. At this point it was still very much a bolt hole for a certain kind of disaffected Conservative. However, in the 2004 European Parliament elections it got 2.6 million votes (16.1% of the total) and came third in share of the vote. In the subsequent UK General Election of 2005, it fell back to 2.2% of the vote, although it did manage to get over 5% in 40 seats. At this point it was still seen as very much a single-issue party, which people would vote for at European elections but not in domestic contests. However, there were several points to note about its position and support at that time. It had started to attract the attention of significant political investors who gave it large donations, more than a fringe party would normally expect. Its surge in support in EU elections showed that already membership of the EU was becoming a significant symbolic issue for voters disaffected from the mainstream on the emerging issue of identity, even though they were not yet prepared to translate that into votes at a General Election. Most importantly, the vote in the 2004 Euro election showed the first signs that it was getting votes from people other than a certain kind of disaffected Tory voter as it performed well in the Midlands and parts of the North (Ford and Goodwin, 2014).

At the same time, after 2001, the first signs manifested of a decay in the loyalty of traditional Labour voters to their party. In 2001, although Labour won comfortably, there was little enthusiasm and there was a widespread decline in vote share and majority size in many of their safest seats. This slide continued over the next decade in the same seats. In fact, Labour's national share of the vote declined at every election from 2001 to 2015. Slowly but steadily, older traditional Labour voters, mostly living in safe seats in the old industrial and mining areas of the country, were abandoning the Party. Many of them could not bring themselves to vote Conservative, as the memory of the 1980s, and the miners' strike were too fresh. Instead, many simply stopped voting. From around 2004 onwards some of them began to vote for other parties, at least in non-Westminster elections. At this point the competition for such disaffected voters was between UKIP and the explicitly far-right British National Party. This fact itself reveals the main driver of the growing alienation of traditional Labour voters: it was not so much economics as questions of culture and identity which were increasingly captured by the two specific questions of EU membership and immigration – with those two issues being conflated for many by the Blair Government's policy on migration after EU enlargement in 2004. The November of that year also saw one other early signal of a disconnection between the New Labour project and Labour heartland voters, which was significant as much for the people involved as anything else. This was the referendum in North-East England on whether to set up a regional assembly. This was a part of the Blair Government's constitutional reform agenda (meant to deal with the big problem with proposals for a federal UK, the overwhelming predominance in population of England). At the referendum the proposal was overwhelmingly rejected by 78% to 22%, effectively killing the idea and stopping further constitutional change. The leading figure in the No campaign was someone who would go on to be a key force in the 2016 referendum – Dominic Cummings.

After 2005 UKIP, still essentially a fringe Conservative group, was competing for the emerging bloc of nationalist working-class voters with the BNP. In 2006 Nigel Farage, who had been the most prominent figure in the party for some time, became leader (he was the first UKIP candidate to save his deposit, in 2001). He consolidated support from important donors and began the process of making the party more than a single issue one by giving it a more rounded and extensive range of policies. At this point the policy suite was still clearly aimed at Thatcherite Conservatives as it combined free markets with social conservatism, along with the core principles of traditional national identity and hostility to the EU. The political context for this move was David Cameron's becoming Conservative leader in 2005 after the Party's third successive defeat. Just as Blair had responded to the Labour Party's four defeats by moving to the liberal end of the economics axis, so Cameron's prescription was to move the Conservatives to the liberal end of the social axis. So, as explained in the previous chapter, both main parties now converged on the upper right quadrant of the voters. Farage's initial project was to voice the views of the voters in the lower right quadrant who were left behind by this, asserting the values of nationalism and social conservatism that Cameron was abandoning. This paid off at the 2009 Euro Election, when UKIP gained 16.5% of the vote, with 2.5 million voters, placing it second overall. Once again though there was a falling back at the subsequent General Election of 2010, with the party getting 3.1% of the vote and 919,471 votes in total. This was though the best GE performance so far.

More significantly, the geographical and social distribution of votes in 2009 and 2015 showed that UKIP had a growing appeal to disaffected Labour voters, as well as to Conservatives who did not like their own party's move to technocratic liberalism. The issue that proved to have crossover appeal was immigration. This expressed the rising anxiety about identity and cultural security that was shared by voters in both of the lower quadrants, by Old Tory and Old Labour voters. The BNP had now collapsed as a serious political force (after Farage had refused categorically to cooperate with them) and so there was no competitor on the scene for the largely working-class voters who had been quietly abandoning Labour over the previous decade. The response of Farage and UKIP was to target those ex-Labour voters, by downplaying the Thatcherite economics (one of the findings of surveys was that most UKIP voters were actually left-of-centre on economics), while emphasising nationalism and cultural politics. In that connection, Farage's public image as a beer drinking smoker was astute politics. It attracted derision from the media but sent a message to the voters he was targeting, that he rejected the prim and censorious lifestyle politics that had become an important part of technocratic liberalism and the consensus. It was at this point, after 2010, that UKIP clearly transitioned from being a fringe party for disaffected Conservatives, into something new, a 'populist insurgency' in the words of the best study of the phenomenon (Ford and Goodwin, 2014). In other words, it became Britain's equivalent of the kind of politics that realignment was producing in most of Europe, a national collectivist politics that was based on the new division of identity, combined with expressing hostility to economic globalism.

The new identity that UKIP developed after 2010 soon started to pay electoral dividends. It reflected and articulated an actual emergent political position and set of opinions that was widespread in certain parts of the country, as much as 20% of the electorate according to some studies. This was not a matter of UKIP or its funders creating that body of opinion. It grew out of actual experience on the part of many voters and as a reaction to the convergent and exhausted politics of the noughties. What UKIP and Farage, an astute political entrepreneur, did was to identify that increasingly coherent political position and set of voter preferences and provide them with a vehicle through which they could find expression. In 2012 the party regularly recorded support as high as 10% in national opinion polls. In 2013 it went on to a strong performance in local elections with an average vote share of 23% in the wards it stood in and a rise in its number of elected councillors from 4 to 147. There were further gains in local elections in 2014. However, the big breakthrough came in the Euro elections of that year when UKIP topped the poll with 27.5% of the vote. It was at that election that UKIP came close to the sweet spot of UK electoral politics by having a vote distribution that was both large enough and sufficiently concentrated. It came first or second in all of the seventy-two council areas that made up the North of England and also did well in traditionally conservative areas of the South and East and South West. It did much less well in Scotland, London and the major metropolitan areas. Geographically it did well in coastal areas and small towns.

At this point UKIP had become a serious political force and posed an important challenge to both of the established main parties, which was also an opportunity for both of them. This became very clear with the two by-elections that were held simultaneously on 9th October of 2014. In Clacton, a rundown seaside town in Essex, the sitting Conservative MP, Douglas Carswell, switched to UKIP and then resigned to trigger a by-election, which he won handsomely. More striking and ultimately significant was the vote in the once-safe Labour seat of Heywood and Middleton in Greater Manchester. Here the UKIP vote went from 2.6% at the previous General Election to 38.7%. The Labour majority was reduced from a solid 5,971 (12.9%) to a narrow 617 (2.2%). Taken together these results were a huge warning sign to both major parties, but particularly the Labour Party. The second was particularly surprising as the two polls taken in the constituency both indicated that UKIP would come in second (as it had in another Greater Manchester by-election earlier that year) but Labour would still have a comfortable winning margin of 19%. This serious underestimation of both Labour's slide and UKIP's surge was partly a reflection of the technical difficulty of doing constituency polls but was more because they missed the late decision of people who had previously not voted to vote this time. In other words, they underestimated the attractiveness of UKIP to the disillusioned Labour voters who had drifted away from the Party into non-voting.

It is worth putting the scale of UKIP's electoral rise after 2009 into perspective. Quite simply this was the largest rise by a new party since the 1920s. Its performance in the 2013 local elections was the best by a party other than Conservative, Labour or Liberal since 1945 and this was repeated the following year. Its first place finish in the 2014 Euro elections was also the first time that a party other than Labour or Conservative had topped a UK-wide election since the 1920s while its increase in vote share in Heywood and Middleton was the seventh largest ever recorded in a by-election. A rise in support on this scale was not simply a transient phenomenon, even if it took the form of what was still a protest vote. What was the nature of this phenomenon though? It was not simple populism. In its early phase before 2010 UKIP was compared to the 1950s French Poujadist movement, which was accurate at the time, but by 2009-10 voting for UKIP was about more than simple hostility to the elite and the system. It had acquired a more definite ideological content. It was the increasingly electorally effective expression of a new political identity that came from an emergent social interest, one that combined social conservatism and a focus on national identity with a mixture of free markets in some areas and economic interventionism in others. This was close to the middle of the lower half of Table 3 and was a pitch that appealed to both National Liberal and National Collectivist voters. In more conventional terms this was a political alliance between Conservative voters who disliked the social liberalism of David Cameron and Labour voters who also disliked the social liberalism while both were very much on the nationalist (and hence anti-EU) side and hostile to the lifestyle politics of the technocratic consensus. The success of this new formation was still constrained however, by the residual historic loyalties of both sets of voters (and the fear in a FPTP system of giving victory to their least favoured option by voting for your first choice), and by the continuing attachment of Farage and other leaders to Thatcherite economics. This was diminishing but not fast enough for the British electoral system.

The 2015 Election and the Decision to Call a Referendum

The General Election of 2010 had seen very large seat gains by the Conservatives but not enough for them to get a majority. The result was the formation of a coalition government between them and the Liberal Democrats. With hindsight the latter would have been better off entering into a 'confidence and supply' agreement in which they undertook to support the government on votes of confidence and money bills while reserving the right to vote against any particular measures or bills. This would have preserved a separate identity for them. In the event they did not and in some sense, it was inevitable they would not. The Coalition government was the final, quintessential expression of the technocratic liberal consensus that had grown up since the previous realignment in the 1970s, socially liberal while 'neoliberal' in economics, strongly supportive of supranational ventures and organisations, and committed to political management of lifestyle choices. The Liberal Democrats defined themselves as the centre of the spectrum of the older alignment, between Labour and Conservative so they had no real principled reason to not support a coalition that would continue the consensus that had finally emerged. This meant that opposition to that consensus began to find a focus, as the consensus was now embodied in a coalition government. On the Left, under Ed Miliband, the Labour Party began to explore departures from the economic aspect of that consensus, with support for a larger economic role for government: they remained strongly supportive of its other aspects however. The context for this was, of course, the huge financial crisis of 2008 and its aftermath. This was, or should have been, a massive blow to the common understanding of the 'neoliberal' consensus in economics but it led in reality to a reassertion of orthodoxy in a programme of fiscal restraint or austerity as it became known. Not surprisingly this began to produce a hostile response from the left and centre-left.

On the right meanwhile, as well as the continuing unhappiness of social conservatives with the social liberalism of the Coalition, there was a belief that the crisis actually resulted from government interference in the monetary system and that the response should actually be a more radical market approach in some ways. At the same time however voters on the right also began to think about government becoming more active, although in different ways to those being explored on the left. The most striking development on the right under the Coalition, however, was an increasingly intense hostility to the radical identity politics of the left. Because the Conservative Party was in government, this all took the form within the party of rebellions and discontent among its MPs and grassroots and a growing propensity by Conservative voters to support UKIP, at least in Euro and local elections. Meanwhile as described, more Labour (or more precisely, ex-Labour) voters also turned in that direction. For the Conservatives this was a serious threat but also an opportunity. They had the problem of losing votes to UKIP from their own base. In the South this did not matter too much because most of their seats were safe. In the Midlands and North however this could be very costly as it could tip seats to Labour or at least stop the Conservatives winning the seats they needed to gain in those regions if they were to have any chance of converting their largest party status into an actual majority. On the other hand, if Labour was losing votes to UKIP in its core seats (as the local and Euro elections, and the Heywood by-election indicated) then this could hamper them and, if the loss of votes was sufficiently one directional, even tip some seats in the Conservative direction. If UKIP gained mostly the kind of ex-Labour voter who would never vote Conservative but did not take too many voters who were Conservative or prepared to vote for them, then its rise could actually redound to the Conservative Party's benefit. Moreover, the possibility was that voting UKIP could be a 'gateway drug' for actually voting Conservative for disaffected Labour voters, provided the Tories came up with policy positions that addressed their concerns. The Labour Party for its part did not see UKIP or the sentiments it represented as too much of a threat, reflecting the insouciance of its leadership and also much of its membership. Faced with this challenge from UKIP and a serious tension within their own ranks the Conservative Party went into the 2015 General Election with a pledge to renegotiate the United Kingdom's membership and then hold a referendum on the question of whether or not the UK should stay in the EU. The thinking was that this would keep enough Conservative voters who would otherwise vote UKIP on board (given the realistic alternative was a hung Parliament or a Labour government) while leaving UKIP to get the votes of people who cared about Europe more than any other issue among Tory voters and picking up votes from Labour and weakening them. The first threat was a serious one as there had been a large-scale rebellion by Tory MPs in 2011 over the question of having a referendum on the Lisbon Treaty (which the party had committed to in its 2005 manifesto but not delivered). The reasons behind the decision to promise a referendum are much misunderstood, and the common misunderstandings reflect the lack of understanding of what was going on in UK political life that would become even more apparent after 2016.

The Realignment in Scotland

Meanwhile though, the realignment of politics was well under way in Scotland. Since before the Blair years the Conservative Party had been destroyed as an effective political choice in Scotland, which left the Labour Party in a hegemonic position, with Scotland close to being a one-party state. In the first Election for the Scottish Parliament in 1999 they won 56 seats, just nine short of a majority. The SNP had its best performance since the 1970s, coming second with 35 seats. This was repeated in 2003 but both the Labour Party and the SNP lost support. The gainers were the Green Party and the new Scottish Socialist Party. This, like the decline in Labour votes in England, reflected a discontent on the part of Labour voters with the move towards a more economically liberal position under Blair – the Scottish Government was a coalition of Labour and Liberal Democrats that was a classic expression of the New Labour politics. Scottish public opinion is slightly but clearly to the left of English on economic matters and this was reflected in a left insurgence, which found representation because of the Scottish Parliament's being elected by PR. However, the Labour-Liberal Democrat coalition remained in office. After 2003 things began to move, just as they did in England, but the form this shift took was different. In 2004 Alex Salmond, who had been leader of the SNP previously between 1990 and 2000, regained the leadership of the party. He adopted (or rather revived) a strategy of orienting the party as clearly left-of-centre (so putting it in line with the bulk of Scottish voters) but at the same time nationalist and so expressing a distinctive and particular national identity. His key move was to redefine that identity. Scottishness was defined in opposition to the British identity of the United Kingdom but located firmly in a European context. This produced a left-wing form of national populism, in which the assertion of national identity was actually combined with support for the supranational politics of the EU and a reasserted social democracy. This was captured in the masterful slogan of 'Independence in Europe.' It meant that the SNP could now appeal to the kind of disaffected Labour voters who were toying with or actually voting for UKIP south of the Border, while at the same time holding on to those who while supporting independence were not so clearly left on economics.

This paid big dividends in the 2007 Scottish Parliament elections. The SNP replaced the Labour Party as the largest single party and went on to form a minority government. The Green and Scottish Socialist parties were swept aside and there was a significant movement of votes from Labour to SNP. At this point the question of separation from the UK versus Unionism clearly became the dominant issue in Scottish politics. The Labour Party's response to this challenge was not so much ineffectual as non-existent; they seemed simply unable to realise what was happening to their Scottish base. They did go on to remain the dominant Scottish party at Westminster in 2010, but in 2011 there was a political earthquake in Scotland – the first real event of the realignment. Despite the electoral system being designed to prevent a single party getting a majority, the SNP achieved that feat, going from 46 seats to 69. The Labour Party meanwhile, had its worst result in a Scottish election since 1931. Since then the SNP has dominated Scottish politics. To strike a personal note, at the time I was trying to explain to people in London where I worked what a total political transformation this was and how far-reaching its effects would be, but I did not find much interest, reflecting the lack of interest the overwhelmingly London-based political class had in Scottish matters (or for that matter North of England ones). During this entire period of Scottish political history from 1999 to 2011 the Scottish Conservatives had flatlined as a residual rump party – their seat scores at Holyrood during that time were 18 – 15 – 13 – 15. Faced with this clear breakthrough for the SNP the Coalition Government under David Cameron allowed a referendum to be held in Scotland on the question of independence, in 2014. The assumption was that this would result in an easy win for the Union option but on the 6th of September a poll showed a 2% lead for the Yes (pro-independence) side – this came after a series of polls that had shown support for that option rising from its historic ceiling of about 38% to around 45%. This led to mass panic in London, very entertaining but hardly edifying, with major party leaders going up to Scotland to plead with voters. The outcome in votes was a clear victory for the Union cause by 55.3% to 44.7% but this was much narrower than expected at the start of the campaign. Moreover, the campaign had completed what the 2011 SP election had started and realigned Scottish politics around the question of independence versus Unionism.

This emerging realignment in both England and Scotland found expression in the General Election of 2015. In Scotland the outcome was a catastrophe for the Labour Party. The SNP went from 6 seats to 56 (out of 59) and got 50.0% of the vote. The SNP had managed to get all of the 45% of Scottish voters who supported Independence to vote for them and that, given the electoral system and the division of the Unionist vote between three parties, gave them almost all of the seats.

The Labour Party lost all but one of its 41 Scottish seats, in many cases to swings never before recorded at any UK general election. This obliteration of the Labour Party in Scotland has transformed the UK political landscape in ways that the wider political class has still not grasped. In particular it makes it as near to impossible as it makes no difference for the Labour Party to win a Westminster majority. Logically the party should now move to supporting electoral reform as a central plank of its policy but that conversation has not even begun yet. The Scottish Conservatives still only had one Scottish seat but they now had an opportunity to become the focus for the other side of the new alignment in Scotland, the Unionist one, which they took once the election was over.

The Breakthrough of A New Alignment

In England meanwhile in 2015, UKIP gained 3.8 million votes in total, amounting to 12.6% of the total. This made them the clear third party in terms of vote share, even though the electoral system meant they only won a single seat, retaining Clacton. Their performance on a seat-by-seat basis saw them rise from an average of 3.6% of votes to 13.8%. They had a rise of more than 10% in 277 seats and came second in 120 constituencies. Their vote was slightly higher in Labour seats than Conservative ones, and that plus the geographical distribution of their vote showed that they drew their new votes almost evenly from Labour and Conservative, with a slight leaning to the former. If people had still been voting on economic policy grounds this would not have happened. However, the voting patterns in 2015 showed there already been a clear shift to voting on identity and cultural grounds, and the rise in UKIP's vote was a key indicator of this. Geographically they did badly in Scotland and London and a number of other places such as Bristol and Liverpool, but very well in the Midlands and the coastal regions, particularly the East coast.

The mirror image of this was the collapse of the self-defined centre, in the shape of the Liberal Democrats who only managed 8 seats and 7.9% of the vote, (down from 57 and 23% in 2010) the worst result for the Liberals in UK politics since 1970. A key factor was their massive loss of support among young graduates and students, formerly a key constituency for them. This was blamed on their policy reversal on the question of student tuition fees together with their participation in the austerity policy of the Coalition. Undoubtedly this was a major cause but as is often the case in politics, the issues had an effect because of the way they captured a deeper social trend. This was a shift to the left on economics among younger graduates, along with a clear move to the more radical end of the identity division. Younger graduates were moving into the upper left quadrant of Table 3. As such, they rejected the economic aspect of the technocratic liberal consensus and voted against the party that embodied it. The decline in the Liberal Democrat vote share was almost an exact mirror image of the rise in UKIP's and the obvious explanation would be that there had been a straight switch. In England and Wales what actually seems to have happened is that about half the 2010 Liberal voters switched to Labour, with a smaller number moving to the Conservatives. The gain to Labour from this was offset by a switch from Labour to UKIP and to a lesser extent the Conservatives. The Conservatives in turn lost votes to UKIP, which balanced out their gains from the Liberals and Labour. It was this movement of votes that produced the big surprise, a Conservative majority for the first time since 1992, when almost all expert opinion expected a hung Parliament. The shifts in votes reflected the workings of the early stage of the realignment, in ways that on this occasion on net helped the Conservatives while hindering Labour and destroying the Liberal Democrats.

In England and Wales, the net effect of the vote shift was that both the Conservatives and Labour improved their vote share very slightly. There was not a geographically uniform pattern of vote movements though. In Liberal seats outside Scotland there was a rise in Labour votes at their expense, which led to the Conservatives, whose vote held up without rising much, winning 27 seats from them. The Liberal

Democrats also lost 12 directly to Labour. In terms of the direct fight between Conservative and Labour the latter actually increased their share by slightly more and there was a positive swing from Conservative to Labour in 222 seats, compared to only 151 that saw a movement from Labour to Conservative. In seats where the two parties cancelled each other out, 9 seats went from Labour to Conservative and 10 the other way. There was a clear geographical and social pattern to these movements however. The Labour Party improved its position in more affluent and metropolitan areas, at the expense mainly of the Liberal Democrats. The problem was that because it started from a long way behind in those areas the rise in its vote did not translate into gains of seats in the UK's electoral system, and handed a swathe of mainly rural Liberal Democrat seats to the Tories. All but one of the seats they won from the Liberals themselves were either in metropolitan areas or had large numbers of university students and there was a similar pattern in their gains from the Conservatives. Their best region by far, where they significantly outperformed their results elsewhere, was the largest metropolitan area, London, where they made extensive gains and increased their share of the vote by 7% to 43.5%. What these figures show is that the Labour Party was becoming increasingly the party of the younger, educated, professional class, living in the major metropolitan areas and university hubs such as Cambridge. The reverse of this was that they went backwards in their traditional core, working-class seats because of voters shifting to both UKIP and the Tories. As a result, they suffered a number of spectacular losses, most notably the Shadow Chancellor Ed Balls being defeated in the solidly working-class Yorkshire seat of Morley and Outwood. In terms of the realignment described in the previous chapter, they were increasingly the party of the upper left quadrant, left on economics and on the cosmopolitan end of the new divide. The slow haemorrhage of older working-class votes in small towns had accelerated. UKIP had established itself as a serious political force even if it had not won any seats and it was in reality the main winner of the election, rather than David Cameron.

To summarise, the 2015 election saw the start of a realignment in England and Wales around the issue of identity and this produced a lot of vote switching. UKIP made a breakthrough in votes if not seats, articulating the position of those who combined a centre to centre-left view on economics with a nationalist and traditionalist view of identity (had they been further to the left on economics than they were, they could have done even better). This UKIP upsurge took votes equally from both the main parties but because the Labour defectors were more geographically concentrated, in smaller, ex-industrial towns and the coasts, it had a bigger impact on Labour, reducing many of their majorities and costing them several seats in their heartlands. The exhausted centre position of the old alignment effectively collapsed as voters increasingly divided on the new issue. This meant Liberal Democrat voters in London, Cambridge, Oxford, and other metropolitan and university towns switching in large numbers to Labour while their voters in places such as the South West (who were more on the national end of the new divide) moved to the Conservatives. The result was a wipeout for them but because of the way the electoral system worked it redounded mainly to the benefit of the Tories, who won enough seats from their erstwhile coalition partners to get a majority. Labour actually advanced significantly in London and some other areas, because of the shift of younger graduates' loyalties, but went back in the North and Midlands, where it had been slowly declining since 2001. The Conservatives came out as winners because their vote held up enough in the South to win large numbers of Liberal Democrat seats while only losing a few to Labour and picking up enough Labour seats in the North to counterbalance that.

From this it would seem that promising a renegotiation of EU membership and then a referendum had been a masterstroke. Indeed, in some ways it had. Why though had David Cameron made that pledge? A common perception among the UK's media class is that this was a frivolous act and an abdication of leadership. He had made this pledge, it is argued, in order to manage the internal party divisions over Europe and placate the restive Eurosceptic wing of the party. This seems plausible but is wrong. Although resolving the Tory party's internal divisions was one concern and goal it was not the major one. For one thing, Conservative divisions over the EU were no worse at that point than they had been for a long time and were less severe than at the peak of the controversy over the Maastricht Treaty under John Major. The decision to pledge a referendum was mainly driven by the need to respond to the voters, specifically those voters who were rallying in ever larger numbers behind UKIP. As explained before, the emergence of a genuine populist insurgency was both a threat and an opportunity for the Conservatives. The main concern though was with the potential threat. One of the great strengths of the Conservative party's position in British politics is its being the only significant party on the right of politics. By contrast, while the Labour Party was in that position from 1931 to the early 1960s, apart from then there has always been a divided vote on the left. It is of vital strategic importance for the Conservative Party that it does not face a real rival on its right. The rise of UKIP's politics threatened to lead to that, so it was hugely important to head that off. Promising a referendum was therefore a response to that threat, designed to mitigate it and as far as possible turn it to the Conservatives' advantage by limiting their own voting losses while allowing UKIP to damage the more explicitly pro-EU and anti-referendum Labour Party. It was the emerging realignment of voter preferences and divisions, as manifested in the surge of UKIP and the SNP and the collapse of the Liberal Democrats, that led to a referendum being promised. In the event David Cameron proved to be a lucky leader – the way the vote switches worked out on this occasion proved to be what he needed to pick up the seats he needed. The growth of the salience of a division in the UK electorate over the questions of national identity and independence (along with related issues such as immigration) had brought about a political situation in which promising a referendum to review and renew UK membership of the EU was the apparently smart thing to do. The election result showed the Conservatives had successfully ridden that wave – for now.

CHAPTER 3

THE REFERENDUM AND ITS RESULT

Why Go Through With It?

David Cameron and the Conservative Party had won the election of 2015 (rather to their surprise) and in the process of doing that had undertaken to renegotiate the UK's membership of the EU and then hold a referendum on whether, given the outcome of those negotiations, the UK should remain a member of the EU. It did not follow from that pledge that they actually had to do it–at one point previously while the Lisbon Treaty was being ratified they had promised a referendum on that before abandoning that promise in 2009 (following the ratification of the Treaty by the Czech Republic, which gave it force). A pledge made in a manifesto is rather more serious though, and politically costly to ignore. Granting that, it did not follow that the process of renegotiation and referendum had to be held immediately after the election, given that the Conservatives now had a majority. They chose not to wait and instead pressed on with presenting the necessary legislation to Parliament and opening negotiations with the EU as soon as the election was over. The legislation, the European Union Referendum Bill, was laid before Parliament on 28th May 2015, and passed its Second Reading two weeks later. Crucially, at that point all of the parties supported the Bill apart from the Scottish nationalists. This may seem strange, given the later behaviour of many of those MPs who had voted in favour of the Bill in 2015. In particular it might seem difficult to understand why the Labour Party, which had opposed the idea of a referendum during the election campaign, now reversed that position and supported the Bill's passing.

The Conservative Government's reasons for pressing on were straightforward and reflected their motives for making the pledge a part of their manifesto in the first place. It was about completing their so-far successful response to the challenges thrown up by the realignment. By getting things done as soon as possible they could see off the threat of UKIP, not allowing it time to continue its growth and to establish itself firmly as a party with organisation and the potential to threaten actual seats. A decisive outcome to the process that the Act provided for would not only, they hoped, remove the threat of populist politics, it would also lance the boil of internal party divisions and arguments that had troubled every leader since Thatcher, leaving them free to concentrate on their domestic policy agenda. The point of course was that while their actions were a response to the continuing progress of the realignment, that response was tactical and did not show that they really grasped what was happening in street level politics. Had they done so they would have realised that a renegotiation and referendum would not put the new issue of identity to bed, unless it produced a massively one-sided result, which the trends of opinion and rising salience of the issue meant it would not do. In this connection the Scottish Independence Referendum, which seems to have made Cameron more confident he could pull off a similar result, should have been a warning. There the referendum had accelerated and intensified a realignment around a new issue, Independence versus Unionism, and destroyed the Labour Party in Scotland in the process. The clear but not overwhelming victory for the status quo, when combined with the actual campaign, had energised and consolidated the Independence side. The dangers of something similar happening in the case of the EU referendum should have been clear and were in fact raised by the Chancellor, George Osborne, who argued against proceeding with the referendum. Cameron, and the majority of the leadership were confident that they could see off this threat.

The Labour Party's reasons for reversing their position and supporting the Bill were more interesting. In the first place, they had suffered their second consecutive severe defeat in a General Election, all the more stinging for being unexpected. Despite their improvements in some areas, they had gone backwards where it mattered in terms of seats, to their worst level since 1987. Some of their members might console themselves by looking at their local advances but that was like football fans seeking solace in their team's having had more possession when the harsh reality was that they had lost 3-0. Most of the Labour MPs had a more realistic view, and were shaken by the way their personal position had in many cases deteriorated sharply. During the campaign while meeting actual voters many had been impressed by the degree of disaffection with the Labour party in its so-called heartlands. In particular, they had noticed the level of hostility to the EU and concern about immigration among Labour supporters, which had led many to switch to UKIP. They had suddenly realised the threat that 'right-wing populism' (as it was usually called) posed to them and they knew it would be politically very damaging for them to resist a referendum. However like the Conservatives, they still did not grasp the fundamental nature of the change underway among the electorate and saw it as a temporary upsurge of concern about those issues, which a referendum could resolve – again the Scottish experience should have convinced them something more serious was going on, but they did not see what was happening in England and Wales as comparable.

The shared factor therefore was that the parties knew there was a popular demand and upsurge of concern about a range of issues that were symbolically united in the question of EU membership but did not realise the extent of that sentiment or the way it reflected a profound change of priorities and therefore political identification among about two thirds of voters. Had they done so they would have realised how risky, from their point of view, having a referendum would be. However, they did see enough of what was happening, thanks to the rise of UKIP, to realise that something had to be done. What they all assumed as a simple and obvious reality was that in any referendum the British public would vote decisively to stay in the EU. Only a few thought it might even be close; most expected a clearcut win for the Remain side. This confidence showed the group thinking and lack of contact with large parts of British society that was to be a persistent feature of the British political and media establishment. In particular, as the campaign was to show, they did not grasp what many voters were now mainly worried about and motivated by. It is worth noting that the Liberal Democrats and the Green MP Caroline Lucas all supported the referendum bill. In their case this was a principled commitment as they had consistently supported a referendum on the Lisbon Treaty but once again, they also had a blithe confidence that the 'right' side would win. One important aspect of this, which was hardly raised at the time, was that there was no requirement for either a minimum turnout or a supermajority (both of which are common requirements for a referendum result to have effect in political systems that make regular use of them). After the event there was much wailing and gnashing of teeth about this, but at the time the prospect of a vote to leave was thought to be so remote that nobody was exercised.

The Renegotiations and the Election of Jeremy Corbyn

David Cameron's strategy began to go wrong almost as soon as the Referendum Act had passed. What he hoped for was sufficient concessions from the EU leaders for him to be able to argue convincingly that the EU had taken account of the UK's detachment from, and unhappiness with, the direction of its development since at least 2001. In particular he was looking for concessions on the question of freedom of movement within the EU, because of its relevance to the pressing domestic issue of immigration. The EU leaders, and in particular the dominant figure of Angela Merkel, were not minded to cooperate, however. The logic of the renegotiations and the British Government's position was for the UK to be given a distinctly different type of membership (perhaps styled as 'associate' to avoid the derogatory implications of 'second tier') in which it would continue the economic integration of the single market regime, and cooperation on other issues on a case-by-case basis, while not participating in the political structures created by the Lisbon Treaty (the UK already had opt-outs from some provisions of that Treaty, as well as some from provisions of the Maastricht Treaty, notably Euro membership). This would have accurately reflected the UK's historic view of EU membership as a pragmatic economic deal and the continued ambivalence or outright hostility of much of the UK's population and political class to the wider European project. However, the other EU leaders would not even entertain this idea, for good reasons from their perspective. To create a novel kind of membership of the kind described for the UK would create a dangerous and destabilising precedent that could well end up undermining or unravelling the entire project embarked on at Maastricht and Lisbon. Once granted to the UK there was the risk that other member states might also seek that status and in almost every member state there were rising political forces (such as the Front National in France for example) that would advocate such a status for their own country. The danger was that instead of being an exceptional status for the UK to resolve its distinctive problems, it would set in train a process that would transform the EU into something like Charles de Gaulle's idea of a 'Europe des Patries' rather than the much closer and integrated political union aimed at since Maastricht.

There was a similar problem with the single topic of migration within the EU (which was what the renegotiation looked at). The difficulty here was that the Single Market regulatory regime, itself a largely British creation, had freedom of movement of labour as one of its four central features (the others were freedom of movement of capital and of goods, and freedom of trade in services). To allow one state to opt out of one of the four while continuing to participate in the others would again create a very dangerous precedent, with other countries also trying to cherry pick in the same way. The end result would be the dissolution of the whole Single Market regime, one of the EU's greatest achievements. The leaders of the post-communist states in Eastern and Central Europe were particularly opposed because of the importance of free movement to their economies. In addition, most of the leaders of the other longstanding EU members found the UK's problems with migration within the EU baffling (they understood perfectly disquiet about immigration from outside the EU as that was a political challenge that they all faced). Other EU countries were able to manage EU migration through rules about residential and employment rights, in particular a widespread rule that you could not stay in another member state for more than a strictly limited time unless you had a long-term employment contract. They could do this because they had national identity cards and rules about recording residence and address that made enforcement relatively simple. The UK could not do this because it did not have those legal institutions – the Blair government had wanted to introduce identity cards but had fallen foul of the visceral opposition of a large part of British society to the very idea of compulsory ID. So, on grounds of both principle and irritated incomprehension there was no prospect of any offer being made on migration.

This meant that David Cameron did not get a convincing or dramatic alteration to the UK's terms of membership, which he could point to as addressing the concerns of many voters (and not just those who had voted for UKIP). He did not even get anything like the more limited concessions he had been asking for. This outcome also had a profound impact on the kinds of arguments that the Remain side felt able to make during the referendum campaign. The effective failure of the renegotiations, even as theatre, never mind substance, meant the whole process had started on the wrong foot from a political sales point of view. In retrospect some European leaders regretted that they had not shown greater flexibility and helped Cameron more but, like everyone else, they could not conceive that a country would actually choose to exit the EU, no matter how discontented its voters might be.

While this failed renegotiation was going on something else

happened, which was to have a profound influence on the subsequent course of events and is also best understood through the lens of realignment – the election of Jeremy Corbyn as Labour Leader. This was another of those events that dumbfounded respectable opinion, taking it completely by surprise. Since as far back as Neil Kinnock's leadership the radical left of the Labour Party had been marginalised, a small group of MPs and party members who guarded the flame of socialist purity but had no impact on the wider party, its leadership, or its policy. This was even more the case under Tony Blair and Gordon Brown and remained the case under Ed Miliband, despite his slight tack to the left on economics. Jeremy Corbyn was first elected to Parliament in 1983, at the peak of the Left's influence on the Labour Party. Throughout his time in Parliament he had remained loyal to the views he had espoused then. These were a combination of radical but rather traditional state socialism, radical egalitarianism, and a view of the world that saw the foreign policy of the Western powers in general and the United States in particular as the source of most of the trouble and conflict in the world. The last of these, radical anti-imperialism as it could be called, led him throughout his career up to this point to be very sceptical of the European Union – he saw it as a capitalist or neoliberal ramp and a key part of the Western global system. During the years he had ploughed a lonely furrow as one of the few clearly left-wing figures in the Parliamentary Labour Party he had also become involved in the kind of radical identity politics that was developing on university campuses and among graduates, although this was never a major interest of his. When Ed Miliband resigned following his election defeat Corbyn was thought by most observers to have no chance of becoming leader but a structural reality plus chance gave him the opportunity.

The structural feature was the hollowing out of the Labour Party described in the previous chapter. Since Blair became leader the party (like its Conservative opponents) had come to be dominated by professional politicians and its grassroots membership had shrivelled away. It had become a shell party, with the apparatus and staff of a professional party and a large number of MPs but few members compared to its past history – it had had a million members at its peak in the 1950s. Throughout the 2010s the membership had been stable at around 200,000. In 2010 Ed Miliband introduced the category of registered supporter, where for a fee of just £3 you could be put on a list as a supporter who could be called upon when needed and, crucially as it turned out, acquire the right to vote in elections for party leader. This was a shell party that, like a shell company, was ripe for takeover. The contingent factor, which has a darkly comical aspect, was this. Under the rules of the Labour Party at the time a candidate for leader had to be nominated by a threshold number of MPs to enter the competition. There were at this point so few Labour MPs of Corbyn's persuasion that although it was his turn to be the left's standard bearer he did not have enough nominations (a similar problem had faced another member of the left, John McDonnell, when he wanted to run against Gordon Brown after Tony Blair stepped down). In the event a number of centre and centre-left MPs nominated Jeremy Corbyn so that he got over that hurdle. They did so of course in the confident expectation that he would stand no chance of winning – they simply thought his tendency within the party deserved a chance to be heard and defeated.

In the event Corbyn's candidacy sparked off wild enthusiasm, much to his own surprise. What followed was a massive rush by his supporters to join the party outright or sign up as £3 supporters. The party's membership more than doubled, to well over four hundred thousand. When the results were announced in September of 2015, Corbyn received 59.5% of the votes cast. In actual numbers 422,664 votes were cast in total, 245,520 by individual members, 71,546 by members of affiliated organisations, and 105,598 by registered supporters. The number of people joining the party continued to increase, rising to over half a million. This was a remarkable result by any metric. It came as a stunning shock to the great majority of the party's MPs. More to the point, it transformed the Labour Party outside Parliament. Essentially, after the 2015 leadership election it was a new party. It still had the name and label of the Labour Party and a connection with that party and its past, through the trade unions and affiliated organisations, but in vital respects it was a new party that had the same name but a transformed identity. What kind of party had it suddenly become?

The key fact was that apart from the massive reality of the unions it was no longer a traditional working-class party. It had become instead a metropolitan, predominantly London-based party with a membership that was overwhelmingly made up of younger middle-class professionals. Many of these soon became organised, in the shape of the Momentum organisation, formed by veteran left-wingers to support Jeremy Corbyn against his stunned critics and opponents. This change in the nature of the Labour Party should be seen as an important part of the realignment process, although a fortuitous one. The Labour Party had quite abruptly become the political vehicle for the economically left part of the rising social formation of graduate metropolitans. This kind of process was taking place across Europe but in other countries it took the form of a rising vote by the same kinds of voters for far-left or left-populist parties (such as Syriza in Greece or Podemos in Spain) at the expense of traditional social democratic ones. In the UK, with its different electoral system that kind of shift was much more difficult – the Green Party was a possible vehicle but it was a serious force in just a handful of seats. So that aspect of the realignment, the movement of a large part of the metropolitan graduate class into the upper left quadrant of Table 3, took the form of a sudden movement of a large number of people into a hollowed out established party. The trigger for this was contingent and accidental but that illustrates the way structural and contingent factors interact in social and political change.

Why though had so many of these younger voters across Europe moved in that direction and why in the UK in particular had there been such a shift, revealed in the 2015 pattern of voting as well as the Corbyn surge? It might seem strange, given that this social group is employed in the networked and globalised part of the economy that is apparently most successful, and live in the large globalised hub cities such as London and Paris that are streaking ahead of the peripheral parts of countries such as the UK and France. Many of them, however, face increasing difficulties as a result of the way the world economy and the labour and property markets of large metropolitan areas are developing both before and since the financial crisis of 2008. The meritocratic labour market is increasingly overproducing qualified graduates for the number of positions available and this, together with technological and regulatory changes, is making employment in the growing sectors of the metropolitan economies more precarious and hence stressful. This is likely to get worse, because automation and the growth of artificial intelligence is predicted to eliminate whole swathes of white collar and professional employment, while leaving manual labour relatively unscathed. The other major problem for this demographic is the real estate market in globally networked metropoles. These markets are increasingly dysfunctional, partly because of restrictive planning laws that benefit the established and older residents by preventing enough new building, but also because of the way real estate in such locations has become a key saving and investment good for transnational capital. This means that the housing market in cities such as London is increasingly driven at the margin by global capital flows rather than local demand, and this severely weakens the connection between the prices of accommodation and local pay levels. This became much more pronounced after the resort to quantitative easing after 2008, which pumped large amounts of highly liquid credit into the world monetary system. The result, of steadily rising rents and house prices in major metropolitan areas, is yet another massive stress for the younger inhabitants of these places. This, along with their perception of their economic position as exploited and precarious, drives many of them to an economically left position. Simultaneously, their cultural perspective, formed again by their everyday experience, and ideas they were exposed to at university, leads them to be strongly on the cosmopolitan end of the new emerging division and also to espouse a very radical form of personal identity politics. In the British context this meant that in general they were very strongly pro-Remain. This, and Corbyn's ambivalent position on EU membership, combined with his effect on voters who did not share his beliefs, were to play a major part in later events.

The Referendum – a Tale of Three (and a Half) Campaigns

The detailed story of the Brexit referendum campaign has been told in several books, one of the best being *All Out War* by Tim Shipman (Shipman, 2017). The day-to-day details of the campaign are not the focus here; rather we will look at the way the form and content of the campaign reflected the realignment going on in British politics and the successes and failures of the two sides in realising what was happening and taking advantage of it. The Leave side was clearly more successful – or at least part of it was. The Referendum Act provided for there to be two official campaign organisations. On the Remain side this was Britain Stronger in Europe, set up in October 2015. On the other side the official imprimatur was given to Vote Leave. However, there was another, rival, Leave organisation, Leave.eu. In one sense the division between the two was a party one, with Vote Leave involving a number of Conservative figures and Leave.eu ones from UKIP but the real division was one of personality and also message and method. During the campaign the hostility and tension between the two Leave organisations was remarkable, with considerable personal animosity. This should have helped the Remain campaign, which also had the advantage of support from most of the British establishment. On the Conservative side, although the party was officially neutral, 25 of the 30 members of the Cabinet endorsed Remain, as did 198 of the 330 Conservative MPs (by contrast on the Labour side only 10 endorsed Leave). All of the leading figures in the Government fronted the Remain campaign. The business community was overwhelmingly pro-Remain, with over 200 leading figures including the CEOs of 35 of the FTSE 100 firms signing a letter to the Times urging a Remain vote. Many large firms openly endorsed or supported Remain, including Airbus, Black Rock, J.P. Morgan, Microsoft, and Rolls Royce. As several of the names suggest, the larger part by far of the UK's financial services sector and the City of London supported Remain. The overwhelming majority of trade unions supported Remain, with the railway unions the only notable exception. Most striking though was the support that the Remain side had from the worlds of art and the media and the 'great and good.' Among the many letters sent expressing support for the

Remain side were ones signed by 200 healthcare professionals (Times 4/4/16), over 150 members of the Royal Society (Times 9/3/16), over 100 University Vice Chancellors (Times 25/4/16), 300 major names in the creative industries (Times 20/5/16), 279 economists (Times, 24/5/16), over 300 leading lawyers (Times 29/2/16), and 300 prominent historians (Guardian 24/5/16). In addition, there were letters signed by 10 Nobel Prize winners in Economics and by 13 winners of science Nobel Prizes.

By contrast, the open supporters of Leave were a much more eclectic bunch. No major party endorsed that side, although 132 Conservative MPs and 5 members of the Cabinet did so. There were a number of prominent business figures, such as Sir James Dyson, but there was no clear section of the UK's business class that supported Leave despite arguments to the contrary by conspiracy theorists. What if anything united the public figures on the Leave side, whether from business or the arts and creative industry, was simply unorthodoxy, whether in business or culture. On the other side what was striking was the way the strongly Remain interests were parts of the social and economic formations that had become dominant over the previous forty years or so; most of finance, globally connected businesses, higher education, globalised science and media, and the creative arts and industries. A common argument (particularly after the result from Remain supporters) was that the Leave side had a disproportionate advantage in media support. Quite simply this was untrue. The major television channels were all neutral and despite heated charges of bias from both sides this was true. The same was true for radio. In the print medium Leave had an advantage in terms of the readership numbers of the major titles supporting it but there were still several major titles from across the conventional left to right supporting Remain, such as the Times, Guardian, and Daily Mirror. The major local newspapers were all either strongly Remain or neutral and all of the Scottish media supported Remain.

Despite the advantage of arguing for the status quo (which normally wins in referenda) and having this overwhelming establishment support there was a general view, even before the votes were counted, that the Remain campaign was badly organised and ineffectual. In some ways this was harsh and reflected the expectation that it would win easily, so when the polls, while still showing a Remain lead, showed a much tighter vote than most had expected there was a feeling that the campaign had missed an open goal. The reality was that the Remain side had a much more difficult fight to win than many thought at the time. The big structural problem it faced was the long-term hostility to the EU of a large part of the public and the lack of a widespread enthusiasm for the EU project. Opinion polls taken over many years before the referendum was even thought of showed there was a persistent 35% or so of voters who would vote to leave the EU. On the other side only about 20% were strongly and enthusiastically committed to EU membership as a matter of principle in and of itself. The largest part of the UK electorate, the remaining 45%, supported EU membership on grudging pragmatic grounds, as an economic arrangement that brought economic and other benefits. This meant that the Remain campaign could not make an argument built around the positive case for keeping EU membership as a good in itself, because that would not appeal to enough voters and would energise their opponents. In addition, the failure of David Cameron's renegotiation efforts meant they could not make a case for a type of participation in the EU project that would appeal to the many mildly to strongly sceptical voters in the 40%. That left them with economic prudence as the only basis on which they could argue. Because they were defending the status quo they could not frame the argument as being about economic benefits that would come in the future from EU membership (as would have been the case had they been making the case for joining), they could only argue that existing benefits would be lost if the UK exited.

The whole Remain campaign therefore had to be negative and minatory, focused on the potential downside and costs of leaving. This 'Project Fear' as its critics called it, was more effective than many realised but it had a huge problem to overcome. The 2008 financial crisis did not work to the benefit of the Remain side as one might have imagined, because that event had seriously discredited expert forecasters in the minds of the public – a point made in a much criticised but accurate comment by Justice Secretary Michael Gove when he remarked that the British public were fed up with experts who were always wrong. Consequently, the warnings from experts like the signatories to the various letters to the Times were discounted or ignored. The response was to ramp up the volume of the warnings and make them even more strident, but this was highly counterproductive as it made the public (or at least the critical target groups) even more sceptical. The major exceptions were Scotland and Northern Ireland but in those two cases the argument about EU membership was also intertwined with ones about the status of both Scotland and Northern Ireland relative to the rest of the UK. In both cases support for the EU was aligned with support for separation from the UK and this meant the kind of identity-motivated voters who in England and Wales leaned strongly towards Leave were Remain-oriented instead. This together with concern about economic costs (particularly in the Irish case) gave a clear advantage to Remain in both Scotland and Northern Ireland.

Another feature of the Remain campaign, which attracted comment at the time, was the minor part played in it by the Labour Party – or at least the leadership of the Party. The Parliamentary Labour Party was overwhelmingly and strongly for Remain, with only a small number of MPs carrying on the once widespread tradition of left-wing hostility to the EU. One of them, Gisela Stewart, was given a prominent place in the Vote Leave campaign, because of that campaign's judgment that while there were only a few Labour MPs who supported Leave, there were many Labour voters who still did so and they were a key constituency to win over. This proved to be completely correct. Jeremy Corbyn had been a strong sceptic where the EU was concerned throughout his time in Parliament since his election on a platform that included leaving the EEC (as it then was) in 1983. There was a widespread suspicion that he still had this view and was in fact a closet Leaver. Whatever the truth of that, his conduct during the campaign and immediately afterwards gave it credence for many. In marked contrast to his performance in the election that was held a year later, in 2017, he did very little campaigning and what he did do was lowkey and low impact. (He actually went on holiday during the campaign). The leadership office and central machinery of the party was not deployed to mobilise members in an active and coordinated campaign so although individual Labour politicians campaigned actively and passionately for the Remain case, there was no real sense that this was a key issue for the party or that it was making a big effort to get the voters it could reach behind a Remain vote. Corbyn himself, when asked during the campaign how he would evaluate the EU said that he would give it seven out of ten. While honest, this did not inspire enthusiasm or indicate it.

Leaving aside any private sympathies he may have had, there were actually good reasons for his position. The Scottish independence referendum two years before was widely thought to have severely damaged the Labour Party in Scotland because of the reaction of left-wing Scottish voters to the spectacle of Labour politicians appearing on the same platform as Tory ones on the pro-Union side. This meant the party leadership was not prepared to cooperate with other parties in a combined Remain campaign. That should not have prevented a forceful and distinctive free-standing Labour campaign however. The problem for the leadership was that, like Vote Leave, they were well aware that a significant part of their electoral base strongly supported Leave. They had become aware of this because of the rise of UKIP at their expense in many seats in 2010 and 2015 (which is why, as said, they had supported the bill to hold a referendum). The danger was that if they came out strongly for Remain, they would alienate that section of their support and drive them into voting either for an energised UKIP or for the Conservatives. Given that they, like everyone else, expected Remain to win anyway, it made strategic sense to effectively sit out the referendum and let the Conservative Party leadership and the establishment do the heavy lifting. More profoundly, this showed the dilemma that Labour was put in by the rise of the new political alignment, a dilemma for which there was ultimately no good answer.

Despite the handicap of not being able to make a positive case for EU membership outside Scotland and the missing in action position of the Labour Party's leadership, the Remain campaign still had considerable advantages, as described, and should have done better than it did. What undid it, and probably turned a narrow win for staying in the EU into a narrow but still clear vote for leaving, was a blindness and lack of understanding of what was going on in British society. This had three elements. The first was a reliance upon the authority of expert and elite opinion. A recurring type of argument was emphasis on official or expert analysis and predictions and on the weight of respectable and celebrity support for the Remain position. Much of the argument did not actually make a case, it rather said "this is what expert opinion says and therefore it is right." This argument from authority is of course a logical fallacy anyway but, in many times and places it is an effective argument because of the respect that most people have for experts and those who know more than they do. What the Remain campaign failed to realise was that today arguments that appeal to expert authority are actually counterproductive; they are less rather than more persuasive. This partly derives from the discrediting of economic experts and forecasters by the financial crisis of 2008 but it also comes from a deeper trend towards scepticism about received knowledge and expertise that precedes that event and has its origins in the nature of the modern media and the way claims of scientific knowledge and the conclusions to be derived from it are understood and experienced by many people. In any event, this was a mistaken rhetorical strategy and it stopped the Remain campaign from engaging effectively with voters.

The second, related blind spot was a firm belief that for most voters it was economics that mattered more than anything else. The mantra of the 1992 Clinton campaign "It's the economy, stupid" was thought to be true for almost all voters in all times. This combined with the inability to make a principled case for EU membership meant a predominant focus on economics, on the benefits of membership and the economic risks and costs of leaving. The operating assumption was that if you could show that leaving the EU would be economically harmful then most voters would not support it. This meant that other kinds of arguments, about Britain's place in the world, and the geopolitical risks of leaving, were underplayed. For many voters this belief in the primacy of economics was indeed correct. However, this approach ignored the realignment. It did not grasp that for an ever-increasing number of voters economics was less important than questions of culture and identity. As a result, the Remain campaign was unable to address the concerns about identity and cultural security that were rising in salience for a critical mass of the electorate. These questions were simply ignored or concerns about them were dismissed as being the product of ignorance and prejudice, rather than being engaged with and debated. The Remain argument was one suited to the old alignment, where economics was central but it lacked purchase in the emerging new alignment where economics was secondary (Kaufman, 2016). It was this that led to the third blind spot, which was a complete tin ear where certain particular issues were concerned, two above all. These were national sovereignty and self-governance, and national identity. (With the ability of the British state to control its own borders and migration policies being the specific issue that united them). These were crucial concerns for Leave voters but were simply not addressed by the main Remain campaign (Menon, 2018. Goodwin and Heath, 2016).

On the Leave side there were, as said, two rival campaign organisations. The official one, Vote Leave, was headed by several prominent members of the Cabinet. Michael Gove and Boris Johnson (not at that time a Cabinet member) were the leading figures in the campaign but they were supported not only by other prominent Conservative figures such as Theresa Villiers, Andrea Leadsom, and Daniel Hannan but also by figures from other parties. Two important ones were the Labour MP Gisela Stuart and UKIP's only MP, Douglas Carswell. The key figures in the organisation were not its frontline representative but its key backroom organisers. These were Dominic Cummings and Matthew Elliot. Both had considerable experience in campaigns of this sort: Elliot had run the successful 'No' campaign in the 2011 referendum on changing the UK's electoral system to the Alternative Vote while, as already mentioned, Cummings had masterminded the 2004 campaign against a North-East regional assembly. They proved to be far more effective organisers and strategists than their counterparts in the Remain campaign, as one might have expected given their record. The rival Leave organisation of Leave.eu was run and organised by the major UKIP donor Arron Banks and had Nigel Farage as its main public spokesman. Although both organisations were on the same side there was much tension between them. This partly reflected personality clashes but also came from different ideas about what to emphasise in the campaign. As a result, there were two rather different Leave campaigns going on, with two different political agendas, and this may well re-emerge in the years to come as two different kinds of post-Brexit right-wing politics.

The campaign of Leave.eu was a populist one that ran explicitly as an anti-establishment one, presenting itself as an insurgency. It had as its central message a combination of radical free market ideas and nationalism, captured in the slogan 'Global Britain.' Another way of understanding that message is as a reiteration of a kind of Thatcherite hostility to the EU that articulated the combination of views that had been successful in the 1980s. This kind of message had a strong appeal to UKIP's original core voters but little or none to either the new voters the party had started to attract or to the ones it needed to win over to be successful in the referendum. Essentially it appealed to the voters in the lower right quadrant of Table 3. The behaviour and remarks of the leading figures in Leave.eu showed that they expected to lose and were campaigning with that as a starting point. (The most notable example was Nigel Farage conceding defeat after the exit poll came out showing a narrow Remain win and saying that the campaign would continue before rapidly backtracking once the actual results started to come through). The organisation and campaign of Leave.eu were aimed not at winning the referendum but at creating the resources and organisation for a longer-term plan of creating a populist politics within the UK – a continuation of the process that had brought results for UKIP in the 2015 election – or alternatively of bringing about a change in the Conservative Party, away from the kinds of position David Cameron had supported and back to a more Thatcherite one. The style or register of this Leave campaign was angry and combative – something that is good for rallying those who already agree with you but a bad look when it comes to persuading waverers.

By contrast the Vote Leave campaign was better based and more effective than either the Remain or the rival Leave.eu ones. It put together a campaign that was in practical terms very effective, and which made use of the new campaigning technologies of social media to great effect. More important though was the way the content of that campaign reflected an understanding of the emerging division in British society and of how to both use it and give it expression. On the surface it was for most of the time a less overtly populist campaign but that is misleading. Rather, it used a language that captured a growing popular sentiment without appearing to be rabble-rousing or extreme. Instead of the angry and combative tone of Leave.eu it adopted one that was reasonable and optimistic – this also contrasted with the increasingly panicked warnings of disaster coming from the Remain side. It also had a different pitch or argument to the Leave.eu campaign, one that was much more effective because, again, it was more in tune with the emerging new divide.

The Vote Leave campaign started from a recognition of the gap between the perceptions and understandings of many ordinary voters and those of the class of media and political experts. Consequently, it did not rely on the argument from authority but made an actual case as to why leaving the EU was a good idea. At the same time, it played up to the growing popular dissent from claims to expertise by attacking the received wisdom of the great and good simply as being the opinion of the establishment, which was out of touch with what ordinary people wanted and thought and also, more importantly, wrong. This was captured in a key moment when Michael Gove remarked that the British public was fed up with experts who were wrong. This led to a stream of attacks upon him on social media and in the press but as the results and subsequent research showed he had captured a real popular sentiment. The central argument of its campaign focussed on the two related issues that the Remain campaign was ignoring or misunderstanding, national self-government and identity. This was captured in its extremely effective slogan 'Take Back Control.'

Quite simply this was a message of genius. In a simple and memorable phrase, it spoke to a whole series of connected concerns and arguments, which were becoming more salient for increasing numbers of English and Welsh voters as the realignment took hold. One was the feeling that policy and politics were being made by a distinct class of technocrats who did not share the concerns of many voters. Another was the feeling that life was shaped by impersonal and transnational economic forces that the political system would not check or would even support and assist. Above all it summed up the feeling that the political community was no longer responding to the concerns and desires of its members. The point at issue of course was what the identity of that political community was and whose interests it should embody and act for. Alongside the focus on national self-governance was an economic argument that was interestingly distinct from the one made by Leave.eu.

Dominic Cummings regarded that and the slogan of 'Global Britain' as catastrophically misguided if the aim was to actually win the referendum vote. Instead the argument was that leaving the EU would make it possible for the UK to act directly in the economic interests of its citizens – by spending the money that would have gone to the EU on the NHS, by supporting UK industry (e.g. protecting the UK steel industry), and by controlling immigration, above all the immigration of unskilled labour. Contrary to the fantasies of Remain campaigners, this was not a message about a radical free market revolution. It was aimed at the voters in the lower left quadrant of the emerging alignment, who were on the national end of the new aligning division but clearly left of centre on the economic one. These were of course precisely the voters who in their disillusionment with the technocratic liberal consensus of the Blair and Cameron years had drifted away from the Labour Party and towards non-voting or voting for UKIP.

The Result

The voting in the referendum took place on 23rd June 2016. The counts were organised by local authority areas except in Northern Ireland, which used Parliamentary constituencies. This gave a total of 399 counting areas (including Gibraltar but not the Isle of Man or the Channel Islands). During the campaign the polls had showed leads for Remain, sometimes quite large ones, but with a narrowing of the gap as the campaign went on. By the end, it was clear that the vote was going to be close but most people expected and predicted a narrow Remain victory, including the normally accurate betting markets. On the actual day of voting the pollster YouGov brought out a poll predicting a Remain win by 52% to 48%. As soon as the first few results came through it was clear that this was wrong. In the event Leave won by 52% to 48%, the exact inverse of the poll prediction. In raw numbers this was 17,410,742 votes for Leave and 16,141,241 for

Remain. Given the turnout of 72% (high by British standards) this meant that 38% of the entire electorate had voted Leave and 35% Remain. The details of how the votes were distributed are revealing. Although the overall result was close Leave won in every region of England except Greater London, where Remain won by 60% to 40%. Leave also won the day in Wales (although by a narrower margin than in England) while Remain had decisive victories in Scotland (62% to 38%) and Northern Ireland (56% to 44%). Of the 399 counting areas 270 voted Leave and 129 Remain, including every single one of 32 in Scotland and 28 of the 33 in London. When this was expressed as estimated constituency results you had 406 constituencies voting Leave compared to 224 going for Remain.

The contrast between the closeness of the overall vote and the marked advantage of Leave in terms of geographical counting areas highlights one of the central features of the vote and the division in British society that it revealed. The Remain vote was large but very concentrated. Where Remain did win it typically did so by very wide margins: 42 counting areas had votes for Remain of over 70%, while a further 64 had a Remain share of between 60% and 70%. This meant that the typical Remain voter lived in an area where almost everyone else had also voted Remain. (This explains much of their subsequent reaction to the vote) (Kanagasooriam, 2019). By contrast, although there were also many lopsided Leave areas, mostly in the North of England and Midlands, there were many with tight margins, particularly in the South East and M4 corridor. There was also a very clear geographical pattern to the vote. In the thirty major cities (defined as having more than 100,000 voters) Remain won overall by 55% to 45% whereas outside the big cities Leave won by 54% to 46%. This however needs to be qualified. Of the 30 large cities 16 voted to leave, some by large margins. The real division in England was between London plus a small number of other cities (Liverpool, Manchester, Leeds, Bristol, Cardiff, Cambridge) that voted Remain by large margins and on the other side the rural areas and small towns and some cities that voted solidly for Leave. In between were some large cities where the result was close (Newcastle and Birmingham for example) together with a large number of more affluent areas, mainly in the South East but with outposts elsewhere, that ranged from heavily Remain to marginally Leave. Geographically the clear division was between large metropolitan areas and affluent suburbs, mainly in London and around it, and the rural, coastal and old industrial areas, mainly in the North and the Midlands but also including much of Wales, and South West England outside Bristol (Evans and Menon, 2017). As we shall see this was associated with very clear social and other divides, which show that this result had been produced by the continuing realignment of British social divisions and hence politics around the new question of identity.

The Result Explained

The vote showed that Vote Leave had judged the feelings and divisions among the English and Welsh electorate far better than the Remain campaign (or, indeed, the Leave.eu one). Initially the reaction of many Remain voters and campaigners to the result was one of amazement and incredulity. The result came as a shattering shock and surprise to most of them and a common refrain was that they could not understand how it had happened because they didn't know anyone who was a Leave voter. This showed something already mentioned, the relative social isolation of Remain voters because of their being concentrated in a relatively small number of places where the overwhelming majority were also Remain supporters (Kanagasooriam, 2019). The next stage of a process that followed the classic stages of grieving, as described by Elizabeth Kubler-Ross, was to come up with a whole range of explanations that were in essence excuses and attempts to come to terms with cognitive dissonance. The classic example of this were claims that the result had been caused by Russian interference in the process (American readers may be familiar with this kind of argument) combined with corrupt behaviour on the part of the two Leave campaigns. The basis for this was findings by the Electoral Commission subsequent to the vote that both Leave campaigns had committed breaches of electoral law and overspent campaign limits. This argument overlooked two crucial facts however; the breaches were highly technical and the amounts involved were small compared to the overall costs of the campaign so the idea that these had somehow swayed large numbers of voters was simply silly.

The very widespread argument that went beyond this was to claim that the Leave campaigns had misled the public with tendentious or simply untrue claims and that explained the outcome. Leaving aside the rather entertaining pearl-clutching shock and outrage that politicians would actually make misleading or tendentious statements, the central argument here was that Leave voters were gullible sheep-like fools who had been misled by cunning and unprincipled operators (unlike the clear- sighted and intelligent critics of course). This condescending and patronising argument was not persuasive for anyone who had voted Leave, to put it mildly, and was essentially a form of therapy for anguished Remain voters. It certainly had no useful explanatory power. The same was true of the closely related thesis that Leave had been brought about by the power of the media. As already explained this was simply not true as far as the mainstream media went and in the case of social media both sides had spent considerable amounts.

It was just that the use made of it by Leave was more effective, not that such media had an inherent bias towards Leave or that only Leave had used these supposedly dark arts.

Initially there were many such spurious and wrongheaded explanations of the result (or rather excuses for the failure of Remain to win its expected victory) (Stocker, 2017). With time though, deeper digging into the patterns of voting, and polls undertaken by various organisations (most notably one by Lord Ashcroft that was done on the day of the referendum and asked people to identify first of all which way they had voted) produced a much clearer picture that made a first-order explanation possible (Ashcroft, 2016; Clarke, Goodwin and Whiteley, 2017; Menon, 2018; Evans and Menon, 2017). These studies showed several strong correlations between voting Leave or Remain and other factors. One of the strongest was age, closely followed by level of education and educational qualifications. The way that university education had grown so rapidly after 1997 meant that these two were so closely connected that they can be treated as the same. Simply, the younger voters were, the more likely they voted Remain. There was an overwhelming Remain majority among the under-30s and an equally lopsided Leave one among the over-65s. Graduates were heavily Remain; non-graduates strongly Leave. The fewer formal educational qualifications you had, the more likely it was that you voted Leave. A common argument, put forward most persuasively by Matt Goodwin and Rob Ford was that the Leave voters came predominantly from 'left-behind' parts of the country. They pointed out that the propensity of areas to vote Leave correlated highly with various measures of economic deprivation and also with both income and class status – generally speaking the middle and professional classes voted Remain, the working classes Leave (Goodwin and Heath,

2016). The conclusion is that the vote to leave was a response to the negative effects of globalisation and transnational integration for many parts of the country plus the impact of austerity. The problem with that reading is that the correlation between income and voting is actually weak, with many higher income people and better off areas also voting Leave. To be fair to Ford and Goodwin, the common reception of their work misrepresents their argument, which was actually more subtle and complex. They argued that the status of 'left behind' was not simply an economic one. It also reflected a perception that as Ford put it, 'Such voters had turned against a political class they saw as dominated by socially liberal university graduates with values fundamentally opposed to theirs, on identity, Europe – and particularly immigration› (Ford, 2016). The status of 'leftbehindness' was thus as much about culture as economics.

Several authors pointed out the very strong correlation between the propensity to vote Leave or Remain and views on apparently unrelated questions, such as the death penalty. Eric Kaufmann pointed out an almost perfect correlation between being in favour of the death penalty and voting Leave as just one example of a series of such correlations (Kaufman, 2016). His conclusion was that the vote reflected a divide between what he called order and openness, which he saw as driving politics in several countries, notably the United States. Another finding of several studies was that Leave voters were very concerned with identity, meaning both national identity, which they saw as threatened by immigration, and traditional kinds of ethnic or sexual identity, which they saw as threatened by the new kind of radical identity politics that had grown up on the left since the early 2000s, and which they strongly rejected. One sign of this was the correlation of voting patterns with immigration and cultural and ethnic mixing. Areas with large numbers of residents who were non-native born were actually much more likely to vote Remain and not only because BME voters and new arrivals tended to vote that way. By contrast, some of the highest votes for Leave were in areas that had relatively little experience of migration but were close to areas that did. The biggest votes for Leave however were in areas that had experienced inward migration that was both large-scale and recent (hence creating the impression of sudden and rapid social change) and where that migration was also largely made up of low-skilled individuals. (This conforms to other surveys that show broad acceptance of immigration by skilled workers such as medical professionals but strong hostility to unskilled and low-paid ones) (Economist, 2016). It was this question that seemed to produce the marked regional divisions, particularly that between globally connected metropolitan areas and less connected cities, small towns, and rural areas.

Perhaps the clearest and most obvious correlation was between voting Leave and a perceived sense of English national identity. Not only did England (or more precisely England outside London) vote heavily to Leave, in contrast to the other parts of the UK, there was a very strong correlation between propensity to vote Leave and seeing Englishness as one's primary identity (Henderson, Jeffery, Wincott and Jones 2017). Respondents who thought of themselves mainly as 'British' tended to vote Remain (that identification correlated highly with other factors such as ethnicity, with BAME voters far more likely to identify as British) whereas those who thought of themselves as 'English' were much more likely to vote Leave. Anthony Barnett argues that the driving force for Brexit was the rise of an English national consciousness that could not find expression through the institutions of the British state, because these had no special or particular place for England, unlike the other nations of the UK (Barnett, 2017). The cultural identity of Leave and Remain voters and their connection with national self-image was best captured by a survey that revealed that the two kinds of voter had very different lists of favourite brands and products. For Remain voters the top ten products in order were: the BBC, BBC iPlayer, Instagram, London Underground, Spotify, Airbnb, LinkedIn, Virgin Trains, Twitter, and EasyJet. For Leave voters they were: HP Sauce, Bisto, ITV News, the Health Lottery, Birds Eye Foods, Iceland Store, Sky News, Cathedral City Cheddar, PG Tips tea, and Richmond Sausages. For anyone who knows anything about Britain the contrast between the two lists is clear and remarkable. (There was a short list of brands liked equally by both sets of voters: Money Saving Expert, the NSPCC, T K Maxx, and Marks and Spencer) (James, 2016).

All of these findings and theories lead to the same broad conclusions. Economic factors such as the impact of the Coalition government's fiscal consolidation played a part but were not the primary reason for the vote. The reason was a division in British society that was about identity, culture, and a profound disagreement over the nature of the British political community and its place in the world. These in turn grew out of divisions that were as much about attitudes, sensibility and character as any thought out and articulated beliefs and those attitudinal disagreements both contributed to and were the product of social and economic changes that had been happening over the previous twenty to thirty years. One feature of this was the way that British voters had been more sceptical of and hostile towards the European project than voters in other countries for many years, with this scepticism increasing with time and particularly after the Maastricht Treaty. Research by Noah Carl and James Dennison showed that by a range of metrics, including sentiments such as how European voters felt, and degree of economic integration as measured by things such as trade connections and investment flows, the UK was consistently in the lowest two or three of EU members across the board. It was clearly less 'European' in terms of both attitudes and actual practice than any of its partners; European but not European enough, as they put it (Carl and Dennison, 2016).

The conscious motives of the voters in the referendum can be gauged quite accurately, thanks to the survey undertaken by Lord Ashcroft on the day of the poll (Ashcroft, 2016). This shows very different concerns and motives for the two sides of Leave and Remain, and also a marked asymmetry in terms of the understanding that each side had of the other side's motives and concerns. For Remain voters it was economic issues that were primary. The main reason for voting Remain, by an enormous margin, was fear of the economic consequences of leaving the EU. There was a minority of Remain voters who had more ideological reasons for their voting, such as a belief in the value of the EU project and a sense of an identity that was European and international as well as British or English. This was very much a minority and was actually a kind of political consciousness and identity that took firmer shape after the result and over the subsequent few years, as we shall see. For most Remain voters at the time of the vote (which is what Ashcroft's poll measured) it was economic caution and anxiety that mattered most. This suggests that the strategy of the Remain campaign of playing up the economic risks and potential adverse economic consequences of Brexit (Project Fear as it was pejoratively dubbed) was the right one: the problem was that it was badly delivered, with too much use of the argument from authority, and that it did not appeal in the end to quite enough people.

For Leave voters economics was a secondary matter. A significant part of Leave voters also thought that Brexit would likely leave the

UK, and themselves, economically worse off. They did not care about this however, or, more precisely, they thought that other questions were more important. Ashcroft's poll showed that for Leave voters there were two issues of overwhelming importance in determining their vote, neither of which were primarily economic. The first and by far the most important was sovereignty or national independence and self-government. This showed that for many voters a key idea was an explicit rejection of the idea of international cooperation through the sharing of sovereignty or the creation of rules and institutions that bound and so limited the decision-making powers of national electorates and governments. That ideal was a core belief of the consensus that had come about in the closing stages of the old alignment: to put it another way, it was a central belief of the technocratic political, managerial, and media classes. This was a radical reassertion of a different political value, that of national self-government and the nation state. The second big issue was immigration. Here further questioning revealed two different reasons for making immigration a priority. For some voters it was a question of newcomers diluting what they saw as an established national identity. The other reason was a concern that immigration policy should be made and determined by an elected UK government, rather than being governed by supranational rules. (It was thus closely related to the aforementioned concern with sovereignty). What united these two slightly different concerns was a feeling that immigration was too high and too rapid, that it was made up of unskilled rather than skilled labour, and that there had been a policy of high immigration that had never been democratically mandated.

What is clear from this survey is that the great majority of Leave voters were not motivated or even concerned by economic matters. Instead, they were moved by issues that were related to the new emerging divide or aligning issue, that of identity and nationalism versus cosmopolitanism and supranationalism. Remain voters were primarily motivated during the campaign and vote by economic concerns but once the result happened it triggered a latent attachment in a significant number of Remain voters (about 20% of the population as a whole) to a different vision of identity. This is why the geographical divide described earlier was so clear and striking – the division of outlook was driven by a physical reality. The division was not simply between affluent areas and deprived ones (many affluent areas voted Leave). Geographically it followed the degree of participation of an area and its population in the globally connected economy and its meritocratic labour market. That is why you find the pattern described earlier, with areas with a higher average age and more retired people leaning to Leave along with places that had a lower proportion of people with formal academic qualifications, above all degrees (often the same places of course). On the other side places with large numbers of students or young graduates voted heavily for Remain. This geographical division was also an attitudinal and cultural one between places where most were 'somewheres' (people with a strong preference for order, stability, the familiar, and attachment to a particular place and its social relations) and other places where most people were 'anywheres' (people with a preference for novelty, innovation, and variety and a focus on longer distance and personal connections).

One of the most striking findings of Ashcroft's poll and later studies concerned the way the two sides viewed and thought about each other. This showed that while Leave voters had a good understanding of the motivations of Remain voters, the same was not true in the other direction (Carl, 2018). There was comprehension and understanding in one direction but not the other. When asked to identify the motives of Remain voters most Leave voters correctly identified worries about economic prospects as the principal factor. When Remain voters were asked to do the same for Leave voters, very few of them identified sovereignty as being the main concern. Immigration was identified as a motive but its importance was massively overstated and the nature of the concern about that issue for most Leave voters was misunderstood. The overwhelming view of Remain voters was that Leave voters were motivated by prejudice and racism, and by a general attitude of xenophobia along with nostalgia for the British Empire. This stereotype was not even close to reality. The lack of understanding and the projection of a hostile stereotype was striking. This kind of one-way understanding, with one side simply unable to grasp or sympathise with the motivations and outlook of the other, is similar to the pattern found by Jonathan Haidt in the United States with regard to the divide there between conservatives and liberals or progressives, and derives from a similar sociological basis (Haidt, 2013). The geographical concentration of Remain voters meant that they typically had little contact with Leave voters; hence the many unintentionally comical comments in the aftermath of the vote. The split in perception also shows the kind of division of ethical perspective that Haidt discusses. Most Remain voters simply could not understand how anyone who was reasonable or virtuous could vote Leave. That meant that, for them, Leave voters were either selfish and malevolent (the leaders) or deluded and prejudiced (the bulk of Leave support). This way of thinking was not found among the people who had run the Remain campaign but it was very widespread, as the poll showed, and it came to dominate the way Remain voters and many of their political leaders responded to the vote and subsequent events. This had important consequences for subsequent politics and was ultimately disastrous for the pro-EU cause.

One interesting counterfactual question is that of what would have happened had the expectations of the professionals and the predictions of the YouGov poll been correct. If Remain had narrowly won what effect would that have had? Counterfactuals are difficult but in this case the answer is clear. A close result, which is what the polls were pointing to, would not have settled the question of EU membership. In the same way that the, actually fairly decisive, outcome of the Scottish referendum energised the supporters of Independence and polarised Scottish opinion around that issue, a narrow Remain win would have stirred up and mobilised the voters who had voted Leave. This would have accelerated the realignment and again made it clear that this was the new division in politics, despite the narrow vote for the status quo (which would probably have been seen retrospectively as a pyrrhic victory). In that hypothetical event there were still two possible paths that subsequent politics might have taken. One, which Nigel Farage and Leave.eu clearly anticipated, would have been a further upsurge in support for UKIP and a genuine political breakthrough for a form of radical national populism, possibly combined with a split in the Conservative Party. The other, which is what eventually happened after the actual result and three years of political mayhem, would have been a decisive shift towards a milder but still clear national populist position by the Conservative Party but in this hypothetical scenario within the EU and as part of a nationalist alliance within that organisation. What we would not have seen was widespread claims that the result was illegitimate or that it should be simply ignored, which is what we increasingly did get in the actual world from the Remain side.

The Referendum Result as a Consequence of the Realignment

Just as it was the emerging realignment and the politics it was producing, combined with political opportunism, that led to the referendum being promised and then enacted soon after 2015, so the result was caused by the way UK politics were realigning. Had politics been dominated still by the old alignment around economics, and the technocratic liberal consensus it had produced, then the result would have been a win for Remain, probably a decisive one as David Cameron and most 'informed opinion' expected. The referendum campaign over the question of EU membership had crystallised the new division in Britain (or at least England and Wales) over culture and identity. The question of British membership of the EU had never been a primarily economic issue, despite the best efforts of the UK political and media class to make it one. The European project, from its foundation at the Messina Conference and the subsequent Treaty of Rome had always been a political endeavour. The aim was to pool or merge the sovereign powers of European states in a new kind of political order and set of institutions, that would make war in Europe impossible and enable European countries to act more effectively together as a unit than they could individually (particularly in a world dominated by two superpowers, or just one after 1989). It had an economic aspect, the integrating of Europe's national economies through free trade and a common regulatory framework but this was a means to an end, not an end in itself: it was always subordinate to the overall political project. Being part of this necessarily involved a surrender of some of the qualities of sovereignty or self-government and in so doing raised questions about how the country doing that understood itself and its identity and its place in the world. From 1973 (when Britain joined the European Economic Community or EEC) to the Maastricht Treaty it was possible to finesse or ignore the ultimate nature and purpose of the project and understand it in purely economic terms, because that aspect was the prominent one. After Maastricht this could not continue as the steps taken there and subsequently were clearly political and part of a political project (for example the creation of a single currency and of a common European citizenship with all of the rights that came with it). The British political class avoided confronting this question but this became increasingly difficult, particularly as the question of identity and the polarity between national self-government and supranationalism came to be an increasingly important division in politics, at least for the public.

As mentioned before, the UK electorate had always been less European-minded than any other national population within the EU. In particular there was far less support for the political project that motivated it and a persistent attachment to the idea of national sovereignty. When the referendum happened the Remain side, which, as has been explained, contained almost the entire political, cultural, and commercial establishment, tried to continue the argument that this was a debate primarily about economics and to ignore the issues of sovereignty and identity. If most voters had still thought of politics primarily through the economic lens then this would have worked. However, the referendum necessarily had to confront the question of what kind of country Britain (or each of its constituent nations) was, and how it understood its status as a political community and its place in the world and relations with other nations and political communities. This was because of what the EU clearly was, and the issues raised by either deciding to no longer be a part of that project or to explicitly commit to it. The Remain campaign tried to avoid this. The two Leave campaigns both focussed on these questions, of sovereignty and identity, for the obvious reason that this was what the whole politics of leaving the EU was about. As such they had to fight a campaign that was not primarily about economics but rather about identity. For the first time in a long while voters were faced with a choice and debate where one side at least was not talking about economics primarily but about a different set of issues, related to identity and the deep question of the relation between the national state and the global order. This divided the electorate in a new way but it also reflected concerns that had increasingly exercised a growing part of the electorate, as the rise of UKIP over the previous decade had shown. Many of these voters had stopped participating in politics because they felt that their concerns and interests were being ignored by the main parties, which they saw as being both the same, committed to a shared ideology of socially liberal internationalism. The campaign therefore mobilised just over half of the voters around a new division and a new question and in doing this it crystallised the new alignment that had slowly been coming into existence. As we shall see, in the aftermath the bulk of the Remain voters also came to adopt a position that was defined by a view of the new aligning issue, and they came to downplay their former focus on economics, although not completely.

The Leave campaigns, and particularly the more effective Vote Leave one, did not completely ignore economics. What they did was to put forward economic arguments that were subordinated to the political ones. The argument was that leaving the EU would free up the British government to do things in economic policy that it was unable to do while a member. Economic policy (which we can think of as including migration policy) was thus seen as a subordinate aspect of the overriding question of sovereignty. For Leave.eu the argument was that it opened up the option of a move to a radical free market and free trade 'Global Britain.' For Vote Leave the argument was that it would enable the government to spend more on the NHS, have an active industrial policy (such as supporting the UK steel industry and using the Government's purchasing power to support domestic producers), and control its immigration policy. This strategy, the brainchild of Dominic Cummings, was critical to the success of the Leave campaign. It enabled the Leave side to make the argument that exiting the EU would make possible a project of national renewal and this had a powerful appeal in parts of the country that felt they had been ignored by successive governments. It also enabled the Leave campaign to appeal to two blocs of voters, who were agreed on the questions of sovereignty and identity but disagreed to some degree on economics. If we think about the kinds of voters who took part in the referendum, we can come up with the four-way division shown in Table 5 below. This clearly is roughly the same as the new political division shown in Table 3 but given a sociological content.

Table 5. The Social Divisions of the Referendum

RADICAL REMAINIA (C 16%)	LIBERAL REMAINIA (C 32%)
Younger, metropolitan and Scottish or Irish, educated. London, Scotland, university towns, Bristol, Liverpool, central Leeds and Manchester.	Younger but slightly older than RR, more affluent, metropolitan and suburban, SE England. Educated but slightly less than RR. Middle-class Unionists in NI and Scotland.
LEAVERSTAN (C 22%)	**BREXITSHIRE (C 30%)**
Older, mainly working-class, living in small towns, older industrial areas apart from Scotland. Working-class Unionists in NI. Less educated.	Older, less educated, slightly more affluent, middle class, living in rural areas, coastal areas and suburbs.

In this table the bottom axis is the economic one while the vertical one is identity and nationalism versus cosmopolitanism, as in Table 3. The strategy of Leave.eu would have a strong appeal to Brexitshire but would not have appealed to enough of Leaverstan to have a majority – some of the Leaverstan voters would have been reluctant to vote for leaving if they thought it would lead to a radical free market policy. By contrast Vote Leave's rhetoric and arguments appealed to both Brexitshire and Leaverstan because they emphasised the question of sovereignty which united these two groups of voters, and subordinated the economics to that issue, leaving voters free to project their own hoped-for policy onto the hypothetical of what a UK government would do after Brexit. In addition, the economic arguments that were made fitted in with the slogan of 'Take Back Control' because they, like the more general arguments about sovereignty and control of the borders, were about giving the UK electorate and government the capacity to act on its own. Moreover, as the 2019 election was to show, the voters in Brexitshire were not as keen on radical free market policies as some supposed, and so the implied policy of moderate government intervention after Brexit appealed to many of them as well.

The referendum of 2016 was caused by a political situation that had arisen because of the decay of an old alignment and the slow rise of a new one. At the time it was called the realignment process and was still in its early stages: many voters (and the great majority of commentators and professional politicians) still thought of their political identity in terms of the old, primarily economic, division and alignment. The questions raised by the referendum related directly to the new emerging division and alignment, because of the way EU membership had come to occupy a central place in that emerging divide (including the new one in Scotland over independence because of the way that had come to be connected in voters' minds with Scotland's being a 'European' country). This meant that, although one side of the debate during the referendum campaign (Remain) tried to frame the argument in terms of the old alignment, the way the argument went, and the strategy of the more effective Leave campaign, meant that the electorate divided in a new way, over the issue of sovereignty rather than economics, with a winning alliance forming between two very different social formations (which we have called Brexitshire and Leaverstan). This appeared to many of the stunned establishment to be a one-off, single issue effect but subsequent events were to show that was not so: the referendum had rather crystallised and firmed up something that had already been coming into existence. The problem was that most of the political class and the institutions of politics such as the parties did not reflect this. The result was to be three years of high drama.

CHAPTER 4

THE AFTERMATH AND THE 2017 ELECTION

Reactions and Immediate Consequences

As said, the initial reaction of journalists, analysts and politicians (and many voters) to the referendum result was one of shock and bemusement. One other feature that was initially prominent was acceptance. Most people, even those who disagreed strongly with the idea of Brexit, accepted the result even if they felt very badly about it. "The people have spoken – the bastards" was a common reaction. What became apparent was that while there was a voting majority to leave the EU, there was no agreement, much less consensus as to what that meant or what form it might take. Anyone who had paid attention to the internal arguments of the Eurosceptic and anti-EU movements over the years would have realized this: people who agreed that Britain should leave the EU had a wide range of suggestions as to what should happen thereafter. In the months after the result a conversation began over what practical form Brexit should actually take.

This was typically presented as a choice between a soft and hard Brexit. The former meant some kind of arrangement in which the UK remained closely aligned with the EU, remaining within the customs union and common external tariff, and remaining within the single market regulatory regime. This could take a variety of forms, such as joining the European Economic Area (like Norway – the two versions were Norway, which involved being in the single market but not the customs union, and Norway+ which meant being in both), joining the European Free Trade Area (EFTA) which was similar to Norway but with more scope for independent action, or having a sector-by-sector trade and regulations deal with the EU (like Switzerland). The 'Norway' option had the advantage of minimizing change and consequent disruption but it meant being a rule taker rather than a rule maker (because while still being bound by EU regulations the UK would no longer have a say in their content because it would have left the political aspect of the EU). For some on the Leave side this option was actually the worst of both worlds, because it left the UK in a position where it was still not able to completely decide its own policy (so the principle of sovereignty was not recognized), while losing the influence it had previously had. In particular most kinds of soft Brexit meant that the UK would still not have control of its own borders, because it would still be in the EU and EEA zone of free movement. These options also meant that the UK would not be able to follow an independent trade and regulatory policy, which for many Leave activists was the main reason for leaving apart from the principled one of sovereignty. (The problem here was not so much being in the customs union as continuing to be in the single market, given that contemporary trade deals are actually more about regulatory harmonization than customs and tariffs). Some Leavers though were prepared to accept it, often on the basis that this could be used as a fixed-time transitional period for maybe five or ten years ('Norway for now,' as it was often called). For the majority of Remain voters at this time this range of possibilities (soft Brexit) was what they could accept and live with.

A hard Brexit by contrast meant that the UK would leave one or both of the customs union and single market, usually both, and would no longer be subject to the jurisdiction of the European Court of Justice. This meant that future economic relations with the EU would be governed by a comprehensive trade agreement, such as the one the EU had negotiated with Canada (as mentioned, such deals are actually primarily about regulatory alignment, even though they are described as trade deals). A Brexit of this kind would give the UK much greater scope for independent action, subject only to the self-chosen limitations imposed by the comprehensive trade agreement. In particular it would give the UK freedom of action in the spheres of trade and regulatory policy, and complete control of its immigration policy. There were two downsides however. The first was that such a Brexit was potentially very disruptive for businesses because of the way it might alter or cut existing business arrangements, including such things as transnational supply chains. The second was that a comprehensive trade deal might prove very difficult to negotiate and take some time to complete. This would create a lot of uncertainty, which business hates, and would therefore stop a lot of investment from happening. It also raised the question of how to handle such a transition.

The hardest of all Brexits would be to simply leave the EU without coming to any agreement, comprehensive or otherwise, not even one on the mechanics of exit. In that case the UK would simply become a third country, on the same footing as any other country that the EU did not have a trade agreement with. It would trade with the EU on the basis of the generic World Trade Organisation (WTO) rules. A WTO exit, usually referred to as a no deal exit, would give the UK the greatest apparent room for manoeuvre but would also be the highest risk option with the possibility of very severe disruption, at least in the short term (meaning several years in this case). Most estimates were that exiting in this way would have an immediate significant negative impact on UK GDP (and possibly long-term growth rates, although this was more debatable). There was potentially a considerable upside but this was hypothetical. This was the favoured option of the hard-core Leavers but anathema to everyone else. It had one thing going for it however. Under the Lisbon Treaty (the EU's de facto constitution) a member state could leave the EU through a set procedure, which was set out in Article 50 of the Treaty. This provided that a member state wishing to leave could submit a formal notification that it wished to do so and by so doing trigger the process. At the point this was done a two year 'clock' began to count down and at the end of that period the state in question would cease to be a member. Crucially this happened regardless of any agreement that had been negotiated in the two years. That meant that a WTO or no deal exit was the default that would apply once Article 50 had been triggered if no deal was arrived at. The only way of preventing that would be for the withdrawing state to withdraw its notification of leaving or for the remaining member states to unanimously agree an extension to the deadline.

In the period immediately after the referendum, as these options were discussed and clarified, a modus vivendi could well have arisen, a broad agreement about a type of Brexit that the great could accept and live with, even if reluctantly. The most likely candidate for this would have been 'Norway or EFTA for now' with a soft Brexit but an agreement that it would be possible, subject to the outcome of future political debates and elections, to go beyond that once a certain time had passed. This did not happen. No such agreement emerged, much less a consensus. The political class failed to perform its function of arguing out the different views held by voters and arriving at something a majority could accept. Had that happened subsequent events would have taken a very different course to the one that did. The obvious question is why, instead of a discussion based around accepting the result but taking into account the views of the 48% who had voted Remain, and arriving at a conclusion that enabled the political process to move forward, there was growing polarisation, the hardening and consolidation of the identities of Leaver and Remainer, and a situation of complete political deadlock. There were several reasons for this, which we shall look at in turn, deriving from the personalities involved and the nature and divisions of Britain's political and media classes, but the main reason was structural: the referendum had crystallised a new division in British politics and, on the specific question of Brexit, had sorted out the voters into two camps. The problem was that this new divide in society was not reflected in the way party politics was organised and the attempts of politicians to deal with that reality meant that a coming together became almost impossible. This in turn opened up an opportunity for a particularly obtuse and self-obsessed part of the UK's elite to adopt a posture that had the effect of deepening the division and solidifying it even further. This was a catastrophic misjudgement on their part, as most of them now realise.

The first thing that derailed any prospect of a consensus developing from discussion was the reaction of the Conservative Party and its leaders to the referendum result. This had many highly contingent (and often comical) aspects, but it was also driven by the same political realities that had led the party to promise a referendum and then deliver it. The day after the referendum David Cameron resigned as Prime Minister and party leader. This was in some ways a serious abdication of responsibility. He felt that since he had led the campaign in favour of Remain, he could not now lead a government that was putting a Leave vote into effect. However, the opposite argument was given that he was best placed to lead the national conversation that would arrive at a negotiating position that was broadly acceptable to a majority of the public. Certainly, his personal qualities should have suited him for that task however difficult it might have been. By resigning he not only triggered an immediate election for the post of Conservative Party leader (and by extension Prime Minister), he also left a vacancy at the centre of the post-referendum national conversation. This had major consequences (which to be fair he did not foresee) because of the way the leadership election went and the personal and other qualities of his replacement.

This was of course Theresa May, Cameron's Home Secretary, but while a strong candidate she did not start the contest as favourite. That position was initially held by Boris Johnson, who had been one of the leading figures in the Vote Leave campaign and the main figure in the minority of Cabinet members who had backed Leave, along with Michael Gove. Initially the confident expectation was that he would become party leader and PM, with Gove as his deputy (and, some unkindly said, his Svengali). The way Conservative Party leadership elections work is that the party's MPs use a series of elimination ballots to whittle down the list of candidates to two, who are then put to a vote of the membership. Johnson's popularity among the members meant that he would be the strong favourite to win that vote, while his position as the leading Leave figure after the referendum meant that he would get enough support from MPs to make the final two, given the number of Conservative MPs who had supported Leave.

As Robert Burns observed, "The best laid plans of mice and men, Gang aft agley." In a weekend of high drama and dark comedy Michael Gove announced that he was going to stand for the leadership himself since he had suddenly and reluctantly concluded that Boris Johnson was not up to the job. ("And it's taken him this long to realise that?" was the widespread sardonic reaction). Johnson himself then announced that he was not going to run and the plans of the group around himself and Gove, which included most of the backroom operatives of the Vote Leave campaign, were thrown into disarray. Gove himself did not benefit from this and was eliminated in the second round of voting among MPs when the vote took place, as many who would have backed Johnson refused to support him because of what they saw as his blatant treachery. (The Conservative Party is typically relaxed about treachery, as long as it is successful and not overt). The Leave-supporting MPs were divided between Gove and two other candidates, the former Defence Secretary Liam Fox, and the junior Energy Minister, Andrea Leadsom, who had also played a prominent part in the referendum campaign. She emerged as the strongest candidate from that section of the party, with Fox eliminated in the first round and Gove the second. This left the way clear for Theresa May, who had the support of the Remain majority of the Parliamentary party, getting exactly half of the MP's votes on the first ballot and 60% on the second. This set up a membership vote between May and Leadsom but then, after severe press criticism of remarks she made in an interview with the Times, Leadsom withdrew with the result that May was elected unopposed. This meant that the overwhelmingly Leave-supporting party membership had no opportunity to make its views known – May had supported Remain though not with any great prominence or enthusiasm (being similar to Jeremy Corbyn, in that respect at least).

Theresa May will probably go down in history as an unfortunate Prime Minister who took office at what was the worst possible time for someone with her personal qualities and character. She was a serious-minded politician with a very strong sense of public duty and devotion to public service. Her political views were actually quite suited to the times, being a combination of a rather old-fashioned kind of social and cultural conservatism, an unreflective but straightforward patriotism, and a paternalistic view of economics and social policy that harked back to a pre-Thatcher kind of Conservatism. Unfortunately for her she was a very poor communicator and not in any sense a 'people person' – many people who had contact with her commented on her inability to do small talk or communicate at a personal level. (This is surprising since these are core skills for a democratic politician). She was hard- working and dedicated but also unimaginative and inflexible and often very secretive. She was also strongly partisan, dedicated to her party and identifying very strongly with it. All of this made her unsuited to the task of putting together any kind of broad, and inevitably cross-party coalition to put through a form of Brexit that would command support from both a majority of Leave voters and enough Remain supporters. Ironically her predecessor, the emollient and flexible David Cameron, was, as noted, better suited to that task. We should not overlook the reality though that she faced a very difficult situation that would have challenged any Conservative leader – Boris Johnson was probably fortunate to have his ambitions derailed and not become Prime Minister at that point. May's own character and the challenges she faced led her to take early decisions about the course of Brexit that were a major factor in cutting short any prospect of a modus vivendi emerging.

The second factor that worked to stop such a broad-based agreement developing was external, the response of the EU to the Brexit vote, and the negotiating posture it went on to adopt. The widespread reaction among leading EU figures, even more than among Remainers in the UK, was one of incredulity combined with deep regret. This soon gave way however to calculation and hard-headed thinking. The immediate consensus view of the EU leaders was that this was a potentially serious threat to the EU that had to be headed off and handled effectively. The starting point therefore was the agreement that the British could not be allowed to have a sweetheart deal that enabled them to have their cake and eat it, to get the benefits of membership without the costs. They had to be clearly worse off than they had been before, not least to deter any other electorates that were tempted to follow the British example. This was not a matter of being vindictive: EU leaders were so convinced and certain of the benefits of membership and the costs of abandoning it that they could not see the negotiations for an exit as anything but a lose – lose scenario (as their chief negotiator Michel Barnier put it). Their concern was to make sure that the UK bore the bulk of the costs. A second point on which there was consensus was that the UK would not be allowed to pick and choose between the various freedoms that made up the single market system (in other words, keeping free movement of goods, services, and capital, while rejecting free movement of people). This was a perfectly reasonable and sensible position, no matter how much some British politicians and commentators denied that. The third, crucial point, was that they were determined to protect and preserve the existing system of regulations that also made up the single market regime – they were not prepared to let goods originating in or passing through the UK have access to the EU market unless they complied with EU regulations. This meant that if the UK government wanted to vary or amend EU regulations in certain ways the price would be that they would not have access to the EU market for goods affected by those regulatory changes.

All of this led to a very clear and united negotiating posture. The starting point was that the EU would not even start negotiating an exit until the question of the UK's contribution to the EU budget had been dealt with (some payments would have to continue for a while after any exit). The second was that they would not deal with the terms of any trade arrangement or detailed agreement (which would cover the kinds of matters relevant to the second and third points above) until after the formal exit from the political arrangements. All they were prepared to negotiate in the time before then was the technical and often complex detail of how the UK would leave a whole range of institutions and rules that had been built up over 43 years and the arrangements for the subsequent transition period that would be used to negotiate the comprehensive agreement. This last did involve a set of guidelines as to what the comprehensive agreement would aim to do but these were just guidelines, they were not binding. The EU were much more relaxed about the exit from the political institutions (including the Common Agricultural Policy) but that was by far the simplest part of the process.

The May Government made a series of decisions in response to this that were the third main reason why no wide-based agreement emerged. Future courses on negotiation for business studies and business school students will probably use this phase of the UK Government's negotiations as a case study in how not to do negotiations of any kind. The more paranoid parts of the Leave side suspected that this was a deliberate conspiracy by Remain-minded politicians and civil servants but nobody with any knowledge of how the UK Government and public sector had negotiated contracts and procurement over the years would have been surprised in the slightest. At the same time the Prime Minister and the Government (including its civil service advisors) were constrained by the still-developing political situation in the UK. The first decision was to hand in a formal notification to the EU President, Donald Tusk, at a relatively early date and so trigger Article 50. This was done on 29th March 2017, meaning that under the terms of Article 50 29th March 2019 became the exit deadline, by which an exit deal (but not a comprehensive final trade agreement) would have to be negotiated and approved by both sides. Subsequently (that is two years later) many people on both sides of the argument complained that this was premature and rushed. There are good reasons for thinking this: in particular triggering the Article and starting the process less than a year after the vote to leave meant that there was no real time to think about the details of the negotiations nor to put in place detailed contingency plans and preparations for a possible breakdown in negotiations or some other event that led to a WTO exit. At the time though the common question was that of why there had been such a long delay in starting the process and there was growing impatience and irritation on the Leave side. This reflected a failure to realise how technical and difficult the negotiations would be and how obdurate and insistent on protecting its interests the EU would be (although neither of these should have come as a surprise to any but the most insouciant). Politically the Government felt that its interests were served by 'getting on with things.' Less forgivably they did not then immediately start on serious contingency planning of any kind.

This reflected another assumption and consequent negotiating decision that May and her advisors made. This was that an exit without an agreement on WTO terms was simply unthinkable and not worth considering (so there was no point in preparing for it). There was also a naïve notion that the EU would be prepared to be much more accommodating to British requests than it proved to be (or should have been expected to be) and so an exit deal was likely to be straightforward to arrive at. The result of this way of thinking was that the May Government ruled out a WTO exit from the start. This was a catastrophic error in negotiating strategy. One of the basic rules in negotiations is that you have to be prepared to walk away from the discussion without a deal – otherwise you are in the position of wanting a deal no matter what, which gives the initiative and all of the aces to the other party. In a negotiation both parties have to have minimum levels or red lines, that they are not prepared to compromise on and therefore be prepared to abandon the negotiation if these are not satisfied or addressed in some way. The EU was very clear and open about its position in this respect but the British Government effectively disarmed itself by saying it would not even in extremis leave without a deal. This handed the initiative to the EU and meant that any deal that did result was likely to be very hard for a large part of public opinion and the Conservative Party to swallow. We will not know for many years exactly why the Government adopted this position, but one reason must have been the intense pressure to avoid such an outcome from the commercial, business, and financial establishment, along with the greater part of the media and cultural elite (which was in any case strongly Remain, as noted previously). This meant that May could not even raise the possibility of a WTO exit as it would have caused mass fury among powerful groups, and triggered a major rebellion in her Parliamentary party from the large part that had supported Remain and would prefer a soft Brexit.

At the same time Theresa May and her Government could not go for a soft Brexit and at a very early stage decided on two negotiating positions that ruled that out. The first was that an exit agreement had to end the jurisdiction of the European Court of Justice over UK citizens and businesses. The second was that there could be no free movement of workers, because the UK insisted on regaining control over its borders with regard to movement from the EU. In response European leaders reiterated the point they had made when David Cameron launched his doomed attempt at renegotiation – this was not compatible with continued membership of the single market regime because freedom of movement was one of the 'four freedoms' and the EU was not prepared to set the precedent of having a country that sought to participate in the single market pick and choose which parts of the package deal it accepted. Participation in this also meant that the Court would continue to have jurisdiction, because it was the ultimate source of authoritative rulings on the working of the single market. Thus, the position May adopted meant that while a WTO exit was ruled out, there was no way of agreeing a deal that would keep the UK in the single market, even temporarily, and so the various forms of soft Brexit were ruled out. In addition, the UK Government entered the process thinking that it would be possible to agree most of the final trade agreement with the EU as part of the technical withdrawal agreement, and that this could be done on a sector-by-sector basis rather than as a comprehensive agreement embodying principles and rules that would apply across the board. The EU made it clear at the first meetings that this was not the case, and that the negotiations could be concerned only with the technical details of withdrawal and the dissolution of a treaty-based relationship.

Theresa May had chosen this route and position, which made creating a broad agreement impossible, for two reasons. The first was personal and peculiar to her: she had always had a particular concern with the control of immigration, which had found expression in her policies and actions as Home Secretary, so for personal reasons she was committed to ending the free movement of EU citizens into the UK. She also believed that this had been a major factor in the vote to Leave and should not be ignored. That connected her personal position with the second reason for the strategy, which was the political position of the Conservative Party and the awareness of Conservative politicians of the continuing shifts in popular sentiment towards a primary concern with issues of culture and sovereignty. There was a large group of MPs, who represented the majority of Conservative voters and the overwhelming majority of members, who had supported Leave. These people might have been open to staying in the single market (and accepting free movement and the ECJ's jurisdiction) if it was a strictly time-limited measure but not if it was open-ended. The more hard-line MPs and voters leaned strongly towards a hard Brexit or even a WTO one. Going for a broad-based agreement would have alienated this section of the Parliamentary party and caused a disastrous split on a par with the ones the Conservatives had suffered in 1846 (over the Corn Laws) and 1903 (over tariff reform). Obviously, as party leader May wanted to avoid this. The other factor was again the one that had led the party to promise a referendum in the first place: as democratic politicians they were aware of the growing feeling among a large part of the electorate that national independence and identity were what mattered and also aware of the simultaneous threat and opportunity that this presented for the party.

The third rock that wrecked the chances of any broad agreement was the reaction of an influential and prominent section of the losing Remain side. While most of the Remain voters had an initial response of resigned or grudging acceptance, a large minority of that vote (about 18-20% of voters as a whole) did not. These voters refused to accept either the legitimacy or standing of the referendum vote and sought from the outset to frustrate it or overturn it. These were often the people who accepted and put about the wilder conspiracy theories that sought to explain the referendum outcome as the result of 'dark money' or Russian interference. The more serious view was firstly that the referendum was only advisory. Legally speaking this was correct because in the British constitution it is Parliament that is sovereign, not the people and so the ultimate decision-making power always rests with Parliament. Politically in 2016 that was a different matter and most elected politicians did not think it would be right or possible to ignore the referendum result because to do so would have disastrous political consequences. The Remain faction we are speaking of here did start by believing that the result should simply be ignored – the people had spoken but got it wrong. This came from the second belief shared by this group, that nobody who was properly informed or rational could possibly vote for Leave: it therefore followed that the ones who did had done so out of ignorance and prejudice or because they had been misled – they had not truly known what they were doing. The conclusion from this was that, if the vote was not simply ignored, then the public must be given a second chance to vote, in the expectation that this time they would get it right. (This had indeed been the practice on several previous occasions in the EU's history, notably in Ireland).

The unreconciled Remain faction was a minority of voters, smaller than the corresponding bloc of hard-line Leavers, but it had several things going for it. It was supported, however covertly, by a significant number of MPs (a slightly larger proportion among MPs than voters in fact), including all of the SNP and Plaid Cymru and almost all of the Liberal Democrats, plus a significant number of Labour MPs. It was also widely represented among the great and good who had been so solidly for Remain. It was not though simply an elite phenomenon, although that was what gave it purchase and both organisation and money. There was also, as mentioned a solid and significant section of voters. These were people who had suddenly realised that they had a sense of identity that was strongly European – for them being an EU citizen with the rights that brought was as important as being a British citizen was for many Leave voters – and that they had a strong commitment to the EU as a project, not just an economic arrangement, and thought that Britain should be a part of that. In many cases this view and sense of identity had always been there but for many it seems to have suddenly become consciously held as a consequence of the result. Just as the campaign had consolidated and crystallised a new and emerging political identity on the Leave side that was broadly nationalist and concerned to preserve a notion of British or English identity, so the shock of waking up to find that something that had been taken for granted was in danger of being lost had abruptly crystallised a different and rival sense of national identity and political allegiance. What this meant was that there was a significant body of unreconciled voters with support in the Establishment who were determined to obstruct and ultimately reverse the referendum decision and were prepared to campaign and organise to that end. This again made creating a coalition for a soft Brexit very difficult, because there was a self-aware group on the Remain side who would not accept that but held out for reversing the decision. The increasingly prominent expression of their views also had an effect on the other side as it firmed up and hardened the views of Leave voters and pushed them towards a harder Brexit position.

The initial battleground for the revivified Remain movement (as it increasingly was), was the question of how Article 50 should be triggered. Theresa May and the Government argued that since this was a matter of negotiating an end to a treaty relationship (the Treaty of Accession and subsequent EU treaties) it fell within the ambit of the Royal Prerogative. The Prerogative is a range of powers that are held by the Crown and which are independent of Parliament and do not derive from it (this is why the sovereign power in the UK is actually the composite Crown-in-Parliament). They are no longer exercised by the actual monarch but by the Prime Minister or other ministers. The Prime Minister of course is someone who commands the support of a majority of MPs and that is supposed to ensure that Parliamentary and Crown powers are aligned but as we shall see this broke down in the context of Brexit. There is no doubt that the making and negotiating of treaties is a Prerogative power, so the Government's position appeared to be a strong one. This would mean Theresa May did not have to ask Parliament for permission to trigger Article 50, and also that the details of the eventual agreement (as opposed to the complete package) would not be subject to detailed Parliamentary oversight. A test case was brought against the government's position by a leading Remain activist, Gina Miller. On the 7th November 2016 the High court ruled in her favour, and stated that Parliament had to give its approval to the triggering of Article 50 and be involved in the subsequent process in a much more detailed way. The Supreme Court upheld this decision against the government's appeal on 24th January 2017. The grounds for this decision was human rights law. The court held that because EU membership had given UK voters certain rights, which would be taken away or amended by exit, the process had to have Parliamentary approval (since only Parliament can rescind or amend legal rights and entitlements). Legally this was well-founded but it had dramatic political results.

Faced with the courts' decision the government introduced a bill into Parliament to give May the power to trigger Article 50 (so complying with the ruling). On 1st February 2017 this passed its second reading by 498 votes to 114. A week later, it passed its third reading 494 votes to 122. The Lords then added two amendments, which the government rejected. The first, on the rights of EU citizens living in the UK, was rejected by the Commons by 335 votes to 287 while the second fell by 331 votes to 286. This second amendment had sought to tie down the government and force it to get explicit Parliamentary approval for any withdrawal agreement at several points. The text read "*(1) The Prime Minister may not conclude an agreement with the European Union under Article 50(2) of the Treaty on European Union, on the terms of the United Kingdom's withdrawal from the European Union, without the approval of both Houses of Parliament. (2) Such approval shall be required before the European Parliament debates and votes on that agreement. (3) The prior approval of both Houses of Parliament shall also be required in relation to an agreement on the future relationship of the United Kingdom with the European Union. (4) The prior approval of both Houses of Parliament shall also be required in relation to any decision by the Prime Minister that the United Kingdom shall leave the European Union without an agreement as to the applicable terms.*" Although thrown out, this was in fact what came to pass, because of subsequent events.

The votes in the Commons highlighted the final factor that made any kind of easy resolution of Brexit impossible. This was the position and attitude of most of the Labour Party and, in addition, the views of its leader, Jeremy Corbyn. As described in the previous chapter, he had made little or no obvious effort to put the Remain case in the referendum. His reaction to the result, one day later, was to argue that Brexit should happen and that Article 50 should be triggered at once. All this enraged his overwhelmingly Remain MPs, most of whom intensely disliked him and his politics in any case and had no confidence in him as leader. (His election had been a matter of the transformed party's new membership voting for him, against the wishes of the overwhelming majority of Labour MPs). On the same day that he made his remarks about Article 50 (24th June 2016) two of his most vocal critics put down a motion of no confidence in him as leader. Four days later it was announced that he had lost that vote by 127 votes to 40. To be repudiated by one's own Parliamentary colleagues in this way was unprecedented for a party leader, particularly for the Leader of the Opposition and potential Prime Minister. This resulted in a leadership challenge, by Owen Smith. The result was that Corbyn was re-elected by an even bigger margin than in his initial election in 2015 (by 61.8% of the votes to 38.2%). He might not have enjoyed the support of his MPs but he still had the enthusiastic support of the party members. He also had the strong backing of several large unions, or at least of the activists who controlled them (their members were another matter). The problem for him and the party were that while he had a large and enthusiastic base, of mostly younger metropolitan professionals and graduates, there were not enough of them to win an election without the support of traditional Labour voters.

Corbyn's particular problem as leader in 2016 and 2017 was the one mentioned in the previous chapter. One part of the party's voter coalition, and the overwhelming majority of the members were passionately pro-Remain (and also strongly pro-Corbyn, despite his own unclear position on that issue). The other half was either strongly pro-Leave or mildly Remain and, according to polls at the time, very hostile to Corbyn. This was not because of economics, where Labour voters who disliked him generally agreed with him, but because of his positions on foreign policy, which were seen as unpatriotic. This was particularly damaging with working-class voters who were already moving towards a politics of nationalism and had shown that by voting Leave in the referendum. The other strategic problem for the Labour Party was the distribution of those voters. Polls indicated that about 75% of Labour voters had voted Remain and only about 25% Leave. However, in terms of Labour Parliamentary seats, 84 had voted Remain (by massive margins) and 148 had voted Leave. This showed that the 75% who had voted Remain were either concentrated in a relatively small number of metropolitan seats or spread out outside those seats, often in ones that Labour had no chance of winning. The Labour Leave voters by contrast were simply and straightforwardly concentrated in the party's traditional Northern and Midlands seats and in South Wales. This meant their electoral effect was potentially greater. Combining those votes with Leave-supporting Conservative and UKIP supporters in those seats had given Leave a lopsided victory in terms of seats and districts. In addition, because of their location, Labour Leave voters could tip a lot of traditional Labour seats over to the Conservatives, if they started to vote consistently as they had at the referendum, on nationalist and cultural lines rather than economic ones. By contrast only 80 Conservative seats had voted Remain, as compared to 247 that had voted Leave so although they also had a problem it was less profound as their voting base was more clearly aligned with the party once the referendum had happened and the majority of Conservative

MPs had accepted it. The problem there was one of a vocal minority of Tory MPs who while accepting the result in principle were determined to water it down in practice.

Corbyn and the Labour Party were therefore in a very difficult position in the aftermath of the referendum, particularly as a vocal unreconciled Remain movement began to take shape. Trying to keep both parts of a fractured electoral coalition happy was a truly challenging task. Given this, it made sense to continue with the policy of ambiguity that had marked the party's half-hearted contribution to the referendum campaign; in fact, to double down on it. It is this that explains the votes on the bill to give Theresa May the authority to invoke Article 50. Corbyn announced that the Labour Party would not only not oppose the bill, it would actually whip its MPs to support it. This accounts for the massive majorities in favour of the principle of triggering Article 50, even though 47 Labour MPs broke the whip and voted against. So, the party's position was that it would not try to block Brexit but would seek to deliver the exit from the EU that the referendum had (in principle) mandated. The fact of so many Labour MPs breaking the whip and opposing acting on the result showed, however, the strength of strong Remain feeling within the Parliamentary Labour Party (with a significant overlap with people strongly opposed to Corbyn's leadership). This, and the feelings of the Remain-supporting part of the party's electoral coalition, was addressed by opposing the actual details that the government came up with; hence Labour support for the two Lords amendments as they, and the second one in particular, provided ample opportunity to vote against whatever actual Brexit the government negotiated. This position, of supporting Brexit in principle while disagreeing with and voting against its actual instantiation satisfied both elements of the party's base – for a while. It also meant that this was one more reason why a national conversation could not converge on a form of Brexit that would command majority assent, because the Labour Party was not prepared to participate in such a conversation, any more than the Conservative Party's leadership was.

So, on 29th March 2017 Theresa May used the authority Parliament had given her to invoke Article 50 and start the withdrawal clock ticking. By this point it had already become clear that the process was going to be more difficult than many had light-heartedly imagined the day after the result. The EU's clear and firm position, combined with the UK government's weak negotiating stance, meant that there was no chance of anything like a final deal, only of a technical withdrawal which left the details for further negotiations after exit had happened. The coming together of a vocal Remain lobby and the position of the Labour Party meant that there would be strong opposition to any deal that was arrived at. The reality of a small but vocal minority among Conservative MPs that was opposed to anything but a soft Brexit added to that challenge. The real problem was that the decisions taken by May, combined with the other factors, meant that there was no chance of a soft Brexit being the outcome and that was the only position that had the support of a majority of MPs (given that even the small majority of Labour MPs who thought the result should be honoured would only support a soft Brexit). However, her own political position meant she had little choice but to take that course and Corbyn's position meant that cooperation between the two main parties would have been very difficult anyway. Had Parliament been clearly divided on the same lines that the referendum had laid bare, a nationalist side and a cosmopolitan one, then it would have been a simple matter to resolve, with the side that had a majority getting its way, but in fact the party divisions were still on the old lines of economics and so the new division was within both parties in Parliament as much as between them. Finally, it had already become clear that Ireland was going to be a seriously difficult problem. Since the Good Friday Agreement that had brought an end to the Troubles the two parts of Ireland had become entirely economically integrated, with the border practically non-existent. Disrupting this would be very damaging economically and would threaten the peace agreement in Northern Ireland, because one essential part of that agreement had been the effective abolition of border controls between the Republic and Northern Ireland. The Irish Republic also had a right under that Treaty to be consulted over any change to the status of Northern Ireland. Because a soft Brexit was not in the cards the question arose of what would happen with regard to the Irish border. The EU was determined that there could be no free access for goods from outside the single market regime into it and that meant a hard border with checks on any land frontier between the single market (which included the Irish Republic) and a country not in it (which would be the UK, including Northern Ireland, unless it opted for continued single market membership, which would mean a soft Brexit). This was therefore a difficult conundrum.

Faced with this challenging situation, Theresa May decided to call an early general election. She did so because, given Jeremy Corbyn's poor opinion poll ratings, and the turmoil in the Labour Party over Brexit and his leadership, she expected to gain a decisive victory. This would give her a majority sufficiently large and beholden to her that she would be able to get any deal through even in the face of opposition from the Labour Party and hard-liners in her own. She would also gain a personal mandate as PM and be able to claim a popular mandate for whatever deal she arrived at. So, the die was cast and an election was called. First though she had to get around something that was to prove to be very troublesome. This was the Fixed Term Parliament Act. This had been passed in the first year of the Coalition Government in 2010, at the behest of the Liberal Democrats. What it did was to remove the traditional Prime Ministerial power under the Prerogative, to decide on the date of any dissolution and subsequent general election. Instead Parliament had to sit for a fixed term of five years, as the 2010 Parliament had. The FTPA was to prove to be a classic example of the dangers and unforeseen consequences of constitutional tinkering and would have a huge, even catastrophic effect on subsequent events. In 2017 nobody realised this. There were some ways of getting around the provisions of the FTPA which were built into the Act itself. One was that a general election could be called before the five years were up, if two thirds of all members of the Commons supported a motion for an early dissolution. This meant Theresa May could get her early election, if the Labour Party supported that call. Much to the dismay of many of his MPs, who feared a heavy defeat, Jeremy Corbyn did so and the motion for an early election passed overwhelmingly.

The 2017 General Election and Its Outcome

The general election of 2017, held on 8th June, was yet another election or vote that produced a shock result, surprising everyone and the experts in particular. When the election was called most people expected a comfortable or even landslide Conservative victory. This included most Labour MPs, who entered the campaign in a state of despairing resignation. The only bright side for many of them was that this might finally rid them of Jeremy Corbyn. When the election was called, on 19th April, all of the signs were that what everyone expected to happen, would happen. The Conservatives had an average polling lead of 21% and Theresa May had an even more dramatic lead over Jeremy

Corbyn on the question of who would make the best Prime Minister. The expectation was that this would be a single-issue election, fought on the question of Brexit, which would benefit the Conservatives in most observers' views, not least because of the continuing divisions in the Labour Party over this issue, which aligned with the one between Corbyn and many of his MPs. The early signs were that Theresa May had made the right call and would indeed get the large majority that would make her task of negotiating Brexit easier. Initially the Tories' poll lead held up and the local elections in May confirmed this. They were a triumph for the Conservatives, who increased their number of councillors by 563 and gained control of an additional 11 local authorities, and a severe beating for Labour, which lost 382 seats and was left with 7 fewer councils. Everything seemed to be set fair for the Conservatives and Theresa May. This continued as the campaign went on, with most pollsters and electoral models predicting a substantial Conservative majority. Three weeks before the vote most sites were predicting a Conservative landslide and a majority of 160 to 180. As the campaign went on the projected majority declined slightly but most were still confident of a still-large Conservative margin as late as one week before the vote. On the day itself, of the published predictions of the seven leading pollsters six predicted a Tory majority (the actual predicted majorities were 82, 66, 64, 66, 24, and 62). The only exception was YouGov, which correctly predicted a hung Parliament with the Conservatives as the largest single party, and had been predicting that outcome since 1st June.

With hindsight there were clear signs as the campaign went on that things were not going well for Theresa May and, in fact, many people had commented on this at the time. What the polls did not pick up was how this was affecting people's intentions to vote and in particular the likelihood that certain demographics would vote. They did show a shrinking of the Conservative lead and a steady rise in the Labour vote share but they did not reveal how close the gap would be nor (importantly) how the votes would be distributed. What though had gone wrong for the Conservatives? One structural problem was the length of the campaign, which made it difficult to keep the focus on the single issue of Brexit and meant that the initial impetus of the Conservative campaign was hard to sustain while the Opposition was able to increase its impact. There was nothing the government could do about this however, since the machinery of the Fixed Term Parliament Act had been used to trigger the election, and that mandated the length of the campaign. What they did have control over was the content and tone of the campaign, and here there were several serious and unforced errors and weaknesses.

The Conservatives ran on an election platform that attracted a lot of comment. As well as promising to deliver Brexit, the party took a distinctive position on economic and social policy – this was thought to be the work of Theresa May's close advisor Nick Timothy. The manifesto advocated a much more interventionist economic policy than the one the party had followed since 1979 when Thatcher became leader, with a clear departure from the kind of free market policy that had dominated since then. Instead there was advocacy of an active industrial policy, and using the greater scope of action available to a UK government after Brexit to pursue a much more expansive role for government generally, with observers noting the similarities with Labour's 2015 manifesto. This positioning was politically astute and showed awareness of the shifting opinions of and divisions within the UK electorate. The target audience was clearly the voters in the lower left quadrant of Table 3, ex-Labour voters who had a clearly nationalist position on the new divide (and therefore favoured Brexit) but were still left-of-centre on economics. In geographical terms this pitch was aimed at voters in small towns in ex-industrial areas in the North and Midlands. It almost bore fruit. The astuteness of that part of the manifesto was destroyed for many voters by another specific policy. This was to address the challenge of providing care for the minority of elderly people who required fulltime and long-term care by raising the threshold for free care from assets of £23,500 to £100,000 while including property in the means test. In other words, people who had substantial property assets should expect to make a contribution out of that towards the cost of care, in most cases via a charge upon the property that would be payable on death. This was a reasonable suggestion for dealing with a serious and intractable problem but it stirred up furious protest. The Labour Party condemned it as a 'dementia tax:' this was highly effective but cynical, given that they had proposed something very similar themselves when in office. (At the time the Conservatives, with equal cynicism, had condemned the idea as a 'death tax'). The problem politically was that this angered a key Conservative constituency, older people without mortgages and valuable properties. Given that none of those voters expected Labour to do well it may have inspired some of them to not vote in protest. After several days of press furore, May then performed a complete U-turn and abandoned the policy, while claiming that she had not. This attracted justified derision and meant the Conservatives were in the worst of all worlds: they had upset a core voting constituency and then made themselves look weak and incompetent in their reaction. Nobody was impressed.

This fed into another feeling that grew as the campaign went on, of a more widespread lack of direction and competence in the running of the campaign and the presentation of the arguments. What the election did was to cruelly lay bare May's weaknesses as a politician, above all her lack of elementary communications skills. Her few public performances were so wooden that when the unkind soubriquet of 'the Maybot' was invented it caught on like wildfire. By contrast Jeremy Corbyn was revealed as a highly effective campaigner, attracting wild enthusiasm from younger voters in particular. The Labour Party's new, motivated, and large membership proved to be both highly motivated and effective at old-fashioned grassroots campaigning. What the election showed was the declining importance of television and the other mainstream media and the revived importance of the actual campaign and things such as knocking on doors and public meetings – we can see a similar kind of phenomenon in the United States in both 2016 and 2018. In this new, or perhaps reborn old, world Labour had a good campaign and the Tories a very bad one and this mattered, contrary to the conventional wisdom that actual campaigns made little difference.

There was one respect in which the Labour Party did particularly well and that was in neutralising Brexit as an issue for the voters the Conservatives were targeting, or at least for enough of them. The Conservatives had promised that Britain would leave the single market and customs union but still have a close relationship with the EU, reflecting the position the Government had arrived at by the time Article 50 was triggered. The Labour Party for its part also undertook to negotiate a Brexit deal but one that kept the UK in the single market and customs union, while ending the principle of free movement. (How this would be done given the EU's categorically ruling it out was not explained). Both parties though had promised that Brexit would happen and this meant that for many voters, who were concerned only with the principle of leaving and not the details of how it would be done, it was not an issue or matter of debate. The exception to this was the large minority of unreconciled Remain voters, who really wanted no Brexit but were certainly not prepared to accept the kind of relatively hard Brexit May was proposing. The neutralisation of Brexit as an issue was thus lopsided and this worked to Labour's advantage when the votes were cast.

As Brexit faded as an issue, other ones came to the fore, above all economic ones. This suited the Labour Party for two reasons. It brought the argument onto terrain where they were stronger given public weariness with austerity and the challenge for the Tories of defending a record in government going back to 2010. It also meant a focus on the questions that united the two parts of their electoral coalition, rather than the one of national identity and independence (as symbolised by Brexit) where they were divided. The most spectacular illustration of this came when the campaign was interrupted by two serious terrorist outrages, in Manchester and at London Bridge. The Conservatives expected that this would be good news for them and very bad for Jeremy Corbyn, given his record of sympathy and support for terrorist groups such as the IRA and Hamas. In reality it actually helped Labour because they successfully made it about the question of austerity and cuts to public services, in this case the police. This was partly due to sheer incompetence on the part of the Conservatives, but more to the way economic questions and the issue of austerity and its effects had come to dominate the debate. Another question that played very well for the Labour Party was that of university tuition fees, which they were pledged to abolish while also writing off student debt. This was a very popular policy with students and young graduates, who were leaning towards the party anyway for other reasons, and it helped to prevent any revival by the Liberal Democrats by reminding younger voters of what they saw as the Liberals' treachery on that question.

This should have been fertile territory for a Conservative response but in yet another example of the incompetence of their campaign they failed to make anything of it and allowed Labour to benefit with a key constituency.

As said, the result came as a massive surprise – terrible for some, euphoric for others and embarrassing for the experts. In terms of seats the Conservatives gained 20 but lost 33, leaving them with a net loss of 13. This meant they ended up with 317 seats, just short of a majority. The Labour Party gained 36 seats and only lost six, all to the Conservatives and so ended up with a total of 262. This was well short of a majority and so this was the third election in a row that they had lost. However, that was not how it was perceived. The expectations for the Conservatives had been so high that the actual result was a crushing disappointment while those for the Labour Party had been so low that to actually gain seats and votes seemed a triumph. To put their performance into perspective, this was the first election since 1997 where they had increased their number of seats, and they received the highest share of the vote since 2001. When we look at the details of the election however the story becomes a more complex one than either Conservative setback or Labour revival.

The most striking result of the election was the revival of two-party politics. Both of the two big parties increased both their absolute vote and their share of the vote. In these terms it was a good result for both parties. It was their highest combined vote share since 1970 and the closest result between them since that decade. The Conservatives increased their share of the vote from 37% to 42% while Labour's went up from 30% to 40%. In both cases this was the best result for quite some time. The other side of that coin was the crushing of the once significant third-party vote. The Liberal Democrats, who had suffered such a catastrophic result in 2015, did not recover, with their vote remaining at pitiful levels compared to where it had been in the 2000s. The other party that saw a setback was the SNP which went from 56 seats (out of 59 in Scotland) to 35, losing 12 to the Tories, 6 to Labour, and three to the Liberal Democrats. There had clearly been a polarisation of the electorate, with many people so concerned to support one side and (more importantly) stop the other that the self-identified centre had been squeezed to near-death. In Scotland the SNP suffered from two factors. One was simply the scale of its success in 2015, which was almost impossible to sustain. The other was the consolidated alignment of Scottish politics around the question of the Union, which led to significant tactical voting against the SNP by Unionist voters, with the result that they lost seats even though their vote held up fairly well. This benefitted both Labour and Conservative but particularly the Tories. Under their charismatic and popular new leader, Ruth Davidson, they had successfully positioned themselves as the main Unionist party and this had already brought significant benefits in the Scottish Parliament election of 2016, when they increased their vote share from 14% to 22% and doubled their number of seats, becoming the main opposition party to the SNP. At the 2017 election the Scottish Conservatives also benefitted from Davidson's being a strong Remainer (she had played a prominent part on that side in the referendum campaign) and supporter of a softer Brexit, which meant the question was less prominent in Scotland and deprived the SNP of an issue that worked to their advantage. At the election the Scottish Conservatives gained 12 seats (making 13 in all) and it was that performance that saved Theresa May and left her in a position to form a new government.

Even more dramatic was the collapse of UKIP. Having had such an impact on the political scene since 2005 and having brought about the referendum in the first place, it now effectively imploded. Its share of the vote collapsed from 12.6% to 1.8% and it lost its only seat in Clacton. This sudden collapse had a number of causes. Nigel Farage had resigned as leader immediately after the referendum result and so the party had lost its most charismatic and popular figure. More seriously it then suffered serious infighting and ended up with a leader (Paul Nuttall) who was compromised in various ways. The basic problem though was this. Even after Farage's broadening of the party's appeal it still remained a single-issue party in the eyes of most voters. It had not been able to establish itself as a true populist party founded on the wider range of issues associated with nationalism and national identity, given the way that in the British context these questions were subsumed into the specific one of Brexit. After the referendum result for most of its voters its mission had been achieved and there was no longer any reason to vote for it. Had the debate over the form and content of Brexit that took place after 2017 taken place before an election then it would have done better, because it could have rallied many of the voters opposed to the deal on offer and in favour of a truly hard exit but in 2017 this division was only apparent to the cognoscenti. What therefore happened within the party was a debate over how to become a populist party, given that its original raison d'etre appeared to have gone, and this proved to be very divisive. As we shall see later though, the appeal of that kind of politics to a not insignificant body of voters remains.

The collapse of UKIP's support was anticipated, as it had been polling at a very low level for some time. What was a surprise was the way its former vote was divided up. The expectation, not least among Conservative strategists, was that the bulk of UKIP voters would plump for the Conservatives, given that Brexit was clearly the primary issue for them and the Tories had a more hardline position on that question. This anticipated electoral bonus, given UKIP's poor poll showing, was one of the factors in May's decision to call an early election. Had things worked out that way then David Cameron's original decision to promise and then have a referendum would have been vindicated, at least in party terms. What happened though was that the former UKIP voters split about 60% for the Conservatives to 40% for Labour with the percentage going to Labour higher than that in many individual constituencies. This was for two reasons. Primarily it reflected the way that the Labour Party's position of constructive ambiguity had successfully lowered the importance of Brexit as an issue at the election. The deeper reason was that the realignment had not fully worked through in many parts of the country. There were still a significant number of voters who had moved away from the Labour Party over nationalism and national identity but were not yet prepared to vote Conservative. Feeling confident that their views on Brexit (and therefore national sovereignty and identity) would be respected (because of the Labour Party's explicit pledge to honour the referendum result) they felt safe to vote on the now secondary aligning issue of economics, and back Labour.

The Labour Party's vote saw a dramatic increase. This was all the more visible for being geographically concentrated rather than spread evenly across the country. Their vote went up, sometimes spectacularly, in London, university towns, and metropolitan areas outside London and the South East such as Leeds, Liverpool, Manchester, and Bristol. It went up by only a very small amount, if at all, in the ex-industrial North, Midlands, and South Wales. The result was spectacular gains in places that had never been happy hunting grounds for the party, such as Canterbury, a seat with a large student population that they won for the first time ever, or Kensington, an affluent area of London that saw another first time ever victory. Basically, the trend that had become apparent in 2015 became even more marked. The Conservative performance was an almost exact mirror image of this. The party's vote share was static or declining in its historic heartland of the South of England with this particularly true in the areas where Labour did well. However, there were dramatic increases in both absolute vote and vote share in the North and the old Labour heartlands. This also brought dramatic breakthroughs in some seats, with Mansfield going Conservative for the first time in the seat's history in an exact inverse of what had happened in Canterbury. The problem for the party was that despite massive increases in vote share in many seats in places like South Yorkshire, the Labour Party started with a significant lead and this was maintained just enough by the way the former UKIP vote divided between Labour and Conservative. So, despite large swings there were only six gains from Labour in those regions, with many near misses as compared to the 28 gains made by Labour, 15 of which were in the South with others (such as Warrington South or Cardiff North) in areas that were also predominantly middle-class professional or with large numbers of students.

The Meaning of the 2017 Election

How, though, should we understand the meaning of the 2017 election? What do the votes and the pattern of results tell us about how British politics was continuing to evolve? The starting point should be to realise that the initial reaction at the time, which has continued to dominate thinking about the meaning of the election on the left, was simply wrong. Because of the expectations, mentioned earlier, people thought that the result was much better for Labour and worse for the

Conservatives than it actually was. The focus on how well Labour had actually and unexpectedly done obscured the undoubted and massive qualification that it still wasn't good enough to win an election or even come close. It also obscured how badly it had done in its historic heartlands and the continued decay of its position there, masked by recapturing some voters from UKIP (which turned out to be temporary). It gave the Labour Party and the left in general false hope, which in politics is fatal. In direct contrast, the relative success of the Conservative Party was discounted or ignored. The results showed that Theresa May and Nick Timothy had had the right strategy and pitch but it had not worked out quite well enough, for contingent reasons. One was the sheer incompetence of the campaign, combined with May's failings as a politician. The other was calling the election when she did rather than waiting long enough for the arguments around Brexit to become clear. Had she done so, subsequent history suggests the result would have been very different. As it was, by calling the election before negotiations with the EU had properly started (in order of course to make them easier) she made it easier for the Labour Party to move the focus from Brexit and maintain its support on both sides of the new aligning divide of cosmopolitanism versus nationalism with its carefully ambiguous position.

In fact, Labour had played a blinder on Brexit for this one election. They had managed to attract support from a lot of angry and anxious Remainers in London and the South by promising to block a Conservative hard Brexit (or even what Theresa May was suggesting in her manifesto). For many of the voters they attracted this was understood as meaning they would block *any* Brexit (or at least any possible one). This benefitted them this time but came back to bite them subsequently. A significant part of the voters they attracted were ones who would normally never support a leftist like Corbyn but did so because they saw Brexit as more important and also did not expect that he would win a majority (they were right of course). At the same time, Labour had managed to reassure voters who combined nationalism with left-wing economic beliefs (the lower left quadrant of Table 3 and Table 4) that they would deliver Brexit – just not a 'Tory Brexit.' At this point most voters were not thinking about the details and so they accepted this. This meant that they did not lose as many voters to the Conservatives in the North of England and the Midlands as they otherwise might have done and meant they recaptured a significant part of the UKIP vote. This meant that while they had large swings against them in places like South Yorkshire, this did not translate into many seats flipping, thanks to FPTP. All in all, it was a Goldilocks strategy. The only problem was it could not be repeated but they failed to realise that.

Another thing we can say about the 2017 election is that it marked the end of a period, going back to 1979, in which public debate and policy had been driven by a kind of increasingly technocratic free market liberalism (neoliberalism in much academic argument). Looking at the two party manifestos, the arguments during the election on economic matters, and the pattern of voting, there had clearly been a shift in the centre of gravity of UK public opinion in a less free-market and more economically interventionist direction. The Overton Window (the range of positions that are taken seriously in political discussion) had shifted to the left. On the Labour side the party stood on the manifesto well to the left of where it had been under New Labour or even Ed Miliband, and it gained the votes of the increasingly economically left-wing young metropolitan voters (the upper left quadrant of Tables 3 and 4). Even more significant was the clear shift by the Tory Party towards a more interventionist economic position. This fitted well with nationalism and was clearly aimed at voters in the lower left quadrant. Theresa May had said that her favourite Conservative politician was Joseph Chamberlain, and there were similarities to her programme and the kind of conservatism he had advocated, particularly after 1903.

The major finding however, once we dig deeper into the entrails of the voting, was that the realignment of voters and voting patterns was continuing and even accelerating (Jennings and Stoker, 2017). Short-term and contingent factors meant that this had not yet reached the tipping point in the UK's electoral system but it came very close and the direction of travel was clear. If we look at the way different social groups voted, the Labour Party made significant gains among middle-class voters, particularly if they were younger and more educated. It was their best ever performance among the middle classes, with Jeremy Corbyn actually doing better than Tony Blair in 1997. Labour had a lead among all age groups below the age of 45, with a lead of 35 percentage points among the 18 – 24 age group. They had a particularly massive lead of 55% among women in that age group (73% to 18%). Amongst 18 – 34 year olds Labour had a lead in every single social class. Among all voters they had a lead of 15% among all graduates, which was much larger among younger graduates, and of 23% and 31% among renters private and public. They had a lead of 64% to 19% among students. The Conservatives' performance was an almost exact mirror image of this, with a lead among all groups over 45 and a massive one among the over 65s. They also did very well among the working classes and had their best performance among the 'lower' socio-economic categories since the 1960s, outdoing Thatcher in that regard. They actually had a lead of 7% among category C2 (semi-skilled workers) and a deficit of only 3% among the D and E category (unskilled and economically inactive).

When you combine the social analysis with the geographical, it is clear that underneath the relatively small change in seats (in both directions) was a major shift in voting patterns, which built on the trends that had already appeared in 2015. The Labour Party had made gains among younger, metropolitan, graduate and professional workers, and among parts of the middle classes in general. Simultaneously it had continued to go backwards among its traditional working-class constituency, except in metropolitan areas and among BME voters. What saved it was that this shift was not large enough to tip many seats and was held back by their astute positioning on Brexit. The Conservative Party had lost ground among the middle classes in general and the metropolitan middle class in particular, while making gains among the traditional working classes. Unlike in 2015, the switch benefitted them less than Labour. The two parties were in the middle of a dramatic switch in the nature and composition of their support, of a kind that had not happened since the 1970s. This came out of the decline of old social divisions and the rise of new ones, in other words the realignment. The Conservative Party was in the process of becoming the party of Brexitshire and a large part of Leaverstan while the Labour Party had become the party of Radical Remainia and (for now) much of Liberal Remainia. In terms of political sociology the Conservatives were caught in the middle of a process of becoming the party of an alliance of older middle-class voters in the South and rural areas, and working-class voters in the old industrial areas, while the Labour Party was moving away from being a working-class party and becoming what Jeremy Corbyn's election as leader had indicated, a party of a distinct part of the metropolitan middle class. What would become clear subsequently was that the Conservatives' new electoral coalition was more coherent and capable of expanding than the Labour party's – at least as long as Corbyn and the ideas he represented were dominant.

The immediate consequences of the 2017 election and its shock result were far-reaching. Theresa May was enormously weakened as a political figure and suffered a blow to her authority from which she never recovered. On the other side Jeremy Corbyn was now unchallengeable as Labour leader and got an enormous boost to his authority over the party. It also gave his supporters a deluded assurance that they were on the right track. The main consequence was that it made the position in Parliament and the negotiating of Brexit even more difficult, having been intended to ease them. Most notably, having lost her majority, Theresa May was forced, in order to continue in office, to enter into a supply and confidence agreement with the main Unionist party in Northern Ireland, the Democratic Unionist Party. This obviously gave them great influence over the course of the Brexit negotiations, and this was to make the Irish border question even more intractable. Outside Parliament the result gave a massive boost to the self-confidence and belief of the once shattered Remainers. This led them to conclusions about their prospects that in the long run proved to be self-defeating. In particular many now came to believe that they had a real chance of stopping Brexit rather than simply amending it and ensuring it was as limited as possible. For the Leave side the result was a blow but they consoled themselves with the thought that Article 50 was now triggered, which they thought meant the UK was certain to leave the EU anyway, and on WTO terms if a deal could not be passed through the (now hung) Parliament. This was equally delusional and led to some truly bizarre fantasies and straw-clutching later on. What neither side grasped was the nature of the political situation within

Parliament that the election result had created, when combined with the Fixed Term Parliament Act. Consequently, neither Leave nor Remain had a coherent and realistic Parliamentary strategy, although there is a good case for saying that such a thing was now impossible. What followed was more high political drama, and a real-life illustration of something familiar only to people who had done university courses in political science or certain kinds of mathematics.

CHAPTER 5

A DEADLOCKED PARLIAMENT AND A POLARISED ELECTORATE

The period between the election of 2017 and the election of December 2019 was a paradisiacal one for political junkies and obsessives. In that period of just over two years there was an almost daily diet of high political drama, with apparently cliff-hanging votes in Parliament on a regular basis. There were splits and divisions within both major parties in Parliament, with many MPs leaving their party to set up new ones or stand as independents. The British constitution, once only of interest to a few scholars, became a central topic in politics and seemed to be at breaking point on more than one occasion. Political correspondents had never been so busy or in demand. Meanwhile, outside Parliament and the Westminster and media hothouse, the public became steadily more polarised, with the divisions that the referendum had brought to light becoming deeper and firmer. For many of the public the high drama at Westminster produced not excitement but exasperation, irritation and ultimately boredom. The drama of this time has been well captured in Tim Shipman's detailed account in *Fall Out: A Year of Political Mayhem* (Shipman 2018). Here we will not give the kind of detailed account of the negotiation process and the Parliamentary and political struggle that Shipman gives but focus instead on the thematic analysis of what went on in those two turbulent years. Once the underlying dynamic is understood, the apparent mayhem and chaos becomes both understandable and, at the time itself, predictable (I myself predicted much of what happened well in advance, although the ultimate outcome was not what I expected). The basic reason for the intractable Parliamentary politics that Theresa May faced was the way the realignment had reshaped British politics without that yet being reflected in its central institution, Parliament, or in the party system there and at the grassroots. The conflict in Parliament consolidated the realignment and eventually gave it a particular form or expression: this was mainly because of a major strategic error made by one group of players, the strong Remainers.

The negotiation process that Theresa May's Government embarked on following the 2017 election proved to be as torturous and difficult as many had feared. The EU stuck firmly to its positions that the terms of the UK's financial contributions to the EU for a time after exit had to be dealt with before any substantive discussions could start, and that details of any future trade relationship between the EU and UK could not be part of the withdrawal agreement itself. Despite the difficulties progress was slowly made on these and other technical details following the formal opening of negotiations on 19th June 2017. However, the major questions of the UK's relations with the single market and customs union remained very difficult politically for the UK, given the EU's clear and inflexible position on this. In particular, the question of Ireland became ever more acute, and came to dominate the discussions. The problem here was simple but difficult politically.

The fundamental reality was that there was a land border between the UK (specifically Northern Ireland) and the Irish Republic. If the UK were to remain a full member of both the customs union and, more importantly, the single market regulatory regime, this would not be a problem. However, for the political reasons described in the previous chapter the UK government had decided that the exit agreement should clear the way for Britain to subsequently leave both of these, during the fixed-duration transitional period that would follow formal exit. Unless some agreement could be reached in that transitional period, there would have to be a hard border between Northern Ireland and the Irish Republic, with checks and customs controls on the movement of goods and people. This was because of one of the EU's 'red lines.' It was not prepared to have open trade and movement between the single market area and a part of the world that was not part of it. The fear was that allowing goods to freely enter the EU that were not compatible with single market regulations would undermine the integrity of that regulatory system. Where the frontier was maritime this was not too difficult as the checks could be done at ports. On a land frontier it was much more intrusive and disruptive, as could be seen on EU land frontiers elsewhere. In the Irish case this had the potential to cause enormous problems, both economic and political. Because of the complete integration of the Irish and Northern Irish economies, a trade barrier would have seriously bad economic consequences, particularly for Northern Ireland but also for the Republic (the Republic stood to be badly impacted by Brexit in general, quite apart from the question of

Northern Ireland). As explained previously, there was also a political element inasmuch as having a hard border threatened to blow up the Good Friday Agreement in Northern Ireland.

One solution to this, which the EU suggested in the Spring of 2018, was for Northern Ireland to remain within the single market and customs union, (and so remain a part of the EU in economic terms), regardless of what the rest of the UK did. Northern Ireland would have a soft Brexit while the rest of the UK would have a harder one. The problem with this was political. It would mean customs checks between Northern Ireland and the rest of the UK and, over time, significantly weaken the connection between the two parts of the United Kingdom. This was completely unacceptable to the DUP, which Theresa May now depended on for her majority so she rejected it. She would probably have done so anyway, because she was a principled politician and this violated what for her was a central part of her beliefs, the importance of the Union. The DUP for its part wanted to have both a relatively clear break with the EU and no hard border in Ireland, a classic example of wanting to have one's cake and eat it. This all meant that something else had to be devised to deal with what was becoming an intractable problem with the capacity to wreck the entire process.

Faced with the difficult negotiations over Ireland and the related core issue of single market membership, a Cabinet meeting was held at the Prime Ministerial country residence of Chequers on 6th July 2018. This approved a plan, which was then published as a White Paper (formal government proposal) on the 12th of July. The discussions were fraught and two members of the Cabinet resigned, the Brexit Secretary David Davis and the Foreign Secretary Boris Johnson. The proposals tried to square the circle of the EU's position, the need to avoid a hard border in Ireland, and the political need to have a Brexit that enough Leave voters and Leave- supporting Conservative MPs would support. They did this by saying that the UK would formally leave the single market but would still observe and adhere to the EU's rules and regulations by having a shared rulebook, but with the prospect of a slow and sector-by-sector disengagement. This effort, like many compromises, ended up pleasing nobody. It enraged many Conservative MPs and bolstered their determination to hold out for a more definite break with the EU. EU leaders for their part were not impressed, and found the proposal regarding Ireland particularly lacking in substance.

Following this more difficult and tense negotiations took place. The EU gave ground in some areas but remained determined over the Irish question. The final outcome was a withdrawal agreement approved by the British Cabinet on 14th November 2018 and by the EU leaders at a summit on 25th November. The position regarding the single market ended up being mostly what the British Government had proposed at Chequers. The solution to the Irish conundrum was what came to be known as the Irish backstop. This seemed confusing but was actually simple. The vexed question of whether there would be a hard border in Ireland was not included in the withdrawal agreement, which would come into effect on 29th March 2019. Instead that question along with the details of the future trade and economic relationship between the UK and the EU was to be negotiated over a transition period of two years. If during that process a way was found to resolve the question of how to avoid a hard border then nothing would happen apart from a long-term agreement being signed. If however, the question could not be resolved then the backstop would kick in: Britain would remain in the single market and customs union (to avoid a hard border in Ireland) until such point as the issue *was* resolved, to the satisfaction of the Irish government. This was open-ended. Essentially the backstop was an insurance policy to protect the interests of the Irish Republic, while also preserving the EU's insistence on safeguarding the single market regime.

The problem for many MPs who supported Leave was that this left the UK at the mercy of the EU in general and the Irish in particular. It meant that there was a high probability that Britain would remain in the single market and customs union indefinitely, in the state of the softest of Brexits. This meant that as soon as the agreement was announced it faced furious criticism from the strong Leave- supporting element of the Conservative Party in Parliament, now organised as the European Research Group (ERG), with Boris Johnson one of its leading members. The DUP also opposed the backstop, and hence the deal. It also attracted strong opposition from the Labour Party. This might sound strange, given that the deal Theresa May had negotiated, including the backstop, was close to what they had demanded. If the backstop had been invoked (as it almost certainly would have been) then the result would have been what many in the Labour Party wanted and what their official policy called for. Although Theresa May faced vehement opposition from a section of her MPs, her loyalists, combined with Labour MPs, would have been enough to get the deal through. Why then did the Labour Party oppose her deal? One reason was simply that they did not wish to support a Conservative government and, like any opposition, were looking to embarrass and humiliate their opponents. There was also the real possibility that the government might collapse, which would clear the way, they imagined, for an election that they would win (given the way they interpreted their performance in 2017).

The real problem though was this: Jeremy Corbyn was leading a deeply divided party in Parliament. A significant minority of his MPs were actually strong Remainers who, in reality, would oppose *any* deal. On the other hand, there were also many MPs, mainly from Northern constituencies who were fearful that blocking Brexit would lead to a furious backlash from Labour Leave voters in their constituencies and very likely cost them their seats (a well-founded fear as events would prove). Outside Westminster there was the division within Labour's electoral coalition between its increasingly passionate pro-Remain younger metropolitan members and its older working-class voters in the North and Midlands (or at least enough of them to be troublesome). All this meant that the leadership of the party was in a very difficult position. The safest course of action seemed to be to continue to pursue a position of ambiguity by supporting the principle of Brexit while opposing Theresa May's deal in the name of a hypothetical 'Labour Brexit' that would miraculously solve all the conundrums May's government had faced in its negotiations with the EU. (This had a similarity to the unicorn, often sighted but never actually found). This all meant that Labour for a long time consistently voted against May's deal, while not coming out as a clearly Remain party or supporting what had become the central demand of the unreconciled Remainers, a second referendum.

The upshot of this was several months of increasing chaos and drama at Westminster. All of this was entirely predictable once the result of the 2017 election was known, or even before then. This state of affairs was caused by three main factors. The first was the increasingly destructive operation and impact of the Fixed Term Parliament Act. Had that measure not been in place, Theresa May could have done what John Major had done in a similar situation with regard to the Maastricht Treaty in the 1990s. She could have made passing the withdrawal agreement a matter of confidence (quite reasonably, given that it was the central element in the government's programme). That would have meant that if it was voted down, she could immediately ask the Queen to dissolve Parliament and call a fresh general election. This prospect would have concentrated MPs' minds wonderfully, particularly in her own party, as many would want to avoid an election at any cost. Even if some Conservative MPs had still rebelled there would have been enough Labour MPs who also wanted to avoid an election and wanted to see Brexit delivered to get a majority. The actual situation because of the FTPA was that MPs could vote against her proposals in the knowledge that this would not bring down the government or trigger an early election.

The second, and fundamental problem was one that has already been alluded to. The division in the country that had produced the referendum result and been made visible by it was not reflected in the division in Parliament or in the party system. There were serious splits within both of the major parties and although Parliament was divided it was not divided in a straightforward way between pro and anti-Brexit sides as it would have been had the party system reflected the division between Leave and Remain. Instead you had a division that led to the third reason for deadlock, which was the existence within Parliament (or at least the Commons) of what is known technically as a Condorcet Voting Paradox. It was this that, along with the incentives produced by the FTPA, produced the shenanigans that so entertained the media and increasingly exasperated the public.

Following the 2017 election and the referendum result, there were three broad groups in Parliament. When the referendum took place, as described in the chapter above, the overwhelming majority of MPs supported the Remain side. There were only about 132 Tory MPs who had openly backed Leave (though the actual number was probably slightly larger if we include those who took that view but thought it not worth publicly supporting it because they expected Remain to win). There were about a dozen Leave-supporting Labour MPs, and the DUP. So the decision to Leave the EU had to be put into effect by an overwhelmingly Remain-supporting Parliament. The people who had always supported Leaving the EU, plus a number of others, formed the first group of MPs, which we may call the strong or definite Leave group. Primarily Conservative, they wanted a harder Brexit and were increasingly relaxed about the prospect of leaving without a deal on WTO terms, to the point that it became the favoured option for many to most of them.

The second group was the diametric opposite of the first. These were the strong or unreconciled Remainers, who did not accept the referendum result and wanted to ignore it or, more often, to let the deluded British public have a second vote so that they could get it right this time. This group included the Liberal Democrats, the Green Party MP Caroline Lucas, all of the Scottish and Welsh nationalists, and a significant number of Labour MPs (probably just short of a hundred). The third and largest group was made up of the majority of Conservative MPs and a narrow majority of Labour MPs and may be described as reluctant Leavers. These were MPs who had supported Remain in the referendum but believed it would be undemocratic and dangerous to ignore or try to reverse the referendum vote. Within this group there was a range of views over exactly what kind or degree of Brexit was acceptable and over time many of the Labour MPs in particular came to feel that a confirmatory second referendum on whatever deal was approved by Parliament was needed, to put the whole matter permanently to rest. What they all agreed was that the referendum decision should be honoured so that there would be some kind of Brexit but that it should not under any circumstances involve leaving on WTO terms, without a deal.

Each of these groups had a preferred outcome. For the strong Leavers that was a no deal exit or at least a very hard Brexit. For the strong Remainers it was staying in the EU. Most of them couched this as a demand for a second referendum but it was obvious to anyone that their expectation was that such a vote would result in a reversal of the first one and staying in the EU, so that was only the mechanism for achieving the real goal, of remaining in the EU. For the reluctant Leavers the preferred outcome was to leave with a deal, although there was some disagreement as to what kind of deal was acceptable. This means three options: hard Brexit/no deal, stay in, and leave with a deal. The behaviour of the three groups of MPs or certainly the core of each group reveals how they ranked these three options, as shown in Table 6. There were two key features of the situation that created a Condorcet Paradox and guaranteed deadlock and paralysis: any two of the groups combined could outvote the third; the way the second choices were ranked meant that there was no majority possible for any one option.

Table 6. The Condorcet Paradox in Parliament

GROUP OF MPS	FIRST CHOICE	SECOND CHOICE	THIRD CHOICE
Strong Leave	Hard Brexit/No Deal	Leave With a Deal	Stay in
Strong Remain	Stay In	Hard Brexit/ No Deal	Leave With a Deal
Reluctant Leave	Leave With a Deal	Stay In	Hard Brexit/ No Deal

If we look at the table, the problem is clear. There was a majority in Parliament against every one of the three options but no majority for anything other than the principle of giving the referendum result effect (because that was backed by two of the three groups, the strong Leavers and reluctant Leavers). If a Hard Brexit or No Deal Exit was proposed both the strong Remainers and the reluctant Leavers would oppose it; if a second referendum or staying in was proposed then both the strong Leavers and (enough of) the reluctant Leavers would vote against it; if any kind of deal that the EU would agree to was proposed then the strong Leavers would oppose it but so would the strong Remainers.

This situation, of having a majority against any particular option from a list of choices but agreement that the choice must be made has been known to mathematicians and political scientists for over two hundred years. It is known as a Condorcet Paradox, after the person who first identified it, the eighteenth-century French mathematician and political writer the Marquis de Condorcet. The root of the problem is that while there are majorities against each option these majorities are composed of different voters for each option (MPs in this case) who have different reasons for opposing the option, reflecting their ranking of the whole range of options. In this case the problem arose because of the preference ranking of one group of MPs – the strong Remainers. Their voting pattern revealed clearly that their preference ranking was as set out here Stay In > No Deal > Leave With a Deal. Had they ranked the options Stay In > Leave With a Deal > No Deal then Leave with a Deal would have had a majority (it would have been what is known as a Condorcet Winner). But their voting pattern did not follow that.

This may seem strange. Why should people who wanted Britain

to remain in the EU support leaving without a deal more highly than leaving with a deal? (This was their revealed position since they voted consistently against any deal even when, as time passed, it became clear that the likely alternative was a no deal exit or hard Brexit). The reason is straightforward once you understand the mentality and outlook of the people involved. They wanted Britain to stay in the EU and not leave; if an exit with a deal was passed then Britain would leave, which they were against. Even a soft exit was not acceptable to them because they felt that even the softest of exits would still not be as good a deal as Britain already had as a member. They did not fear a no deal exit because they knew that the great majority of MPs were opposed to that no matter what. They also made two critical judgment calls. The first was that opposition to a no deal exit was so strong that if they could eliminate the option of leaving with a deal, faced with the choice between staying in and no deal MPs would vote to stay in or more likely approve a second referendum. The second was the combined call that there was a majority in Parliament for a second referendum, if only they could kill off the option of a deal, and that in the event of a second referendum Remain would win it easily.

The last part of this came from the outlook we have already described. They simply could not believe that people could possibly vote again for leaving the EU, once they knew what it involved and once they really understood what it was about (the assumption being that many or most of the Leave voters were misled or confused while those who knew what they were doing were unregenerate bigots who should be ignored). Quite simply, these beliefs were delusional. Even if there would have been a majority for Remain in a second referendum (the polls indicated that there would be but a narrow one) there was never a prospect of a majority for a second referendum in Parliament.

There were too many MPs (a majority in fact) who believed strongly that having a second referendum would be politically catastrophic, not only for themselves personally but for the country as a whole, because it would leave the country even more bitterly divided than before and open the door to extremely unpleasant radical populist politics. Crucially, this majority included not only the great bulk of Conservative MPs but a significant number of Labour ones. These were mainly MPs who represented Northern and Midlands seats with large numbers of Labour Leave voters (who were concentrated in these seats) and who both feared for their own prospects if they were seen to block or overturn Brexit and were able to judge from contact with their constituents just how angry many of them would be if their vote to leave was ignored or sent back to them with an implicit instruction to think again and give the right answer. The strong Remain MPs mostly represented the kinds of seats that had voted Remain by massive majorities and consequently suffered from the bubble effect of thinking that the views of their own constituents (and the media world they inhabited) were more common than they actually were. By the end of the negotiating process in 2018 they were also influenced to an ever-greater extent by the mobilisation of the Remain vote outside Parliament, which we discuss below.

The practical consequence however was that an unholy alliance of strong Leavers and hard Remainers prevented Theresa May's deal from getting through Parliament. In blocking this deal while holding out for a second referendum the strong Remainers were pursuing a mirage that they were never going to get and in doing this they gave up what should have been their second choice. They went only for the big prize and ended up getting effectively nothing. This was an amazing display of arrogance, entitlement, and lack of judgment that cost them dearly, but it reflected the beliefs and outlook of a large and self-reinforcing part of the UK's social, political, and media Establishment. On the other side the strong Leavers were also revealing high levels of delusional thinking. One example was the persistence of the idea that the EU would change its mind and renegotiate the deal it had approved in December 2018, even when the EU reiterated (in words of one syllable almost) that there was no chance of this, or the persistent notion that there had to be some way of getting May's deal but without the hated backstop. As time went on the delusions took the form of thinking that however often an actual withdrawal agreement was defeated in Parliament Britain would still leave the EU because there was a hard deadline to the Article 50 process that would ensure this would happen – and without a deal. This again completely ignored the reality of the situation in Parliament, that there was a solid majority against a no deal exit.

The withdrawal agreement that Theresa May had negotiated with the EU was due to be voted on in Parliament on 11th December 2018. In the debate held on 10th December it became clear to May and the Government that the agreement would be rejected, with a series of Conservative MPs expressing vehement opposition to it, above all to the backstop. May announced that the vote would be postponed and went to the EU to ask for the backstop to be renegotiated. On the 14th December the EU reiterated in very blunt terms its position that the agreement was final and could not be changed or amended. Meanwhile, enough Conservative MPs had written to the Chairman of the 1922 Committee of backbench Conservative MPs to trigger a vote of confidence by Conservative MPs in May as leader of the party. This was held on 12th December and May won by 200 votes to 117 (had she lost there would have been an immediate election for the post of party leader. And, by extension, Prime Minister). The 117 votes against May indicated the strength of the strong Leave faction in the Parliamentary party. Subsequently May put back the date for a vote on the withdrawal agreement to January (to allow the Christmas break to be available for attempts to persuade MPs to support the deal and for the whips to practice their dark arts).

The vote (a 'meaningful vote' as it was called because the Government was bound by it) took place on 15th January 2019. May's proposed agreement was voted down by 432 votes to 202, the biggest margin of defeat ever suffered by a Government in Parliament. The vote against included almost all Labour MPs plus all of the 10 DUP MPs and no less than 118 Conservative MPs. The majority thus consisted of strong Leave Conservatives, strong Remain MPs (some Labour plus all of the other opposition parties), the DUP and a large number of reluctant Leave Labour MPs, for the reasons set out earlier. Normally such a crushing defeat on a central Government policy would have led to the immediate resignation of the Government, but these were not normal times. The following day Jeremy Corbyn put down a motion of No Confidence in the government but this was defeated by 325 votes to 306. After a great deal of Parliamentary argument Theresa May brought her agreement back for a second meaningful vote on 12th March 2019. This time it was defeated by 391 votes to 242. The number of Conservative rebels fell to 75, still a substantial number for any Government. The day afterwards there was a vote against a no deal exit under any circumstances by 312 votes to 308.

After the second vote on the 12th March it was clear that the supposedly fixed deadline of 29th March would not be met but also clear that there was no majority in Parliament for allowing the clock to run down and let a no deal exit happen. The result was that Theresa

May was forced to go to the EU and ask for an extension of the deadline. She wanted an extension to 30th June, because that was the latest possible date that would not require the UK to take part in the European Parliament Elections in May. However, the EU leaders would not hear of this and instead offered an extension to the 22nd of May if a deal was passed, or the 12th of April if it failed to pass. The May government reluctantly accepted this and a vote to extend the deadline was held in Parliament on 14th March, which resulted in a majority in favour of an extension, by 412 votes to 202. This motion had several amendments attached to it, one of which called for a second referendum; this was defeated by 334 votes to 85, with most Labour MPs abstaining.

After this there was a complex period of Parliamentary activity, in which the divisions between parties were seriously weakened, to the point of almost breaking down but not completely. Theresa May's humiliation with two crushing defeats and her having to beg the EU for an extension, when combined with the FTPA (which meant the chance of an early election was minimised) meant a period of Parliamentary fluidity, in which party loyalties became severely strained. During this period the actual divisions described earlier between strong Leave, strong Remain, and reluctant Leave, became almost as important as the party ones. There was a great deal of cooperation across party lines, by people who were united in a determination to avoid a hard Brexit and, in many cases, to so obstruct the process that a second referendum would happen, as (they hoped) despairing MPs conceded it as a way of breaking the deadlock. On the Government side Theresa May and her loyalists were in a difficult position but were equally determined not to give up. Her own position was massively weakened, with many of the MPs who had supported her in the December vote of confidence now regretting their decision. She was able to survive because of the common understanding of the Conservative Party's rules, which meant that if a leader was challenged unsuccessfully a year had to pass before another could be mounted. Plus, there was no obvious successor and replacing her would force the party to decide clearly where it stood on Brexit and the new aligning issue, which it was not yet prepared to do. The other side of that coin was that as a lame duck leader she had little to offer in the way of carrots, while the stick of threatening an election was removed by the FTPA. Her strategy became one of enduring humiliation and hoping that if the now coalescing cross-party movement for some kind of softer Brexit became strong enough the threat of its success would spook enough of the strong Leavers in her party to swallow their opposition to her deal and back it because they feared ending up with their worst option of a second referendum and Brexit not happening. This strategy largely worked, with a series of prominent strong Leaver Tory MPs, including Boris Johnson, abandoning their resistance to her deal. The reason why many had begun to think that way and become more flexible was that their comfort blanket of a supposedly immovable exit date had been removed. There was still a hard core of Leavers however (the so-called Spartans) who would not settle for May's deal on the grounds that this was in some ways worse than still being in the EU. For them a no deal exit was the best option but they would rather take staying in than a deal with the backstop.

In March a series of complex Parliamentary manoeuvres took place, led by the emerging coalition of people who wanted at the very least a very soft Brexit or even none, with considerable assistance from the Speaker, John Bercow, who delighted Remainers (of which he was one) and enraged Leavers and the government by making a series of controversial rulings. These allowed the majority of MPs in Parliament to gain control of the Parliamentary business agenda (the order paper as it is known) so as to allow time for debate and voting on motions that the government itself had not put forward or approved. The idea behind these 'indicative votes' as they were called (because they were not binding on the government) was to make clear if there was a compromise position that would command the support of a majority of MPs on a cross-party basis. It was hoped that this would then provide a basis for the May government or even some kind of new government formed on a cross-party basis to approach the EU and negotiate a new deal, almost certainly a softer one than the deal May had negotiated and which would be acceptable to the EU because it would minimise the effect of the UK's leaving and make the Irish question moot, while preserving the principle that the UK was visibly worse off for having left. Many or most of the MPs behind these manoeuvres supported the idea that this renegotiated softer deal would then be put to a confirmatory referendum, with a choice between the deal and staying in.

On the 25th of March a motion (technically an amendment) put forward by the Tory MP Sir Oliver Letwin, allowing time for a series of indicative votes, was passed by 329 votes to 302, against the government's wishes. The votes were held on 27th March. The votes considered a range of options. At one extreme was a motion to simply revoke Article 50 and stop the entire process. At the other end was a motion calling for a no deal exit and another calling for a 'managed no deal' in which the exit would be drawn out rather than being abrupt. In between were four motions calling for some kind of softer Brexit than May's deal, all of them involving much closer alignment between the UK and the EU on a long term basis. One of these was the Labour Party's still nebulous official alternative to May's deal. The final motion called for a second, confirmatory referendum on any deal. The outcome of the votes is set out in the table below.

Table 7. First Round of Indicative Votes

MOTION	AYES	NOES	ABS.	MAJORITY
NO DEAL	160	400	74	-240
COMMON MARKET 2.0	189	283	162	-94
EFTA MEMBERSHIP	64	377	193	-313
CUSTOMS UNION	265	271	98	-6
LABOUR EXIT	237	307	90	-70
REVOKE A 50	184	293	157	-109
REFERENDUM ON DEAL	268	295	71	-27
MANAGED NO DEAL	139	422	73	-283

Several things did indeed become clear from these indicative votes. The number of MPs prepared to either accept a no deal exit or to straightforwardly block Brexit by revoking Article 50 was large in both cases but well short of a majority. However, the two hard line groups together had a majority against any softer Brexit. There was a small but clear majority against a second referendum. In the event this was 27 but there were 71 abstentions and all of the indications are that most of those 71 would have voted against a second referendum if they had thought it had a chance of succeeding, so the real majority against a second referendum was more like 70. This was produced by the combination of almost all Conservative MPs plus a substantial number of Labour MPs. This reality shows the delusional thinking of the strong Remainers, who would not accept that they had no chance of getting their desired outcome, no matter how long they kept the process going. The main point though was that there was a majority against every single one of the proposed options. This was a perfect illustration of the Condorcet Paradox that existed in Parliament, with the two hard line groups able between them to block each and every one of the compromise options, even though they did so for very different reasons.

Following this May had a third attempt to get her withdrawal agreement passed, on what had been the deadline day of 29th March 2019. This time the deal was defeated by 344 votes to 286. Her strategy of wearing down the strong Leavers in her party had almost worked but not enough. The 'Spartans' led by Steve Baker would still not accept her deal and 28 of them rebelled on that third vote, which was enough to defeat that (as it proved) final attempt to get it through. Following that third defeat there was a second round of indicative votes after a further insurrection within Parliament. This set of votes on the 1st April 2019, on a more limited range of options, produced the outcome shown here.

Table 8. Second Round of Indicative Votes

MOTION	AYES	NOES	ABS.	MAJORITY
CUSTOMS UNION	273	276	85	-3
COMMON MARKET 2.0	261	282	91	-21
REFERENDUM ON DEAL	280	292	62	-12
REVOCATION	191	292	151	-101

The majority against revocation hardly shifted. That against a second referendum fell but there was still a clear and large majority of MPs not prepared to vote for it. The two surviving soft Brexit proposals both improved their position and the option moved by the former Chancellor Kenneth Clarke, of staying in the customs union, fell short by the agonisingly narrow margin of just 3 votes. Even here though there were 85 abstentions, so once again there was a clear majority of MPs who could not bring themselves to support it. Once again, MPs had voted against all of the options put before them. This provoked much caustic comment about how appropriate it was that these votes had been held on April Fool's Day and reflections about the uselessness of MPs and indeed of Parliament as a whole. This however was very unfair. Individual MPs were desperately trying to find a resolution to the deadlock and their failure to do so was a reflection of the structural collective action problems they faced, which they were not able to overcome.

The question of why they were not is an important one and the answer to that question shows how it turned out that the mismatch between the division in the country and the one that existed in Parliament could not be resolved within Parliament itself. It also shows how the alignment process was working out and the form that it took: this was contingent since, had some things that were not structural been different, the way it worked out and the form that the realignment took in the end would also have been different. The dynamics of Parliament and the increasingly fraught debates over what to actually do about Brexit led to the emergence of a cross-party coalition of MPs. They had two goals: the first was to ensure that a no deal exit on WTO terms did not succeed, the second was to get a majority in Parliament to rally around and support some kind of soft Brexit that could be then offered to the EU as an alternative to May's positions and which, they hoped would resolve the national division. This second goal was essentially a reluctant Leaver one, in terms of the three-way typology set out earlier, but with a softer form of exit than May's version of that position.

This informal coalition succeeded in the first goal but not the second. The first was much easier, because well under 200 MPs were prepared to consider a no deal exit. In opposing that they had the support of all of the reluctant Leavers, plus the strong Remainers. Why though did they fail in the second? Before we answer that, it is worth considering what success in that endeavour would have meant. It would have meant a coalition of MPs supporting a particular position on a central issue of public policy that was not the position of either the Government (given Theresa May's deal had been roundly rejected but the Government did not support any of the options offered as an alternative) or the official opposition (given that the 'Labour Brexit' option was also solidly defeated and again the official party position was not to support any of the particular options). This would mean a cross-party majority coalescing around a specific soft Brexit position as a statement of Parliament's preferences. What though would happen thereafter? One possibility is that the Government would adopt Parliament's position and go back to the EU. This though would have meant a split in both the Conservative and Labour Parties – the Conservatives because of intensified opposition from the hard Leave faction, the Labour Party because a majority for a specific soft Brexit option would depend upon a significant number of Labour MPs supporting it (to make up for the Tories opposed to it). So, in practice, for Parliament to take control and force through a specific alternative softer Brexit there would have to be a split in both major parties and the emergence of a new majority drawn from both of them. This would mean almost certainly a new government and the effective appearance of a new kind of party alignment in Parliament with the three-way division described earlier becoming much clearer.

In this counterfactual, Brexit would have brought about a realignment in Parliament that would then have gone on to see a restructuring of the party system outside Westminster, with a hard Brexit nationalist party, a soft Brexit 'centre' party, and a coalition or collection of parties that favoured rejecting Brexit outright. This pattern, of a reconstruction of the party system inside Parliament and the political elite followed by a reorganisation and reordering of political structures in the wider country, is the way that realignments happened in the 19th century – we can see this in both 1886 and 1846. In 2018-2019 we came very close to seeing this happen again, mainly because of the effects of the Fixed Term Parliament Act which had removed one of the main weapons that the executive used to control the legislature in the British system. The point at which it seemed a real possibility was March and April of 2019 but in the event the votes in Parliament fell just short of what was needed to trigger it – had any of the specific soft Brexit options (notably the customs union one) gained a majority it would almost certainly have provoked a crisis, which could not be resolved by a general election and which would have produced the dramatic party splits described. The margin by which it did not happen was greater than the headline votes suggest, once we take the abstentions into account.

Why though did it not happen? There were several reasons. The first and most obvious was the strength and persistence of existing party loyalties and divisions. Both Theresa May and Jeremy Corbyn had made holding their fractured party coalitions together their top priority, for obvious and respectable reasons, given that was their job. This meant neither of them was prepared to cooperate in putting together a soft Brexit cross-party coalition, since to do so would have split their parties in either case. Also, parties since the mass expansion of the franchise in 1918 are more powerful and 'rooted' organisations than their nineteenth century predecessors. It is much more difficult for MPs, even acting as a coherent group, to reconstruct the party system, given the electoral system. This is why the last realignment in the 1970s took the form of a transformation of the parties in response to shifts in the electorate, rather than being driven by splits at the top and the emergence of a new party (although there was an attempt to do this, with the SDP). Realignment of political debate and structure are now driven by changes in the outlook and behaviour (above all voting) of large numbers of ordinary voters, and the way politicians respond to them.

A second problem, which became very clear later on in 2019, was the way Corbyn's election had transformed the left and the way it was viewed by other shades of opinion. Many MPs in both parties who were deeply unhappy about Theresa May's deal and terrified of a no deal exit while thinking the referendum vote should be respected (at least in form) were also totally unable to accept having Jeremy Corbyn and the people around him anywhere near power. A different Labour leadership would have been much more acceptable to a significant number of non-Labour MPs and would have been much better positioned to take a lead in putting together a coalition. A critical mass of Labour MPs, because of party loyalty and Corbyn's relative success in 2017 and crushing victory in the 2016 leadership election were not prepared to abandon him or make a deal with dissident Tories and other parties. Thinking about that counterfactual shows though how this was still unlikely anyway. There were always two large groups of people in the Labour Party who would not accept taking part in some kind of soft Brexit compromise. The first were the Corbyn loyalists. The other were the strong Remain tendency on the Labour benches.

That brings us to the third and main reason why a cross-party coalition that could break the deadlock by supporting a soft Brexit did not in the end come together. This was the arrogance and intransigence of the strong Remainers in Parliament. As set out earlier, they refused to settle for what any reasonable person would have thought was their second-best option and held out for their first choice. Apart from the hard core of 25-30 'Spartans' the same was not true on the strong Leave side, with most of them moderating their position and being prepared to settle for a less than first choice option, as shown by their votes for May's agreement. The Strong Remainers in Parliament did not show the same flexibility. Nowhere near enough of them were prepared to support one of the specific soft Brexit options. Instead they held out for their main demand of a second referendum. Getting a second referendum was not one of the goals of the informal alliance of MPs that took control of the agenda in March 2019, for a good reason: not all of them supported the idea. There were many MPs who were against no deal and supported a soft Brexit but were opposed to a second referendum, as the votes showed – at least, they were against the kind of referendum on offer.

The idea of a second referendum, as proposed by its advocates, was to have a confirmatory second referendum in which a deal approved by Parliament would be put to the public with a choice between the deal and staying in the EU (on the quite reasonable grounds that having made a choice to leave in principle the public should be asked if they still felt that way once they knew what it actually involved). The difficulty, which was elided by those advocates, was that you could not do this until you actually had a deal that was passed. The logical course of action for supporters of a second referendum in Parliament was to vote for a soft Brexit option and attach a confirmatory referendum to it. However, the strong Remainers did not do this and so those options failed. Instead they argued that May's Brexit agreement should be put to a popular vote, with the only alternative being to stay in the EU, even if it had not been formally passed. Their reasons for insisting on that are revealing. They were confident that in such a case they would win the popular vote, because May's deal was unpopular with a significant number of Leave voters who would either vote to stay in (on the grounds that that was better than a botched exit) or, more probably, not vote. The polls indicated that in such a hypothetical case Stay In would win by about 53% to 47%. What they did not address was the fear of many MPs, particularly Labour MPs representing constituencies in the North and Midlands, that a second referendum on those terms would be politically catastrophic and would provoke a massive popular backlash against what disgruntled Leave voters would perceive as an establishment stitch-up. That is why, despite their delusions, there was never a majority in Parliament for a referendum on those terms. By holding out for that and not supporting a soft Brexit they missed the chance of getting something they should logically have preferred to the kind of Brexit they got in the end.

The Remainers were not prepared to vote for May's exit deal and then try to get it put to a second referendum after it passed because they did realise that in that specific case there would not be a majority in Parliament for doing that – it would have been opposed by almost all Conservative MPs and a large number of Labour ones. The same was true if a soft Brexit option had got through, although that would have been much closer. What would have gotten a majority in Parliament for a second referendum would have been to propose a three-way choice, between staying in, leaving with a deal, and leaving without a deal. (This would have been a preferential vote). In that case even some of the hard Leave MPs would have supported it and it would not have run the same risk of provoking a populist backlash (because the populist voters' first choice would have been available for them). Almost every person advocating a second referendum was adamant however that no deal could not be an option in any referendum under any circumstances. There was a simple reason for this: the same polls that showed a majority for staying in if the choice was that or a deal showed that if it came down to a choice between no deal and staying in, it was too close to call. They were not confident that they would win the vote. There was a similar problem from their point of view with a choice between staying in and one of the soft Brexit options.

In reality, the advocacy of a confirmatory referendum was profoundly disingenuous. The actual goal and purpose of such a measure was to reverse the outcome of the first referendum and remain in the EU. In the meantime, every effort had to be used to stop any agreed exit from happening that might have a chance of commanding popular support. Just as May's strategy was to hold up the threat of no Brexit so as to wear down Leaver opposition to her deal until they reluctantly passed it, so the Remain strategy was to hold up the threat of a no deal exit and block any movement until MPs gave up on the idea of passing a deal in despair and either gave up on the whole process or agreed, eventually, to a second referendum on terms that would mean Stay In would win. That they ever thought they could get this and were prepared to frustrate attempts to create a Parliamentary majority for a moderate Brexit in pursuit of it showed a staggering level of wilful self-deception. Where had this come from? Partly it came from the smug insularity and self-confidence of the British establishment and the professional middle-class elite it was drawn from (Gray, 2019a). It also had a source in the continuing developments in the electorate outside Westminster – or at least one side of them.

As explained before, the 2017 election result had emboldened and reinvigorated the part of the public that supported Remain – which had been recovering its mojo and determination anyway. Following the election, in June and July of 2017, several grassroots organisations were set up and a number of MPs and political figures who were unreconciled to the referendum result such as Caroline Lucas, Chukka Umunna, and Anna Soubry began to formally cooperate together. The various separate grassroots and political organisations came together in early 2018 in an umbrella organisation called People's Vote, which was launched on 15th April 2018. As well as commanding the support of a number of prominent political and media figures it also had support from significant political investors, so it was not short of funds. It rapidly became a genuine mass movement and was able to hold a series of mass demonstrations in London in 2018 and 2019 that attracted hundreds of thousands of people (for some of them People's Vote claimed attendance of a million but independent estimates were in the 400,000 plus range, which is still very impressive). The main focus of its campaign was a demand for a second referendum - now called a 'People's Vote' as though the first referendum had not been a popular vote – but more generally it was an organised expression of the kind of identity and set of attitudes that had become consciously held on a large part of the Remain side in the immediate aftermath of the referendum. Obviously, there is nothing wrong with organising to promote a particular view and to campaign to have that view reflected in public policy or Parliamentary votes: people on the losing side had every right to organise and campaign to have that vote reversed, if they believed that it was a catastrophically wrong and harmful decision. The problem was the way they did this and the arguments they used.

What the People's Vote movement focussed on was mobilising

the Remain voters and intensifying their attitudes and identity. There was no effort to engage with and debate their opponents among the Leave voters. This meant there was not a serious argument made about how the concerns Leave voters had did not need leaving the EU to be addressed, or to the effect that there were ways the EU needed to change and could change that would assuage the feelings of Leavers. Partly this was because of something described earlier, the focus of many leading Remain figures on economics. The only supposed Leave concern they would address was that of being economically left behind so there were arguments about how Brexit would make the economic problems of places like the North of England worse or about how the real solution was an end to austerity. This missed the actual main concerns of Leave voters, which were national self-government and identity, with immigration control the symbolic issue that united them. Clearly these could not have been addressed in the same way as economic concerns because they went to the heart of the new division over identity: for the Remain side to have addressed them by making compromises or concrete policy offers would have meant compromising a core belief, in this case in the value of pooling sovereignty. What People's Vote could have done was to engage in debate, to make a positive case for their own values and argue in a respectful way against the core values of their opponents. They did not do this. Instead the views of Leave voters were disparaged as the product of ignorance, prejudice, or mendacious propaganda and therefore not worth addressing, even to criticise. The underlying belief was that in the first referendum people had not known what they were doing. By contrast, the Remain side was composed of people who were rational and informed (Bickerton, 2019. Jones, 2019).

What this did was to mobilise Remain voters (or at least a large part of them) and to give them a strong sense of a political identity. What it did not do was to change people's minds or bring significant numbers over from the Leave side to the Remain side. One result therefore was the creation of a large, passionate and vocal constituency of voters that was strongly opposed to Brexit and united in demanding a second referendum to reverse it as the most important goal in Parliament (Cohen, 2019). This fed through into Parliamentary politics and was the other big reason (in fact the more important one) for the obdurate hard line taken by the strong Remainers in Parliament, which prevented a soft Brexit coalition from winning. Another consequence was to harden and intensify the identity of Leave as a political position, in reaction to the campaign against Brexit and the rhetoric of the People's Vote movement. Studies done in 2019, by Populus and by Evans and Schaffner show how by the late Spring of 2019 Remain and Leave had become clear political identities for most people, with a wide and established range of associations in the minds of most people (Populus, 2019. Evans & Schaffner, 2019). They also revealed how for many voters these identities and labels had become more important than traditional party ones. Thus, the Populus poll discovered that while 66% of voters had a party identity, with 47% rating that identify as 'strong' or 'fairly strong' no less than 88% of the public identified as either Leave or Remain with 72% rating their attachment to that identity as 'strong' or 'fairly strong.' Even more dramatic was the finding that for a large number on both sides the Leave or Remain identity was more important than any party identity they had. The findings were that about 36% of voters identified as strongly Leave with the same proportion identifying as strongly Remain and the proportion saying that the question of Leave or Remain was more important to them than party identification was 77%. What this captured of course was the realignment, with voters now sorting themselves out by and identifying with positions on the new dividing issue of identity. With neither party clearly identified with one side or the other (due to the divisions and disagreements within the two parties in Parliament) it is not surprising that attachment to parties by voters was suddenly more fluid.

The campaign by People's Vote also had another consequence when combined with the structural deadlock in Parliament, which was to polarise the electorate, with both sides of the new divide moving towards more extreme positions. In the immediate aftermath of the referendum few Leave voters or even activists saw a WTO terms no deal exit as their first choice (partly because many thought getting a deal would be easier than it was) while few Remain voters wanted a second referendum much less simply revoking and ignoring the outcome. At that point, as explained earlier, the big middle ground position, that Theresa May was unable to own, was for some kind of soft deal such as 'Norway for now.' By April 2019 no deal had become the most popular choice for self-identified Leavers and a second referendum the overwhelming first choice for self-identified Remainers but with strong support for revoking Article 50. The public had become polarised and had moved towards the most extreme versions of the Leave and Remain positions, as a result of the campaign of People's Vote and the deadlock and failure to agree any deal in Parliament. One consequence of this was a strong sense of ingroup identity and negative stereotyping of the rival group, which gave the whole national debate an increasingly shrill and vitriolic quality (Evans & Schaffner, 2019). One of the reasons for this, which is revealed by the stereotypes and in the increasingly intemperate arguments used by both sides, was that Brexit was a proxy or signifier for other, deeper divisions. These were the divides that had started to emerge over the previous decade or less, over security both economic and cultural, identity, the location of government and lawmaking power, the relationship of the law to public opinion and the popular will, and the relation between the specific, national and local on the one side and the global, general and, universal on the other. Brexit had not caused these divisions, as many thought. Rather it had been caused by them, and the way people had responded to them. The process of Brexit had made them more apparent and intensified them.

This brings us to the final point to make about the failed attempt to create a cross- party agreement around a soft Brexit in Parliament in the Spring of 2019. The large group of reluctant Leaver MPs who supported that project to some degree or other were the representatives of the public as it was in the Summer of 2016. By Spring 2019 they represented the views of at most a quarter of the population, with that share shrinking. They were not aligned with one of the two main factions in the country, both of which were increasingly unwilling to compromise and insistent on having their first-choice option with those first choices by now moving to the extremes of the new aligning division. It would be easy to typecast the stranded centrists (on this question) in Parliament as the defeated Establishment but that would be only partly true. What they represented was the realistic and pragmatic element in the Establishment, which was prepared to make at least some concessions to the popular insurgency of the Leave vote. The other part of the Establishment, which refused to do that or to even engage with the views of Leave voters, much less accept them, was represented by the strong Remainers in Parliament and the leaders of the People's Vote movement (often the same people).

The polarisation of the electorate and the solidifying of the identities of Leaver and Remainer added to the challenges facing the leaders of the Labour and Conservative Parties. Theresa May and Jeremy

Corbyn were both in a very difficult situation and deserve sympathy rather than criticism. The challenge for May and the Conservatives was more acute in Parliament, because that was where the division within the party was greatest. In the country as a whole the Conservative Party was united in supporting Brexit and in wanting a fairly hard one. In terms of political strategy, the challenge for her and the party was that many of the people who now identified mainly as Leave voters were former Labour identifiers or still identified as Labour while prioritising Leave when that issue came up. The question for the Conservatives was how to appeal to them as voters – this would almost certainly require abandoning the free-market position the party had had since Thatcher, at least to some degree. May's manifesto in 2017 showed that she realised this, and the results showed it had been successful, just not enough. The other part of her problem was that there was a significant minority of Conservative voters (as compared to party members) who were pro-Remain and the challenge was that of retaining their support while appealing to Leavers. This was also tricky because the Tory Remain voters were also the most pro-market of any group of voters. The risk therefore was that for every vote they gained from Leave-identifying former Labour voters they would lose one from pro-market Tory Remain voters. That both of these groups of voters were concentrated, the Leavers in the North, the Remainers in London and the South added to the challenge.

The Conservatives' problems paled into insignificance when compared to those facing Jeremy Corbyn and Labour. As already set out Labour faced a serious electoral dilemma. Most of its voters and a large majority of its voters in the South East and in metropolitan areas defined themselves strongly as Remain voters. To the extent that the People's Vote campaign heightened that identity, they would be more likely to abandon the Labour Party for other left but pro-Remain parties, such as the Greens or the Liberal Democrats or (in Scotland) the SNP. Even more problematic from Corbyn's point of view, the bulk of the Labour Party's members had come to identify strongly as Remain with the People's Vote campaign consolidating that. This added to the pressure he faced in Parliament with his membership and many MPs pushing ever harder for a move to an explicitly anti-Brexit position or at the very least support for a second referendum. Corbyn and his team however resisted this pressure for a very long time. They had good reasons for this from their point of view. The main reason was the one described earlier, the 25% or so of 2017 Labour voters who were concentrated in traditional Labour seats. It was all very well to say that the majority of Labour voters in those seats were still Remainers: if the large minority of Leave Labour voters acted on their increasingly strong identity and switched to the Conservatives, that would topple many Labour majorities. This was a simple matter of mathematics but apparently beyond the grasp of some people. The secondary problem and reason for resisting the push engendered by the People's Vote was that most of the Labour figures associated with it were strong critics of Corbyn and his leadership and so they saw it as a mobilisation of a political tendency opposed to him and even perhaps to the Labour Party itself. This made the Labour leadership and MPs supportive of it very reluctant to move the way the People's Vote wanted. The problem was that this strategy of ambiguity and triangulation worked up to some point in the Spring of 2019. After that it became a liability, pleasing neither of the new voter identities and leaving the party vulnerable to erosion of its vote in both directions. As we shall see, by that point there were no good options for Labour.

As the debates inside and outside Parliament became more fraught the People's Vote organisation began to take on the quality of a political party in embryo. Simultaneously there was a succession of defections from both of the main parties, mainly by people who were strongly opposed to Brexit. The most serious and organised of these took place in the Labour Party when in February 2019 seven MPs left the party in an organised resignation. They were joined by three MPs from the Tory Party's Europhile wing and adopted the name of Change UK (with the extremely unfortunate acronym of CUK). This might have led to the coalescing around them of a genuine Remain party that would represent one of the emerging political identities, possibly using the apparatus of People's Vote as its basis but they did not get anywhere near that. One reason was that the whole process was mishandled but the real case reflected the strategically difficult position of the Remain side, had they realised it. Change UK and the whole Remain campaign had the central demand of a second referendum, which made them into a single-issue movement and party, in the way that UKIP had been when it started out. What they needed to do was to make that simply the obvious conclusion to a wider political position that would embody the views and interests that led to a Remain stance as a conclusion. However, it was too soon to do this and the big problem (which we will return to in the final chapter) was that the Remain and pro-second referendum side was still deeply divided over the secondary question of economics. There was still a profound split between socialist Remainers who identified also with the Labour Party and those of a centre-left or centre-right disposition who did not.

The failure of Change UK did not mean however that there was no prospect for a party to round up at least a large part of the self-identifying Remain vote. The more likely vehicles were established parties, specifically the Liberal Democrats, SNP, and Greens (with hindsight the defectors should have simply gone directly to the Liberal Democrats). At the same time the campaign for a second referendum and the growing prospect that Brexit would be blocked indefinitely in Parliament began to produce a response on the Leave side. All of this amounted to a huge problem for the two main parties, possibly an existential one. By the end of April of 2019, the process of trying to pass a deal through Parliament had reached an impasse with no apparent way forward. That debacle and the campaigns outside Parliament (increasingly from both sides) had polarised the public and produced a febrile political situation. Politics now descended into a Summer and Autumn of intensifying crisis, which ultimately resolved itself.

CHAPTER 6

CRISIS AND RESOLUTION – 2019

A Summer of Crisis – The Party System on the Brink

The failure of Parliament to resolve its internal divisions by the end of March 2019 led to a crisis of the party system in the Spring and Summer of that year. This was a crisis in the original sense of the term, which referred to the high point of a fever that resulted in either recovery or death. British politics in 2019 was indeed feverish as the realignment of the electorate pushed up against the established party structure and in the Summer of that year at least one of the two major parties had a near-death experience before suddenly bounding back at which point the fever broke and rapidly abated. Following the failure of the second round of indicative votes, on 3rd April Parliament narrowly passed a bill proposed by the Conservative MP Oliver Letwin and the Labour MP Yvette Cooper, which obliged the government to get Parliamentary approval for either an extension of Article 50 or a decision not to apply for one. The bill passed by 313 votes to 312, the narrowest possible margin. The point of the Act was to force the government to ask for a further extension to the deadline for exit, given that the failure to either pass May's withdrawal agreement or establish clearly what Parliament wanted meant that the deadline of 12th April would now apply. On the same day there was an attempt to authorise a third round of indicative votes, to be held on 8th April. If this had passed, there might have been a majority for one of the options for a soft Brexit and the EU would then have had an idea of what Parliament and (possibly) the British government would use a further extension to negotiate. However, the vote to have a third round of votes was tied at 310 votes either way and the Speaker was obliged (according to established precedent) to vote against so the third round did not take place.

The government though was bound by the Cooper-Letwin Act and knew that given both continuing opposition to May's deal and the big majority against no deal they would have to approach the EU and ask for a second extension to the EU deadline. The high drama and high jinks at Westminster were providing great entertainment for political obsessives and much excited news coverage but the response of the general public was different. Rather than being interested or enthralled by the drama, they were irritated, exasperated and frustrated by what they saw as the inability of MPs to arrive at a conclusion and deliver some kind of Brexit – any kind of Brexit in fact. Leave voters in particular, already irked by the vocal People's Vote campaign and what they perceived as the refusal of people who had lost a vote to accept the result, became slowly ever more enraged by what they saw as a deliberate obstruction of a popular mandate by a political elite. This frustration and irritation with the inability of the UK's political class to get its act together was shared by the EU's leaders. While they had all regretted the UK's original decision to leave by this point, they wanted the whole torturous process finished, not least so that they could move on to other urgent matters.

The British government asked for a further extension, again suggesting 30th June as the date, at an emergency EU summit on 10th April. It was not clear that they would actually get this. The French President, Emmanuel Macron, took a very hard line, arguing that the British would be unable to make any effective use of an extension (he was proved correct in this) and that it was better for both sides to bring the whole saga to an end sooner rather than later. The German Chancellor Angela Merkel took a more emollient line and argued for giving an extension and after much very tense debate she prevailed (the extension required the unanimous consent of the 27 member states so if Macron had held out and vetoed it, it would not have happened). What they agreed to was an extension much longer than the one May had asked for, to 31st October. This had important consequences: it meant the UK would have to participate in the European Parliament elections in May and that there would be enough time for important political developments to happen in the UK as a result of those elections, without the immediate threat of a no deal exit.

The need to ask for a second extension to what had been presented as an immovable and fixed date of exit was too much for the Leave part of the Conservative Party and set off a crisis. The common understanding of the party's rules was that, having survived a vote of confidence by her MPs in December 2018, Theresa May could not be challenged again until December 2019. Given that assumption, May's plan was to bring back her deal for a fourth time, in May or June, with the expectation that continued erosion in the ranks of the 'Spartans' would give her a majority. It is not clear that she was correct in that as indications were that opposition to her deal had actually hardened within the ranks of Conservative MPs, but in the event that was moot. There was in fact another, little known way, in which she could be challenged as Conservative leader. If the chairs of at least 65 Conservative Associations formally asked for it an extraordinary general meeting of the party's associations would be held at which a motion of no confidence in the leader could be discussed and voted upon. This was non-binding but clearly there was no way a leader could survive such an adverse vote. On the 22nd of April it was announced that 70 associations had asked for such a meeting and vote, so initiating the process. It also became clear at this point that there was no chance of May's deal being passed.

On the 2nd of May the UK's local elections were held, with very bad results for the Conservatives; their vote share fell by 7% compared to the last time these seats had been contested, to only 28%. The Labour Party also did badly with an identical decline in vote share (because of the nature of the seats that were up this translated into a big loss of seats for the Tories and a comparatively small loss for Labour). The Liberal Democrats and Greens both did well. The Conservatives lost over 1,300 seats, their worst performance at a local election since 1995. The seats had been contested last in 2015 when the Tories had benefited from the effect of UKIP's vote, with many of that party's voters switching to them, but those voters now abandoned the party and abstained, in protest at the May government's failure to deliver Brexit; hence the large losses. This took place against a backdrop of an increasingly febrile public debate. March 2019 saw several very large public demonstrations by the People's Vote movement demanding a second referendum, the largest of which had several hundred thousand attendees. At the same time an online petition asking for a second referendum soon attracted over six million signatures, in a record short time. The Remain voters being mobilised by the People's Vote were steadily losing patience with the ambiguity and triangulation of the Labour Party and its leadership and demanding a clear anti-Brexit party they could vote for or at least one that would give them their central demand of a second referendum.

On the other side of the divide, the ever more infuriated and exasperated Leave voters were also becoming organised and mobilised. The constant demonstrations outside Parliament and elsewhere by Remain supporters led to the formation of a rival campaigning group, Leave Means Leave, and by April 2019 there were always two groups of vocal protesters in Parliament Square, reflecting the growing self-consciousness and mobilisation of both sides. Nigel Farage meanwhile, had not been resting on his laurels following the referendum result and the subsequent implosion of UKIP. Despite stating publicly that he was going to leave public life and retire from politics, in December of 2018 he incorporated a new party, called the Brexit Party. The idea was that this would advocate leaving the EU on WTO terms and would become active and run candidates if the original deadline of 29th March was not met. As it became clear that this was indeed the case, on 5th February it was formally registered as a political party. Nigel Farage became the formal leader in March, replacing the initial organiser Catherine Blaiklock. The new party did not run candidates in the local elections but did do so in the European Parliament election on 26th May, which the UK was now obliged to participate in because of the duration of the second Article 50 extension.

Those elections produced a political earthquake. The turnout was 37% so only the most committed on both sides voted. However, this actually gave the vote a greater significance because these were the kind of voters very likely to turn out in a general election and also likely to cast the vote according to the symbolic issue of Brexit. The results did not make good reading for either Labour or the Conservatives. The big winner was the Brexit Party, which came from nowhere to top the poll with 31% of the vote and 29 seats. It won every region of England and Wales except for London. This was at the expense of the Conservatives who suffered their worst ever result at a national election, with only 9% of the vote as compared to their previous share of 24% while their number of seats went down from 19 to just 4. The Labour Party did almost as badly, coming third in the share of votes with 14% (down from 24% also) and with its number of MEPs halved from 20 to 10. In addition, it suffered devastating losses of votes in both directions, to the Brexit Party in places like the North East and to the Liberal Democrats and Greens in London and the South. Apart from the Brexit Party the other big winners were the clearly Remain parties. The Liberal Democrats came second in vote share, putting their vote up from 7% to 20% and increasing their MEP count from 1 to 15, while the Greens vote increased from 7% to 12% and their seat count went up from 3 to 7. Just as the Brexit Party's success came mainly at the expense of the Conservatives but with some gains from Labour also, the Greens and Liberal Democrats gained mainly from Labour but also from the Conservatives. In Scotland the result was a clear win for the SNP, who topped the poll with 38% (up from 30%). The Conservatives did relatively better in Scotland, although their vote share did decline by 6% to 12%. The real loser in Scotland was Labour, as they managed only 9%, a decline of no less than 17%. The Brexit Party meanwhile got a respectable 15%.

These results led to justified panic in both the Conservative and Labour Parties. They showed that the whole party system was in crisis and that both parties faced a potentially existential electoral threat. The electorate was polarising and sorting itself out around the two new identities of Remainer and Leaver, as the realignment around the underlying divide that Brexit had come to signify firmed up. It was still unlikely that the kind of result seen in Euro elections would be repeated at a UK general election – a European Parliament election was precisely the stage on which Brexit identities would be most clearly expressed – but if a significant number of voters switched at a general election because of their prioritising Brexit and what it represented over economic questions then the results for both traditional parties would be both catastrophic and wildly unpredictable, because of the nature of the electoral system. It would only take about 15-20% of voters overall to do that for there to be dramatic results and the polls described in the previous chapter showed that there were probably more voters than that who would vote on Leaver versus Remainer lines. To spell out the likely consequences, the Conservatives would lose many seats to the Brexit Party, but also to the Liberal Democrats because of split votes in the South. The Labour Party would lose seats to the Brexit Party in the North and Wales but also become very vulnerable in its new strongholds in the South, because of switching to the Liberal Democrats and Greens. Both parties would take seats of each other on an unpredictable basis, because of the vagaries of FPTP. The bottom line was that no MP could be sure their seat was safe.

The seriousness of the threat posed to the two existing parties by the realignment of voters and their failure to resolve Brexit in Parliament became clear in a series of opinion polls after the European Parliament elections. These showed an almost exact four-way split in general election preferences between Brexit, Conservative, Liberal Democrat, and Labour, with the Greens a very strong fifth. Under the UK's electoral system the outcome of any election was almost impossible to predict and the outcome of each and every seat was highly unpredictable. If reproduced at a general election it would have meant many seats being won on less than 30% of the vote, a situation last seen on a widespread scale during the realignment that took place in the 1920s. These kinds of polls were not simply a one-off; they persisted for several months and probably would have firmed up if the two traditional parties had not responded.

Even before the European Elections it had become clear that Theresa May's position was untenable. Faced with rising pressure from the party rank and file and many of her MPs, she announced on the 24th of May (two days before the Euro elections but at a point where the scale of the impending disaster was clear) that she was stepping down as Conservative Party leader on 7th June. The ensuing election for a new leader would not be concluded until late July so she stayed on as Prime Minister until the outcome of the contest was clear. This meant of course that an entire two months was taken up with this so that Brexit was put on hold for the duration, using up a considerable part of the extension granted by the EU. The contest for leader of the Conservative Party saw many candidates putting themselves forward or allowing themselves to be canvassed, a true feast of ambition, but in the event, it was completely one-sided, not quite a walkover but nearly that. It was clear from the start, as it had been in 2016, that if Boris Johnson was one of the two candidates to survive the elimination ballots of MPs, he would comfortably win the members' vote. Before the Summer of 2019 it was not clear that he would make the second phase because a large number of Tory MPs did not trust him and had doubts about his character and judgment, so that there would have been machinations to stop his getting into the final two candidates. As he did not stand in

2016, following Michael Gove's sudden enlightenment, we will never know what would have happened at that point. He would certainly still have had a decent chance of making it. By June 2019 there was no problem for him. Faced with the threat posed by the Brexit Party, Conservative MPs swallowed their doubts and took decisive action to preserve their party's prospects and its position as the only effective party on the right of British politics.

Boris Johnson announced on the 16th of May that he would stand as leader, even before Theresa May formally stepped down (he was actually the third MP to make such an announcement). Following the various elimination ballots, throughout which he had a comfortable lead among MPs, he went into the membership election facing the Foreign Secretary Jeremy Hunt. He won that by the massive margin of 66% to 34% having topped the fifth and final ballot of MPs by 160 votes to 77 for Hunt (Johnson's vote was 51% of all those cast in the MPs final ballot). The outcome was decisive and never in doubt, despite the desperate hopes of most of the liberal commentariat. This meant that the Conservative Party both inside and outside Parliament had made a clear and categorical choice.

What though was that choice? It was more than just choosing a particular person as leader, in the hope that he would restore the party's electoral fortunes. By going solidly for Boris Johnson, the Conservative Party had removed any ambiguity about where it stood on Brexit. It had come down clearly on the Leave side and not in any reluctant fashion, as had been the case under May. It was now clearly the party of not just Leave but a significantly harder Brexit than even May's withdrawal agreement had envisaged. The decision was about more than Brexit however. The Conservative Party had effectively decided to make itself the party of one side of the new political division that was realigning politics. It had chosen to become the party of nationalism as opposed to cosmopolitan globalism, of national identity as opposed to a more global or European sense of identity (of 'somewhere' as opposed to 'anywhere'), and of a politics that prioritised popular will and opinion over expertise and the rule of both experts and lawyers. It had clarified and changed its political identity to fit in with the realignment. Part of this was a downplaying of its formerly central concern with economic liberalism and free markets and a move towards a more expansive and active but also reformed and reconstructed state and administration. This had been foreshadowed in May's administration and the 2017 manifesto but became even more marked.

This clearcut and decisive action should not surprise anyone familiar with the history and record of the Conservative Party over the centuries. In its long and successful existence, it has had many ideologies and positions and has shown great willingness to change and discard these as the occasion requires. The core principle that has persisted is simply that there are many things in life more important than politics and that therefore the scope of politics should be restricted. To that end the main goal of the party has always been to win elections and hold power, no matter what (Ramsden, 1998). Holding office is an end in itself, because it keeps the other lot (who do want to use politics to change the world) out of office and stops them doing things. This is rather like football teams who base their play on retaining possession of the football: even if you are not scoring yourself, the other team can do nothing while they don't have the ball. This all means that the party will ultimately do whatever it takes to be electorally successful and to respond to changes in the demands of the electorate. This quality, of ruthless pragmatism, was clearly on display when Johnson was chosen. The other vital principle, which we have referred to several times, is that the Conservative Party should be the only serious party on one side of politics. It was this that had led David Cameron to promise a referendum and deliver it, when the emerging realignment led to the rise of UKIP. When the deadlock in Parliament meant that May's deal could not be delivered and the public reaction consequently saw the sudden upsurge of the Brexit Party, the reaction of the Conservatives was to recognise the new division in British society and politics and move to identify themselves clearly with one side of it.

This became very obvious, if anyone had doubted it, when Johnson announced the makeup of his Cabinet, immediately after becoming PM. No fewer than eleven cabinet ministers were sacked with another six resigning. This was the biggest purge of a cabinet either numerically or proportionally since World War II. The new cabinet was much more ideologically united and uniform, being composed entirely of people who supported a tougher line on Brexit. Almost immediately afterwards a series of increases in public spending were announced, with a pledge to recruit another 20,000 police officers particularly eye-catching. Even more significant was the announcement that Dominic Cummings had been appointed as the Downing Street Chief of Staff. This brought not only a very astute political tactician into the centre of the Government (as his record in both referenda he had worked on showed) but also someone with a very clear longer-term political strategy. The obvious conclusion, looking at the cabinet and the appointment of Cummings and others to backroom positions, was that this was a Government set up to provoke and win a general election on a particular kind of platform, to pursue a thought out longer-term strategy. Many commentators on the left and liberal centre however completely missed this and preferred to focus on Johnson's personal failings and his supposed unpopularity. This was a classic misjudgement. One of the immediate effects of Johnson's becoming Prime Minister was a recovery in the Conservative vote in opinion polls, which began almost immediately and continued steadily thereafter. This was much more than a 'new leader bounce,' because of its sustained nature. Rather it was caused by a steady decline in the Brexit Party's figures, as the Conservatives became clearly and definitely the party of choice for Leave voters. Much of what happened thereafter was part of a deliberate attempt to stage-manage events so as to strengthen that perception and the Opposition parties fell into the trap of playing up to that.

The Labour Party meanwhile also adjusted its position to take account of the reality made clear by the European elections. In response to the overwhelming pressure from its members and the clear threat of a huge haemorrhage of votes to pro-Remain parties such as the Liberal Democrats and Greens, the party moved to change its Brexit position. What they did not do was make the same kind of decisive choice that the Conservatives had done, and become an explicitly and openly Remain party. Instead they agreed to support a second referendum but not in an unambiguous way. The policy they finally arrived at was that if Labour were in office, they would renegotiate a new exit deal with the EU and then put that deal to a referendum that also had an option to Remain in the EU. In some ways this was a reasonable and sensible policy but it had several crippling drawbacks as a political move. The deal they were looking to negotiate was of a kind that the EU had repeatedly said it would not entertain so that part was implausible. Secondly, almost all of the leading figures in the party indicated that even after concluding a renegotiated deal they would campaign to stay in the EU at a subsequent referendum. This struck voters on both sides of the Leave-Remain divide as preposterous: why try renegotiating if you were then going to campaign against the deal that you had negotiated? Finally, this was a complicated position that could not be summed up snappily and went over very badly on the doorstep. The two consistent positions would have been to renegotiate a deal and then argue for it or to simply say they were going to call a second referendum and then campaign to stay in. The second would have made them a clearly Remain party. As it was, the Labour Party did stop the loss of votes to the explicitly Remain parties but not completely. They had once again failed to arrive at a clear position on the new divide.

It would be easy but unfair to be harsh in our judgement of the position the Labour leadership adopted during the tense Summer and Autumn of 2019. The brutal reality was that they had no good options, because of the split in their electoral coalition and the way those divided votes were distributed geographically. If they had moved to a clear Remain position, they would have stopped the loss of votes to the Greens and Liberal Democrats in the South and maybe even picked up some from the Conservatives in that region (although that would have been limited by Jeremy Corbyn's electoral toxicity with those voters). However, they would have suffered a massive loss of voters in the North and Midlands with big effects on seats because of its geographical concentration. Conversely, had they leaned more definitely to Leave, albeit with the pledge to negotiate a different kind of Brexit, then they would have done better in the North but suffered an even larger loss of votes to Remain-supporting parties elsewhere, which would also have been costly in seats. They literally could not win. From that perspective the position they finally adopted was one of damage limitation but at the time many did not see things that way and actually thought it was a position that could win. If they had written off the election everyone knew was coming by the late Autumn and focussed on the longer term then they might have adopted a clear Remain position, taking losses now to bounce back later, but nobody was thinking so strategically. In any case, because of the internal divisions in the party and the wider Labour movement, any attempt to settle the question of the party's orientation decisively, as the Conservatives had done, would have caused a massive and disastrous split.

The events of the Autumn of 2019 surpassed even those of the Spring for political drama, leading some people to seriously talk about the dissolution of the UK's constitution and political order. There was a critical difference though between the events of March and April and those of September and October. In the first case Theresa May was trying to hold together a party with very different ideas about what Brexit should be and was at the mercy of events – she did not control her destiny. In the second, Boris Johnson was leading a party that had made a definite choice and was now much more united and he had a very clear idea of what he wanted to do (or Dominic Cummings did). Despite the way they were understood and presented at the time, the Parliamentary votes and events of the Autumn should be seen as being responses to or engineered by an agenda that the Government knew it had and was deliberately pursuing. Johnson was much more in control of the course of events, although he did require help from one party (the SNP) at one critical point.

The most dramatic of these events was the Prorogation controversy. On the 28th of August Johnson announced that the Queen had agreed to a request from him to prorogue Parliament from the 9th September to the 14th of October. Prorogation is a suspension of Parliament, which is regularly and normally used, to mark the end of one session and the start of another. Technically only the monarch can do this and so this is a Prerogative power but it is exercised in fact by the Prime Minister (he or she has to ask the Queen to do it but as long as she is sure that he or she has the support of a majority in Parliament she is obliged to grant the request). This sparked off furious protest and reaction, not only from the Opposition but also from dissident members of the Tory Party. Proroguing Parliament at this stage of the year was normal but a prorogation of such length was unprecedented. Furthermore, the strong suspicion amounted to certainty on the part of the PM's opponents that this was being done to minimise the time available for any attempt to delay or stop Brexit. This was almost certainly true, but it also had another original intention, which was precisely to provoke a response and in so doing serve two ends: to flush out the hardcore opposition within the Conservative Party and force them to make their position clear, and to make the Opposition parties seem clearly intent on stopping Brexit, as far as the Leave-voting part of the public was concerned. It succeeded in both of these.

When Parliament met in September after the Summer recess, on the 3rd of September Oliver Letwin moved a motion to allow time for discussion of a bill introduced the previous day by the Labour MP Hilary Benn. This bill ordered the Prime Minister to seek a third exit deadline extension from the EU if there had been no Parliamentary approval for either a withdrawal agreement or a no deal exit by 19th October. The extension that the bill mandated the PM to ask for was one till 31st January 2020. The government argued very strongly against this, on the grounds that it removed the threat of a no deal exit on 31st October, and so weakened the government's negotiating position in any discussions with the EU. It was described by Boris Johnson as a 'Surrender Bill.' The Government undoubtedly did think that the law weakened its position but the inflammatory language used also showed that they saw how the bill could be used against its proponents, by stirring up Leave voters and mobilising them. Their first choice would be to have the bill not pass, but failing that they could see how it could be used to their advantage. Letwin's motion, to allow time for the Benn Bill, passed by 328 votes to 301 after a very emotional and dramatic debate. Twenty-one Tory MPs voted for the motion. Their numbers included several leading figures in the party including people who had served in May's cabinet, such as the former Chancellor Phillip Hammond. They were all immediately stripped of the whip, which meant that they could no longer stand as official Conservative candidates at a general election and so were effectively purged from the party. This act of unprecedented and decisive ruthlessness showed both the purpose of the Government's provocative stance and language, to force internal critics to break cover and expose themselves, and the degree to which the mass of the party in Parliament was now united around a clear Leave position. The removal of the whip when combined with another MP's defection to the Liberal Democrats meant the government had clearly and decisively lost its majority – it was now in a minority by a margin of 43. This however did not concern it. In some ways it freed the government from constraints because it meant they no longer depended on the DUP – even with their support they did not have a majority. As an election was what they wanted being in a minority was irrelevant.

The following day on the 4th of September the Benn Bill passed by a vote of 329 to 300. It completed its passage and became law on the 9th of September. On the 4th Boris Johnson asked for Parliament to pass a motion under the Fixed Term Parliament Act for an immediate general election. Such a motion had to have the support of two-thirds of the members of the Commons to be effective. This time it passed by 298 votes to 56 but failed because it did not get the required supermajority.

There was a second attempt to get an election on the 9th September after the Benn Act passed into law which attracted 293 votes in favour, so once again it failed to reach the required level of support. The reason why it failed on both occasions was that the Labour Party abstained. All of this struck many of the public as laughable: the Government wanted an election, and was in a minority but the main Opposition party that had been calling for an election at regular intervals over the previous two years now did not want one. Boris Johnson and the Conservatives knew perfectly well that they would not get the required level of support at this stage. Their purpose in trying to get an election was precisely to make the Opposition look weak, ridiculous, and obstructive and they succeeded in that. Getting an election was indeed their primary goal but they also wanted to stage the process of getting one in a way that damaged their opponents. The longer an election that the Government wanted was delayed the better for the Conservative Party.

The Opposition for their part did not want to give Boris Johnson an election at a time of his choosing, quite reasonably on their part, and they did not want to have an election until there was a definite extension of the deadline and so no chance of a no deal exit happening during the campaign – at least they said that and many believed that. Some though had a different motive: they wanted to keep the Government in office for as long as possible, without a majority and unable to get its business through until eventually there would be a majority for a second referendum to avoid a no deal exit, given that a decisive general election could not be called. This was the culmination of the strategy the Remain forces in Parliament had pursued for two years. That they still thought this would work shows the level of self-deception and delusional thinking that had set in for many of them. Quite simply there was no chance of a majority for a second referendum under those circumstances. There were still too many MPs who saw that as a prospect to avoid at any cost and who would have split ranks and voted to bring about a general election to prevent it. Moreover, the longer this went on the more enraged the Leave voters became and the more this consolidated support for Leave behind one force – the Conservative Party. Boris Johnson and Dominic Cummings were well aware of this.

All of these debates and votes in Parliament took place under the shadow of the Prorogation and Parliament was duly suspended on the 9th of September. The battle over that issue meanwhile had moved to the courts. Two separate cases were brought before the Court of Session in Edinburgh (Scotland's highest court) and the High Court in London. On the 4th and 6th of September respectively the courts ruled that because the Prerogative power was a political matter it was not justiciable, and so the Prorogation stood. This was in accordance with the long-established view of the Prerogative power, which was that in most cases its exercise was not justiciable and so it did not attract much comment. The plaintiffs however appealed their case. On the 11th of September the Inner House of the Court of Session (the Scottish court of Appeal effectively and the highest possible jurisdiction in Scotland) ruled that in fact it was justiciable and that this exercise of the power was unlawful. To resolve the conflict between the High Court and the Court of Session, the Supreme Court of the UK heard the case, brought by Gina Miller (who had previously won the case that obliged Theresa May to seek Parliamentary approval for invoking Article 50). In its decision, on the 24th of September, the Supreme Court found that the use of the Prerogative power was justiciable and that this particular use of it was unlawful because it was for an improper end and had involved misleading the Queen as to its purpose. This was a dramatic and extraordinary decision. Obviously, it humiliated the Government and put a spanner in the works of its plans, but it did much more than that. In its ruling the Supreme Court did not find against the Government on relatively narrow grounds, mainly because it had the problem that if the use of the power was explicitly political then it must be non-justiciable. Instead it effectively recast an understanding of the scope and nature of the Prerogative power that had built up over the previous two hundred and fifty years by stating that the Prerogative power and its exercise was entirely justiciable and that therefore its use had to conform to a number of established legal principles. This was a dramatic assertion of the power and role of the judiciary against both the executive and the power of a Parliamentary majority (given that is the source of the Government's authority). It moved the UK much closer to the kind of model found in the United States or the German Federal Republic. One may agree that the Prerogative power gives the UK executive too much scope for arbitrary action and that it should be more explicitly subordinate to both the legislature and the judiciary and still think that this was a very strange way to bring about such a major constitutional change.

In the event, the effect of the decision on the actual progress of events was minimal, given that the Benn Act had already passed into law. Parliament resumed sitting the day of the decision but then proceeded to only debate uncontentious measures and, to adapt a W S Gilbert line, "Do nothing in particular, and do it very well." The Supreme Court decision had no substantive effect on what took place or the final outcome. However, its future significance is likely to be great and it will almost certainly come to play a major role in politics in the future and it also did so in 2019. The Supreme Court's decision set off wild rejoicing among the UK's liberal intelligentsia and was generally seen as a huge humiliation and setback for Boris Johnson and Dominic Cummings. There was also much gleeful comment about the way that since he became PM Johnson had lost every significant vote he faced in Parliament. All of this missed the point and showed the self-regard and lack of awareness of those celebrating. This meant controversy and debate on exactly the terrain that Johnson and Cummings wanted. One of the latter's central beliefs was that the increasing scope of judicial review and the expanding reach of the courts, particularly as regards human rights law, was a serious dysfunction of the British state.

More important was the reality that this was one of the main divides in the new political alignment. The same voters who were exercised by questions of identity and national self-government were also strongly opposed to the increased power of the judiciary and the way that human rights law in particular, as they saw it, worked to thwart and obstruct the common sense wishes and beliefs of ordinary people. The law and the people who administered it were seen as the quintessential expression of both the power and the beliefs and attitudes of the class of liberal professionals that they disliked so intensely. For a party and a Prime Minister who had located themselves firmly on the populist and nationalist side of the new alignment this was an ideal topic to have covered in the press, one that would further enrage their voters and make them even more convinced that they were the victims of an elite conspiracy to frustrate their democratically expressed wishes. This was shown by Boris Johnson's response to the Supreme Court's decision in Parliament on 25th September, when he used very inflammatory language and refused to make any apology or concession to the views of his opponents and the Court. This shocked many of his critics but was astute politics.

There was an uncontroversial and short Prorogation between 8th and 14th October. While this was going on negotiations continued with the EU. To many people's surprise a new and significantly different withdrawal agreement was reached and agreed to on the 17th of October. Why though had the EU backed down and renegotiated the deal, having refused to do so several times when Theresa May had asked them to do it? The answer is that they had not backed down. What Boris Johnson did was to come back to the EU with precisely the offer that the EU had made to Theresa May over a year before, to resolve the Irish border question by having Northern Ireland remain in the EU's economic arrangements (and hence the customs union and single market) after Brexit. This means a customs barrier, however moderate, between Northern Ireland and the rest of the UK and as such was a betrayal by Boris Johnson of the undertaking he had given to the DUP. Basically, he had thrown them under the bus. However, he did not care as, given he no longer had a majority anyway, he did not depend on them for a majority, and wanted a general election anyway so was not concerned if they voted against him on a vote of confidence. By doing this he got a deal with the EU that he could be sure the overwhelming majority of Conservative MPs would support, as it no longer contained the hated backstop. There were a number of other changes to the agreement mostly of a minor technical nature and more significant changes to the political declaration about the future agreement between the EU and UK, to be negotiated following the UK's formal exit. The deadline for completing those talks was now set to be the end of 2020 and the revised agreement made for an exit that was slightly harder than Theresa May's, although the details remain to be filled in.

On the 19th of October following another passionate debate another amendment moved by Oliver Letwin passed by 322 votes to 306, forcing Boris Johnson to follow the Benn Act and apply to the EU for a third extension to 31st January. Again, there was much celebration on the Remain side with many arguing that this was a humiliation Johnson would not recover from given his pledge soon after becoming PM to 'die in a ditch' rather than seek an extension past 31st October. All this self-congratulatory bubblethink missed the key point. The only people who felt that way were Remain voters who were not going to vote for Johnson anyway. Leave voters did not blame him for the delay but rather Parliament and the Opposition and it only confirmed their view that there was a systematic and disingenuous attempt going on to frustrate the decision of the referendum and block Brexit. Again, this all played into the hands of Johnson and Cummings. Outside Parliament many activists on both sides had apparently lost their reason with all kinds of delusional fantasies and feverish speculation going on as to whether Johnson would write the required letter, what would happen if he did not (a common delusion among Leavers was if he defied the law and did that then the UK would simply leave on the 31st, overlooking the reality of a massive no deal majority in Parliament that would stop that), and about possible political upheavals such as the formation of a national unity government.

Instead, Boris Johnson did ask for and get the extension. On the 21st of October his deal passed Parliament by 329 votes to 299. This was a critical moment because it was the first time that a deal had passed since the whole process began. It meant that Johnson could now tell the country that, unlike May, he had a deal that had passed and so could conclude the whole saga (of which most voters were now thoroughly fed up). It showed also that the Conservative Party was now united, with many even of the 21 rebels supporting the deal. In fact, the Conservative Party in Parliament and the country was now more united than at any time since the early 1990s – its long agony over Europe had finally ended. Having a deal that had passed also cut the ground from under the strong Remain faction, because they could no longer present things as a choice between a second referendum and no deal. There was a deal now and one that was already more popular than May's. They still had one last throw of the dice however. Having passed the deal they then refused to pass the motion for an expedited timetable - the motion for that was defeated by 322 votes to 308. This meant the bill would not complete its stages in time for the end of October. This was presented as assuring full time for Parliamentary debate but in reality was a transparent attempt to delay matters so as to have discussions continue past the end of October. Once the extension had been fixed it became hard to see what the point of this was. The government then suspended the bill and left it lying on the table while they had another (this time) successful attempt to get what had been their main goal all along, a general election.

The granting of a third and final extension also cleared the way for a general election. The Labour Party now came around to supporting the idea and on the 29th October a vote that would allow a general election was passed by 438 votes to 20. Much subsequent comment has argued that the Labour Party should have refused to go along with this and continued to block an early election. This comment is not only misguided but ignorant. In the first place the Labour Party's stated reason for not agreeing to an election had been removed by the extension to January 31st. To continue to block one could be defended if the party was clearly and explicitly a Remain party because it could be justified in terms of holding out for a second referendum. The Labour Party was not an explicitly Remain party though, for very good reasons, and so that line of argument was not open to it. By continuing to block an election it would only have infuriated even more of its Leave-supporting voters and driven even more of them into voting Conservative. The reason why such criticism is ignorant is simple. The Conservatives had another way of getting around the FTPA, which was to introduce a short bill that would set its provisions aside and call an election. This is what they did and it was a bill of that kind that passed. That kind of measure only required a simple majority. There was clearly a simple majority for such a bill because not only did most Conservatives support it, it was also backed by the SNP for reasons of its own and the combination of Conservative and SNP MPs plus a number of independents meant a majority for it. So, Boris Johnson was bound to get his early election at that point: for the Labour Party to have still voted against it would have been futile and made a bad situation for them even worse.

It is worth asking another question, which is why the only hypothetical alternative to a general election with any chance of happening did not happen. This was the much-canvassed idea of a multi-party Government of national unity, formed with the sole purpose of preventing a no deal Brexit and then setting up a second referendum. This was the great hope of Remainers and the great fear of Leavers. In reality it was never on the cards for several reasons. In the first place, it was never clear that there was a majority for such a Government, given that not only the great majority of Conservative MPs were opposed but also a non-trivial number of Labour MPs because of their opposition to a second referendum. The other problem, which was impossible to resolve, was the question of who would lead such a Government. Precedent suggested it should be the Leader of the Opposition but the difficulty was that that position was filled by Jeremy Corbyn. He was simply not acceptable to most of the MPs who would have to support such a Government for it to be even hypothetically possible. The alternative was for it to be headed by a neutral figure who commanded respect across the party lines, such as Kenneth Clarke or Margaret Beckett. This however would mean Jeremy Corbyn stepping back and would have both provoked and only been possible with a split in the Labour Party. The political credit he had from 2017 meant this was not going to happen and so the whole idea was ultimately a fantasy. In reality, the peak time of opportunity for something like that had been around the time of the indicative votes in March and April when it did seem briefly possible that both major parties would split and a centrist coalition form around some kind of very soft Brexit but that had not happened for the reasons set out earlier, above all the obdurate intransigence of the strong Remain MPs and the loyalty of too many Labour MPs to a leader who was never going to be acceptable to anyone else. By the Autumn it was too late.

So, as the Autumn drew to a close a general election was called with the date set for 12th December 2019. The Parliaments elected in 2015 and 2017 were incapable of delivering what the popular vote in the 2016 referendum had requested because firstly it was not clear what kind of exit was wanted even though the principle had gained a narrow majority, and secondly because the divisions in Parliament were not sufficiently clearcut and binary to allow for a majority to rally around a specific option. This was because, until the very end of 2019, the divisions in Parliament did not match the hardening division in the country between Leave and Remain. The strategy followed by Boris Johnson and Dominic Cummings from the moment Johnson became leader was to deliberately heighten tensions and bring about a situation where Parliament was dissolved and an election called. Had they been able to get a deal through before the deadline they would have taken that and then gone for an election but they knew this was unlikely. In the event a crucial stroke of luck for them was that the SNP also wanted an election for reasons of its own (to capitalise on its position in Scotland and to have an election before its former leader, Alex Salmond, went on trial on a charge of sexual assault).

Johnson and Cummings had taken a calculated gamble. This was that by clearly identifying with one side of the new aligning division they would win a majority, and transform the composition of Parliament to one that would pass the deal they had got. The electoral calculation was that they would be prepared to lose a tranche of middle-class Remain voters in Scotland and London and the South and maybe even shed a non-trivial number of seats in those regions but more than compensate for this by picking up large numbers of working-class Leave voters in the Midlands and the North. This was effectively a re-run of the strategy Theresa May had followed in 2017. One critical difference was that by 2019 the gloss had gone off Jeremy Corbyn: voters who had voted tactically for Labour in 2017 to stop a 'Tory Brexit' were horrified at the (now apparently realistic) prospect of Corbyn becoming Prime Minister. So, the downside risk of losing votes again in the South was less than before. Even so, it was allowed for.

In this election there was no shock with the polls being shown to be incorrect, unlike several previous ones. Throughout the campaign they showed a clear and substantial lead for the Conservatives. Both Conservatives and Labour improved their predicted vote share throughout the campaign but they did so at the same rate, so the gap remained constant. Commentators and pollsters however had been severely chastened by their experience in 2017 and so were much more cautious in their predictions. The experience of that election also meant that Conservatives were much more nervous and Labour supporters much more hopeful than they should have been on the basis of the polls.

The campaign had its occasional moments but was largely low key – the impression grew as it went on that most voters had arrived at a conclusion and were merely waiting for it to all be over so that they could vote. This meant that the campaign itself did not shift the balance much as it had in 2017; instead it tended to confirm and strengthen already formed opinions. This all came from the underlying reality, which had been shown by the Euro election result. The realignment of voting patterns had now begun to consolidate and firm up. The only question was which party was better positioned to take advantage of that.

That was obviously the Conservative Party once it had made that clear decision and purged many of the Remain-supporting MPs and candidates from its ranks. Its predicted vote share rose steadily once Boris Johnson had become leader and, as said, this was primarily at the expense of the Brexit Party. That party had lost its main reason for campaigning once a deal had actually managed to pass through Parliament. It could still make the case for a WTO exit but that appealed only to the obsessives. Had there been time it could have tried to combine hard-core Euroscepticism with other messages that would appeal to the national collectivist quadrant, as UKIP had started to do, but having an election so soon after its formation meant that it was stuck in the trap of being a single issue party that had lost its defining issue for most voters. As the Autumn went on and in particular once the election had been called its vote was squeezed mercilessly. Faced with this Nigel Farage was forced against his wishes to announce, on the 11th November, that the Brexit Party would not run candidates in any of the 317 seats the Conservatives had won at the previous general election. He had previously asked for an electoral pact with the Conservatives, to maximise the effect of the Leave vote but the Conservatives had categorically refused to do this. This made perfect sense since one of the main aims of everything the party had done since May resigned had been to respond to the threat of the Brexit Party and destroy it as a credible political force. The whole aim was to be the only serious party on one side of the new divide.

On the other side of the new divide there was no such clarity. Instead of having one serious party and a fading fringe one there were several serious contenders. In Scotland the SNP were obviously the main choice if you were a Remain supporter. In England and Wales, Plaid Cymru, the Greens, and the Liberal Democrats entered into a limited electoral pact, which also involved several onetime Conservatives now running as independents, such as the former Attorney General Dominic Grieve. This though had only limited effect because of the refusal of the Labour Party to take part. This came from the Party's long-time resistance to pacts of any kind. The reason was exactly the same as for the corresponding position on the Conservative side – the Labour Party aimed to be the only serious party on the left side of politics. The problem with this historically was that apart from a period in the 1930s to the 1950s they had been unable to do this because there was a significant bloc of voters that was opposed to the Tories but would not vote Labour for various reasons (principally because those voters were liberals and would not vote for a socialist party, even if the socialism was nominal). So, the left side of politics was normally contested in a way the right was not. This was even worse in 2019 because of the Labour Party's ambiguous position over Brexit, which many Remain supporters could not accept, and because of their leader, who was unacceptable to liberal left voters. Even more fundamentally the Labour Party was not only impaled on the fence over Brexit: it was not clearly positioned on one side or the other of the new alignment in the electorate (the other Remain parties clearly were) and so it was engaged in the hopeless task of trying to reach across that divide. The end result of all this was that one side of the new divide was almost united while the other side was split between several parties.

The Conservatives' campaign was a stripped down one with few promises or headline policies. It was made clear that there would be significant increases in public spending, with austerity and fiscal prudence forgotten, and there was an explicit pledge to review the balance between the legislature and the courts, with a view to restricting the scope of judicial review. The central overriding theme though was summed up in another very simple but brilliantly effective slogan: "Get Brexit Done." This simultaneously identified the Tories as the clearly Brexit party and appealed to the widespread weariness with the long delays and wrangling and irritation at Parliament's inability to do what many of the public thought was a simple job. The election saw a major change in the Conservative Party's candidate list. Many of the 21 MPs who had had the whip removed either retired or stood as independents and there was a wave of MPs standing down and not seeking re-election. These almost all came from the pro-EU and technocratic liberal wing of the party, so this meant the Party's new identity as a party of the national right was consolidated. In essence the Party ran a repeat of the 2017 campaign but with a much clearer and simpler message and a much better run campaign.

The Labour Party had by general consent a disastrous campaign. Its ground game, in the shape of its many young activists, was better than ever and extremely well- organised but this had no effect in the face of the two crippling problems it faced. The first was the challenge it faced over Brexit. Its compromise position worked as damage limitation because it stopped large-scale loss of support to the Greens and Liberal Democrats but that was a purely negative benefit. It only stopped a bad situation from getting even worse. As it was, it still suffered a serious loss of support to clearly Remain-supporting parties and only regained about half of the voters it had lost in the Spring. On the other side, in the North and Midlands and traditional working-class areas it faced a major loss of support from Leave voters who saw it as having helped to obstruct Brexit. It was thus squeezed from both sides, with the loss of Leave support smaller in absolute numerical terms but more significant in terms of the impact on results in seats, because of the way those losses were geographically concentrated. All this was made worse by the second problem which was the massive unpopularity of Jeremy Corbyn as leader. He was still adored by a certain section of the voters but they were massively outweighed by those who since 2017 had come to a settled and strongly negative view of him. He was in fact the most unpopular opposition leader ever recorded, with record negative ratings. The negative view of Corbyn took two forms. Among middle-class voters, particularly in the South, he was seen as an economic extremist who had crazy ideas about how to run the economy. More serious though was the second source of hostility, which was found everywhere but was particularly strongly felt in working-class areas. This was that he was unpatriotic because of his support over his career for radical anti-Western organisations, including ones involved in terrorism. Quite simply Labour suffered because it was unable to locate itself clearly in the new alignment and its economic pitch to traditional working-class voters was overshadowed by the new division over identity, which Brexit symbolised. For many Labour voters Corbyn was very much on the wrong side of that new divide, being identified with a view of the world (radical anti-Westernism) and a kind of 'woke' politics, both of which they detested.

In that connection it did not help that the policy prospectus of the party did not impress the voters it was aimed at. There was a whole series of radical economic proposals, announced at regular intervals throughout the campaign. Some of these were individually popular but there were too many of them and they were not united by a single obvious theme or vision that would help voters make sense of them. Instead the impression was given of a financially reckless approach that most voters found deeply unpersuasive and unconvincing. They would have been better off making fewer promises that were more clearly connected to an overarching theme. It did not help that the mechanics of the campaign were seriously incompetent, almost on a par with the Conservative one of 2017, and that in several cases this was clearly driven by the factional interests of the Labour leadership group rather than serious electoral calculation. Finally, there was the poisonous legacy of the party's shocking failure to deal with the emergence of anti-Semitism within its membership following Corbyn's becoming leader. This had a bad impact everywhere because it added to the fatal perception that the party was both unpleasant and intolerant and incompetent. The whole thing was a fatal combination of a lack of a clear identity in terms of the new political alignment, an incompetent and deeply unpopular leadership, a mismanaged campaign, and being on the wrong side of several major aspects of public opinion – a perfect storm in fact.

The Liberal Democrats had, if anything, an even more disastrous campaign than Labour. This should have been a great opportunity for them, to take advantage of Jeremy Corbyn's unpopularity and Labour's unsatisfying triangulation over Brexit, to gain votes and even in many parts of the country to establish themselves as the alternative to the Conservatives in the new alignment, by capturing a critical mass of the liberal cosmopolitan vote. Their campaign had two main problems, both of which were self-inflicted and indicative of the way liberal politics had moved away from the position of the mass of the public, even on the Remain side of the new divide. The first was their decision, taken at the party conference in September, to move to the policy position of not even asking for a second referendum but to simply revoke the Article 50 notification and stop Brexit, so ignoring the referendum result. This was a policy that even many Remain supporters thought both extreme and arrogant and, above all, anti-democratic. It appealed to the hard core 20% of the electorate who were strongly Remain with an awakened sense of European identity, but it alienated everyone else and made it impossible for the Party to play a constructive part in debate because of the extreme nature of their position. At the point when they adopted it it seemed to make sense because of the perception that there was no way a deal could get through, and so adopting a clearcut and radical position seemed to make sense. A moment's reflection however should have told them this was not going to go over well outside the seventy or so Remain citadels. The Party however was full of people who, to quote Jonathan Swift, "It is the folly of too many to mistake the echo of a London coffee-house for the voice of the kingdom." The other thing that derailed the campaign was the move to adopt positions on some issues that were from a radically 'woke' position, in particular that people should be able to simply assert a sexual identity and have it recognised and protected in law. This was far out of line with public opinion and a completely unnecessary distraction from the issues voters were actually exercised by. Finally, it turned out that their leader, Jo Swinson, did not go over well with the public, as polls showed that voters (who knew little of her before the campaign) had a worse opinion of her after finding out about her.

In Northern Ireland and Scotland there were two almost separate campaigns. In Northern Ireland there was a complicated electoral pact around the issue of Brexit with deals on a seat-by-seat basis between Sinn Fein, the Social Democratic and Labour Party (SDLP) which is the other main party on the nationalist side in that province, and the non-sectarian Alliance Party, which is neutral on the question of the unification of Ireland. The media paid almost no attention to the campaign there but it had a striking and potentially historic outcome with a massive rise in support for the non-sectarian Alliance Party. In Scotland, the SNP fought a campaign that hardly mentioned Brexit. Instead they chose to focus on the aligning issue in Scottish politics, that of Independence and on their demand for a second independence referendum. At the start of the campaign the expectation was that they would sweep the board because of their commanding lead in the polls but as the campaign went on the indications were that the Conservatives in particular were doing better north of the border than many expected and a common view was that the SNP leader, Nicola Sturgeon, had made an error in choosing to focus on an Independence referendum. In the event she was vindicated.

The result of the election was not so much of a surprise as, by the polling date, almost everyone apart from terminally optimistic Labour supporters expected a Conservative victory. What surprised most people was the scale of that victory and the form it took. The consensus expectation was for a Tory majority of around 30 seats with the predicted majorities ranging from 28 seats to 52. They actually achieved a majority of 80, the largest such margin since 1987, winning 365 seats with a net gain of 48. Their share of the vote came in at 43.6 up from 42.4 in 2017. This was only a small increase (of 1.2%) but that needs to be put into perspective. Theresa May had achieved a significant rise in the Conservatives' vote share in 2017 and to actually improve on that, even slightly, was impressive. It was in fact the highest share of the vote gained by the Conservatives since 1970. It was also the sixth general election in a row that had seen the Tories improve their vote share. For the Labour Party this was a disastrous result: their vote share fell by 7.8% compared to 2017, from 40% to 32.2%. That was still higher than they had achieved in 2015 and 2010 but that was small consolation given that the Party lost 60 seats and was reduced to 202, its smallest number since 1935. Labour supporters cheering themselves up by pointing to vote share statistics were like football fans taking consolation in their team having had more possession or shots on target while ignoring the fact that they had lost 5-0.

What was striking about both the Tory gains and the Labour losses was where they happened. All through the campaign there had been talk of a Red Wall of traditional Labour seats in the North of England that the Conservatives had to capture if their strategy was to work. These were the seats that had seen a major swing to the Conservatives in 2017 but in that year they only made six gains. This time although their own vote only went up slightly, Labour's fell back and the Red Wall was shattered. Conservative candidates won seats that had never been remotely competitive for decades, such as Blyth Valley and the nearby seat of Bishop Auckland, which had never voted Conservative in its 134-year history. A succession of apparently rock-solid Labour working-class seats turned blue on the electoral map. There were many where the Conservatives did not win but turned once-impregnable safe Labour seats into marginals, in places such as Hull, Coventry, and Sunderland. In places such as Barnsley in Yorkshire it was only a strong vote for the Brexit Party that saved Labour and had the Brexit Party stood down in all seats, Labour would by most calculations have lost another 30+. The Labour Party did less badly by comparison in the South and managed a consolation gain in the seat of Putney in London but the less commented on but still noteworthy feature of the result was how badly Labour also did in the South, with its vote falling back right over the region. The losses in the South-East that Conservative strategists had allowed for did not happen. One way of looking at the campaign and result was that the strategy was a repeat of what Theresa May had tried in 2017, the difference being that this time it had worked. Maybe this was because of competent campaign management as opposed to incompetent but a more generous way of understanding this would be that May had laid the foundations for Johnson's triumph.

The Brexit Party's performance was mostly disregarded, except for its role in acting as a 'spoiler' in some seats and preventing an even larger number of Conservative gains. The headline figures would suggest that it had been crushed, as it only got 2.0% of the overall vote (644,257 actual votes) and did not win a single seat. However, it only stood in 276 seats and its performance in some of the seats it did stand in was much stronger than the headlines would suggest. Thus, in Hartlepool it got 25.8% of the vote, in Barnsley East and Barnsley Central it came second, getting 29.2% and 30.4% respectively. The party had strong and respectable performances in a range of seats across the North of England, which showed an appetite in those areas for a kind of national collectivist and radical politics that was not Conservative. This means that the project of Nigel Farage and others such as the people associated with Leave.eu, of a breakthrough for a genuinely radical kind of populist politics cannot be written off.

For the Liberal Democrats and the 'centre' in general this was a poor result. Here though there were definite silver linings, even if heavily disguised. The Liberal Democrats got 11.6% of the vote, which was a rise of 4.2% from 7.4% in 2017. This was not a bad performance given the low starting point following two disastrous performances in 2015 and 2017, but it was still a disappointment given expectations and the levels of support recorded in polls as late as September or October when the Party was getting around 20%. This was partly an example of the squeeze on third parties that is a regular feature of UK elections, as voters vote negatively to stop their least favoured option, rather for their first choice. However, as noted earlier, they had a great chance to position themselves as the clearest party of one side of the new alignment, in opposition to the Conservatives' clear identification with the other side, and they failed to do this. In terms of seats they ended up with a net loss of one seat, and Jo Swinson lost her seat in Scotland to the resurgent SNP. They did have a number of near misses and significantly increased their number of second places, to 91 from 38 in 2017. All of this was poor consolation however and will mean nothing if not built on. One notable feature was that all of the dissident MPs who stood as independents, typically on a no-Brexit platform, were defeated, and by clear margins. This shows something we shall return to, the exhaustion of the category of the centre as the alignment took hold.

In some ways the most historic results other than the Conservative gains in the Red Wall came in Scotland and Northern Ireland. In the former, Nicola Sturgeon's strategy was hugely vindicated, with a stunning victory for the SNP. They won 45% of the vote in Scotland, up 8.1%, and gained 13 seats to end up with 48. Labour was reduced again to only one seat while the Conservatives lost many of the gains they had made in 2017 and were reduced to six seats. In Northern Ireland both the DUP and their Republican counterparts Sinn Fein lost ground. Some of this was to the nationalist SDLP but the big winner in vote share was the Alliance

Party, which improved from 7.9% of the vote in the province to 16.8%. Because of seat changes this was the first election ever when a majority of the constituencies in Northern Ireland had voted for non-Unionist parties and there were the first signs that, for some voters at least, the communal allegiances that had existed since 1912 were finally breaking down.

All in all, this was a truly decisive result. It meant that all of the plans and manoeuvres of the opponents and critics of Brexit had come to nought. It had settled also what form that would take – Boris Johnson was now the unchallenged leader of his Party and Prime Minister and could put through his deal with no difficulty. The question of Brexit as a principle was finally settled. What though was the meaning of this result at a deeper level, particularly when viewed in the perspective of the time since 2015 or even 2010? The simple answer was that it showed that the realignment of political argument and of voting allegiance and behaviour had finally broken through and become obvious, on one side of the new divide at least. What that means in detail and its likely implications for the future are what we will finally examine.

CHAPTER 7

WHAT NOW?

The 2019 election showed that the realignment of British politics is almost complete. A new political and social division has become apparent and one of the two poles of that new division is now established and its nature is known. What remains to complete the realignment is the consolidation of the rival pole and the determination of its precise nature, but this will happen sooner rather than later. The election will be recognised (and for some is already recognised) as the moment when one alignment and political era gave way to another. As such it is on a par with elections such as those of 1886, 1922, and 1979, all of which saw major changes of voter allegiance and a shift in the social basis of parties and the nature of the main political division in UK politics. The story that led up to the election is the one told in the previous chapters, of how the tectonic plates of politics slowly but remorselessly shifted over several years and produced firstly a situation where a referendum on EU membership became politically necessary, then a vote to leave the EU, followed by a period of stalemate and intensifying and clarifying polarisation, and finally a moment of resolution when the new division in British society and the new political alignment it was producing became manifest.

The headlines of the election obviously concentrated on spectacular individual results and in particular the success of the Conservatives in capturing seats that had been Labour citadels for decades in some cases. It is the sociological and geographical analysis that shows what lay behind those results and the way in which this was a realigning election. If we dig deeper, we can see that 2019 saw a continuation of trends going back to 2010 and which were already very clear in 2017 – the difference between the election of 2019 and the previous ones was that this time the shifts in voter identification and loyalty produced by a realignment of debate reached a tipping point, where they were large enough to shift a significant number of seats. Geographically the Labour Party declined most dramatically in working-class small-town areas, many of them the places where the Party had originally been founded in the 1900s. This translated into a severe loss of ground in the North and the Midlands, and also in parts of Wales. It was already on life support in Scotland and this was confirmed. All of this was a trend going back to at least 2010. The Conservatives saw a mirror image geographically, making advances in places like County Durham that had been hostile to them for over a century and reappearing as a serious force in places like Doncaster where they had not been competitive since the 1960s. In Scotland they fell back compared to 2017, but not by as much as they themselves probably expected. Although Labour did badly everywhere London saw by far its least bad performance, just as in 2015 and 2017. It also had not-so-bad performances in places like central Greater Manchester, Leeds, Merseyside, and Bristol. Outside those metropolitan areas it did worse than expected and the Conservatives less badly than they had feared in the suburban areas of the South. Here the negative effect of Corbyn's unpopularity seems to have held back what would otherwise have been a counterbalancing performance to their dire showing in the North, Midlands, and Wales.

These geographical variations were caused by quite striking shifts in the class basis of the two main parties' electoral support, with an intensification of what we saw in 2017. The age at which the Conservatives became the most popular party fell compared to 2017, from 49 to 39. The Conservatives led in every single socio-economic category and for the first time ever had a lead in the category of DE (state pensioners, unemployed, unskilled labour). Labour actually did less badly among the more affluent and professional categories. The really dramatic aspect of the social distribution of the vote was that the Conservatives had their largest leads among the poorest and most working-class groups. Their lead among category AB (upper middle class and professionals) was 10%, among C1 (skilled workers) it was 9%, but among C2 (less skilled workers) it was a massive 18% and in the 'lowest' category of DE it was 13%. They led in every single band of household income. The one single social group where Labour had a lead was graduates: here they had a commanding lead over the Conservatives, by 43% to 29%. When this is combined with the geographical distribution the conclusion is clear. The Conservatives had become the party of some parts of the middle classes (the older and less educated basically) and of the larger part of the working class. They had become, as far as their electoral base went, a much more working-class and plebeian party than for a long time – you would have to go back to the 1950s or even the 1930s to find such a wide social base. The Labour Party by contrast was rapidly losing its working-class identity and becoming the party of the educated and young, of professionals, metropolitans and BME voters. Their leadership meant that at this election their scope for gains in the middle-class demographic was limited but if this trend continues, we would expect to see the Conservative Party becoming even more lower middle-class and plebeian and the Labour party even more middle-class and professional. The problem for the Labour Party in that scenario is that while there are many such voters, they are very geographically concentrated, so that is a recipe for having about 170 extremely safe seats but not much else. The class and geographical division, which started to appear in 2010 and became steadily more marked over the next three elections, reflects a genuine and severe conflict of interests, experience, and outlook between the two parts of the country and the population. It is this that has led to new questions coming to dominate politics and has consequently realigned political divisions around them. The result is lifelong Labour voters suddenly voting Conservative and many people from an affluent or professional background who would have been Conservative a couple of decades ago now being strong Labour supporters.

This new alignment and division in British society, which had led to the referendum and produced its result can also be seen very clearly in the way the identities of Leave and Remain played out in voting decisions (Electoral Calculus, 2020b). If we look at Leave and Remain voters and compare the choices they made in 2017 with the ones they made in 2019 a striking pattern of shifts becomes apparent. Of Leave voters who had gone Conservative in 2017, 92% stuck with the Tories. Among the Leave voters who picked Labour in 2017 52% remained loyal but 33% switched to the Conservatives. These switching voters were highly concentrated, in seats that had voted heavily Leave in 2016 and since most of these were once-safe Labour seats, the result was devastating. Among Remain voters who had gone Conservative in 2017 65% stayed Conservative while 22% moved to the Liberal Democrats and only 8% to Labour. Labour's more pro-Remain stance this time was not enough to outweigh the hostility these economically liberal voters felt for Jeremy Corbyn and Labour's economic proposals. Among Remain voters who went Labour in 2017, the party held on to 79% but lost 12% to the Liberal Democrats and 3% to the Greens – enough to explain their poor showing in much of the South. The Conservatives had made themselves clearly the party of Leave and what that stood for whereas the Labour Party presented a confused image on that and was unable to see off competition from other parties for that side of the new divide in the way that the Conservatives were on the other.

There have been a number of studies in recent years by pollsters and social research firms, looking at the ways in which the UK electorate divides into a number of discrete tribes, sharing certain demographic features and fairly coherent views and outlooks. An early one was the Opinium Survey 'Dead Centre' which used diagnostic surveys to identify a number of coherent opinion clusters (Opinium, 2016). Another, which was carried out just before the 2019 election was done by Datapraxis (Datapraxis, 2019). Both of these are useful and informative, particularly for sociologists (and marketing specialists, including political ones) but they are not quite as useful for understanding broad shifts in politics or the overall outcome of elections, because their fine-grained approach divides the electorate into too many sub-groups when an approach that identifies a smaller number of groups has greater explanatory power. The third model, which does this, is the one developed by Electoral Calculus (Electoral Calculus, 2019). Not coincidentally, that site had the best record in anticipating the result of the General Election in 2019 being closest to the actual result of all the major predictions. Their model divides the electorate up on three axes. These are economic left and right (markets versus government), social conservatism versus social liberalism, and nationalist versus globalist. This is very similar to the analysis used in this book, except that it still gives a role to the divide between social conservatism and social liberalism, which I would argue is no longer a serious divide in British society. (Their model would work very well as a way of understanding American politics, given the continuing salience of that axis there).

In theory the Electoral Calculus model should generate 16 voter groups but in their actual findings there are seven: Strong Left, Traditional Labour, Progressives, Centrists, Somewheres, Kind Young Capitalists, and Strong Right. (This is because of the limited salience of the social conservatism versus social liberalism axis with only one of their groups having strong socially conservative scores on that). In terms of the analysis used in this book and set out in Table 3 Strong Left are Radical Cosmopolitans who combine very left-wing economics with strong cosmopolitanism and radical identity politics, Progressives are also very cosmopolitan and left on economics but in a much milder way, Kind Young Capitalists are free market on economics and cosmopolitan and so go into the Cosmopolitan Liberal quadrant. Strong Right are National Liberals who combine nationalism with free markets, while Somewheres are National Collectivists who combine left-wing economics with nationalism. Traditional Labour are on the nationalist side of that divide but not by as much as the Somewheres and on the left end of the economic one but not as much as the Strong Left (although by more than the Progressives). The Centrists are the apolitical group of voters but they tend to be slightly left on economics and slightly more nationalist than globalist. The way the Electoral Calculus groups play out in the political categories of the new alignment is set out here.

Table 9. Distribution of Voter Tribes in the New Alignment (From Electoral Calculus)

LEFT COSMOPOLITAN	LIBERAL COSMOPOLITAN
Progressive (11%) Strong Left (4%)	Kind Young Capitalist (24%)
NATIONAL COLLECTIVIST	**NATIONAL LIBERAL**
Traditional Labour (10%) Centr Somewheres (12%)	ists (24%) Strong Right (15%)

Several things should become apparent from this. One is that there is a left majority on the now secondary economic issue (the scale of that depends on how the Centrists divide, given that in the population as a whole 37% are clearly on the economic left as compared to 39% on the economic right). On the nationalism versus cosmopolitanism scale there are 37% on the nationalist side to 38% on the cosmopolitan so again it depends on how the Centrists divide; here the indications are that they lean to the nationalist side, giving it the majority. This means that the winning electoral position is one that leans left on economics but nationalist on culture and identity. This was exactly the position that the Conservatives finally arrived at in 2019. The work of Electoral Calculus brought out how these 'tribes' were distributed on a constituency-by-constituency basis, even down to local government ward level. There were some interesting findings here such as that

Scotland had more Strong Left voters proportionately than anywhere else (although still very much a minority), that Somewheres were highly concentrated in the coastal areas and certain parts of the old industrial regions (but not all) while Kind Young Capitalists were very regionally concentrated, mainly in affluent parts of the South East, with local pockets elsewhere. Progressives and Strong Left were concentrated in London.

This model captures the nature of the realignment and the way it drove the election result, particularly when we combine it with follow-up work done by Electoral Calculus on migration of voters between parties correlated with 'tribal' identity (Electoral Calculus, 2020). This shows which 'tribes' showed gains for the victorious Conservatives and shows the kind of pattern to it, which shows how the realignment worked out and why it had the actual effects it did. The Conservatives lost some votes among the Kind Young Capitalists and even the Strong Right with most of those going to the Liberal Democrats. This shows how cosmopolitan voters were put off by the nationalism of the Tories' Brexit position, and also by their position on other questions that were part of that bundle, such as the role of the judiciary. Their losses though were limited, because these two kinds of voter were too far down the free market end of the economic axis to be attracted by the Labour Party's programme. The Conservatives made significant gains among the Somewheres (where they had already advanced in 2017) and among Traditional Labour. This was clearly due to their position on Brexit (and so on the nationalist – cosmopolitanism scale) but also because of their neutering hostility to them among those 'tribes' on economic questions. They had become the predominant party of the lower half of the table, on the nationalist side of the now aligning issue. In the future they will likely lose more votes among the

Kind Young Capitalists and even some of the Strong Right but have scope for further gains among the Somewheres and (even more) the Traditional Labour 'tribe.' To do so though, they will have to shift some distance to the left on the economic axis. The trick will be to do that without putting off too many of the Kind Young Capitalists. The Labour Party, according to the work of Electoral Calculus, went backwards in every single 'tribe' and lost ground to both the Conservatives (among Traditional Labour in particular) and the Liberal Democrats (among the Progressives and Kind Young Capitalists). The question for the future of UK politics is this: there is clearly now a completed or almost completed realignment on the right, with the Conservative Party the one that has captured it. The realignment on the other side is incomplete and has not yet settled on its final form. What shape it takes will depend on how the Labour and Liberal Democrat parties respond to this new political world.

What though is likely to happen? Detailed prognostications are a mug's game, but we can make informed speculations, given the state of play now and what we know. Clearly Brexit is done. There will still be negotiations between the EU and UK over the final trade deal and these will have their fraught moments, not least because of the Johnson Government's decision to impose a deadline for completing them on 31st December 2020. The dynamics however have changed as compared to when Theresa May was in charge and there will almost certainly be a decisive outcome, even if it is one that horrifies many people. The most likely course of future events is that the UK's economic connections with Europe will diminish slightly, with many supply chains being brought back into the UK, but not by as much as many imagine or fear. What will continue is the reorientation of UK exports away from the EU, which has been going on for over a decade already. On the other hand, cooperation between the UK and EU on security and defence matters will almost certainly become closer and deeper, because of the slow but steady parting of the ways between European countries and the United States in these areas, which is already becoming apparent. The idea that the UK will become a client of the US is wide of the mark – what is far more likely is that the famed 'special relationship' is likely to get cooler and less close, something of which there are already early signs.

The right in terms of the new alignment is currently victorious, and things look rosy for the Conservatives – provided they can keep their electoral coalition together and satisfied. That however is always tricky (Gray, 2019b). They have captured one side of the new alignment but that means they have to appeal to voters in the National Collectivist quadrant, who lean to the left on economics. Electoral incentives mean that they will have to continue to tack slightly to the left of centre on economics. The idea, found on both sides before the referendum, that Leaving the EU was part of a project to carry through a radical free market revolution and create a Hong Kong or Singapore on the Thames will be revealed as the fantasy it always was. There simply never has been the electoral basis for such a project. What we will get instead is something much more like South Korea or Taiwan on the Thames, with a still capitalist economy but one with a much more activist and interventionist state, often spectacularly so. Fiscal prudence has certainly gone and we may end up in the novel situation of its being the left of politics that is calling for fiscal restraint and less spending. All this means the now-dominant Tories will run the risk of losing voters from their free market side, particularly if the left side of the new alignment settles around a broadly liberal position. One response will be to tack towards that side on specific questions such as trade. The other side of this though is that the declining salience of economics as an issue will mean that other ones come to the fore, related to the new alignment.

The other side of right-wing politics in the next decade at least however, is likely to be the deliberate highlighting of issues and policies that will enrage the liberal cosmopolitan left but consolidate and enthuse the new nationalist right coalition. Two will be the old standbys of immigration policy and criminal justice policy but the scope for these to yield significant electoral gains is actually more limited than many imagine. The more significant ones, which we should expect to see making headlines, are these. Firstly, a range of cultural issues concerned with the arts media and broadcasting and including questions such as the future and status of the BBC. The new model Conservative Party is likely to take aim at the BBC and the arts, seen as the centre of opposition to its worldview and so a cultural war is likely, fought out mainly over questions of public funding. Politically this will cost the Tories support in West London but play very well elsewhere. The second issue we can expect to see is one we have already referred to and it has a good chance of being the defining one of the next decade. This is the question of the role and power of the judiciary and, beyond that, the question of how far democratic majorities and popular sentiment should be checked and constrained and ultimately overridden by laws and regulations, above all human rights laws, as interpreted by the courts or quasi-judicial bodies. This is an issue that divides the two broad social formations described earlier more sharply than almost anything else. It is also the issue that perhaps most clearly splits liberal cosmopolitans from nationalists apart from that of migration (which is related to it because of the way human rights laws and international conventions impact on migration policy).

If things do not go well for the Conservatives for whatever reason, most likely contingent events, there is always the prospect of a revival of the populist insurgency that once found expression in UKIP. One of the results of the way the Conservative Party has successfully adapted to the new alignment (even if only at the last minute) is that in the UK the realignment has not seen the emergence of a genuine radical national populist party with mass support. Instead that tendency has been captured by a transformed party of the centre-right. This will most likely persist, but there is a chance it will not. Nigel Farage has already registered a new party under the aim of the Reform Party, with an agenda of pushing radical constitutional reform so as to give more direct and effective expression to popular opinion and majorities. At the moment this is just a paper party but he and others such as Arron Banks have clearly not given up on the longer-term project that inspired both UKIP and Leave.eu, of a more profound transformation of UK politics by a genuine popular insurgency. Some of the results obtained by the Brexit Party in 2019 indicate that in certain parts of the country there is still an appetite for that kind of politics and these embers could be blown back into flames if things go wrong for Boris Johnson or if the Conservatives are seen to have let down the new voters they attracted in those areas in 2019. Farage seems to believe that the key to attracting those voters is political radicalism combined with social conservatism. The missing ingredient so far is economic populism and nationalism; if that were to be added there is great electoral potential, if the stars align.

Meanwhile on the left of the new alignment there is confusion and disarray (as there is in most countries apart perhaps from France and Spain) (Gray, 2020; Kaufman, 2020). In terms of the new alignment the big problem on that side is that a dominant and coherent pole has yet to emerge, to challenge the coherent Conservative one that has appeared on the other side. One reason for the incoherence of the left as compared to the right is the long-standing and historic divide between liberalism and socialism, which has plagued the non-Conservative side of British politics on and off since the 1920s. This has now been joined by a new and increasingly bitter division between the traditional liberal left and the newer 'radical woke' left which is having very disruptive and divisive effects on that side of politics. In terms of the actual actors, the Labour Party is faced with an existential decision, much more important than that of who leads it. In this it is no different to any of its European sister parties, or the Democrats in the US, all of whom face the same choice. What it cannot do is avoid it – parties that have tried to do that such as the French Socialists or the Dutch Labour Party have been destroyed as a result. The challenge and choice are this. Social democratic parties such as the Labour Party now have an electoral coalition that is being split down the middle by the new alignment. On the one side are older, less educated, working-class voters (the Somewheres and Traditional Labour). On the other side are younger, more educated, professional, metropolitans (the Strong Left and Progressives). Keeping these two groups together when economics is declining in salience is close to impossible, particularly when your political opponents play on the disagreements with wedge issues.

There are now two options for the Labour Party. If it wants to keep its working-class base and also its left economics, then it will have to move to the nationalist end of the new divide. That would mean aiming to have a coalition of Traditional Labour, Somewheres and Strong Left. A central element would have to be recapturing the language of patriotism and national identity that was once a central part of Labour politics, as David Edgerton shows (Edgerton, 2018). The alternative is to accept that the working-class base of the party is a wasting asset, try to keep as much of it as possible for as long as possible but to accept that it will be eroded and go for the newer and growing part of the left coalition, the younger left. That however would require two things. Firstly, a move away from conventional socialist economics towards some kind of egalitarian economic liberalism, because there are simply not enough voters in the Radical Cosmopolitan quadrant to win an election on that basis. What such a strategy needs is a way to appeal to enough of the Kind Young Capitalists as well as the Strong Left and Progressives, while holding on to as many as possible of the Traditional Labour voters in the meantime. The Labour Party cannot continue to push both economic leftism and cosmopolitanism – one of the two will have to be sacrificed. Either the Party keeps the economic leftism in which case it has to move towards nationalism or it keeps the cosmopolitan liberalism which means moving towards economic liberalism. The people who are guaranteed to lose out are the Strong Left, mainly because they are easily the smallest group. The other thing the Party cannot do is continue to try and appeal across the new divide. If it does that it will eventually suffer the same fate as the Dutch Labour Party or the French Socialists.

The alternative to a reinvented and redefined Labour Party is the emergence of a self-consciously liberal force in UK politics. There are many obstacles to this, most notably the electoral system and the stubborn attachment until now of working-class voters to the Labour Party. On the other hand, there are demographic realities that mean a liberal party could become a serious force. The obvious core demographic for such a force or party is the Kind Young Capitalists who are both the second largest tribe (at 24% of voters) and geographically concentrated. Such a force would also appeal to the Progressives, particularly if the non-economic issues of the new alignment become really dominant. The obvious question is that of whether the Liberal Democrats could become a party of that kind or the core of one. In the aftermath of the election one of Britain's leading psephologists, Sir John Curtice, said that the party's problem in the 2019 election had not been so much its extreme Brexit position but rather that its leader had not come over well and, most importantly, that it had an unclear identity: voters were unsure as to what its ideology was and what it stood for other than being very anti-Brexit (Curtice, 2019). What this, and the defeat of all of the defecting MPs who stood as independents, shows is the futility of defining one's politics at present through the category of the centre.

As used by people like the Liberal Democrats' former leader, Vince Cable, centrism means the centre as defined by the old alignment, the technocratic and redistributive liberalism that became politically dominant in the 2000s under Tony Blair, Gordon Brown, and David Cameron (Cable, 2019). That kind of politics is exhausted and does not speak to any significant or sizable constituency. Under the new alignment the policy package associated with that kind of centrism has limited appeal because it does not speak to any part of the new divide – with one exception. One curious fact is that people who were in the centre on the old alignment defined by economics are on one pole or end of the new one as defined by nationalism versus cosmopolitanism when it comes to questions such as migration and supranational governance. That suggests what the way forward is, which is to put forward and articulate a politics that is clearly and self-consciously liberal and therefore opposed to both the national politics of the right (as embodied in the current Conservative Party) and the combination of left economics and radical identity politics that currently animates the left. What nobody putting such an ideology forward should do is to present it as being 'moderate' or 'centrist' because it is not, particularly in the new alignment. The other thing to avoid at any cost is technocracy and the rule of experts.

Another thing that is much discussed is the future of the Union and therefore of Scotland and Northern Ireland. As far as Scotland goes, it is clear that the separate realignment that has taken place there is now completed and has been for some time. For now, the overriding issue is the division between Independence and Unionism, which increasingly pits two different visions of Scottish identity against one another (so here as elsewhere the question of culture and identity has become primary, but in a different way as compared to England and Wales). The SNP may seem to be effortlessly predominant, and Nicola Sturgeon monarch of all she surveys, but the SNP actually faces serious problems, many coming from the simple fact of its having been in power in Edinburgh for a long time, which brings increasing attention to its performance. However, as long as the question of Independence is dominant this will not have the effect it would in most polities or, indeed, in an independent Scotland. The common reaction to the 2019 election is that it has made Scottish independence more likely, because of the Scottish electorate's strong support for Remain. The idea is now that Brexit has happened there will be a move to get independence so that Scotland can rejoin the EU.

In reality, Brexit makes Scottish independence slightly less probable and makes the prospect of Scotland being in the EU once more much less likely, whether it is independent or not. If Scotland leaves the UK and then joins the EU or even the European Economic Area (like Norway) then there will have to be a hard border with England, given that the rest of the UK will be outside the EU on the terms of Boris Johnson's deal. There is no avoiding this since the EU will insist on it, as they did in the case of Ireland. A hard border between Scotland and England would have a simply devastating effect on the Scottish economy and will be a seriously intimidating prospect for that and other reasons. This makes leaving the UK much less attractive, if the main reason is so as to be in the EU (as it is for some Scottish voters). If however Scottish independence is seen as an end in itself or as the primary point, with EU membership a secondary matter, then Scotland could still vote for independence: it would simply not rejoin the EU and probably have the same kind of relation with the EU as England and Wales. That would make independence a different kind of project to the one it has been since Alex Salmond had his second spell as leader. Independence of that kind would still attract a large part of Scotland's electorate, because of the growth of national feeling and the increasing divergence between the political cultures of England/ Wales and Scotland. However, it is less likely to command a majority, although that prospect should not be ruled out. Also, given the inevitability of close cooperation between an independent Scotland and England and Wales over trade, foreign affairs and defence, independence outside the EU would not be that much different from full Home Rule, which the UK Government may well offer.

All that assumes that the UK Government will concede a second Scottish Independence referendum – something it has said it will not do. However, that is very much a political judgement and may change if circumstances do. Right now, it suits both the SNP and the Conservatives to polarise Scottish debate around this question, at least until the Scottish Parliament elections in 2021. What happens thereafter depends on how the balance of political advantage lies. The same is true in Northern Ireland. That province is now much more closely linked economically to the Republic than the rest of the UK and this is likely to become more marked over time. The 2019 election indicated that for a part of the Protestant community there (the middle-class part basically) economic questions are now becoming more important than ones of political allegiance. This means that if a Border Poll were to be held under the terms of the Good Friday Agreement there is a much better chance than heretofore of a vote for a united Ireland. Such a vote, particularly if it was close (as it would be) would cause all kinds of problems but these would be problems for the Irish government in Dublin to deal with, not the British one in London.

There is one big and sweeping question that we need to ask. Are we at the end of a liberal era, in Britain and elsewhere? There will no doubt be a spate of books in the next few years arguing that this is so, and that we are now moving into a post-liberal era of politics. In one sense in the UK case at least this is true. If we look at the political divisions of the old alignment as set out in Table 2 and think about the way that alignment finished up in the 2000s we can see that over the course of that alignment there was a convergence on a certain kind of liberalism. The Conservative Party came to be defined by economic liberalism, from Thatcher onwards while the Labour Party was increasingly defined by social liberalism, maybe from as far back as Roy Jenkins (while combined with egalitarianism). Under Blair the Labour Party moved a long way towards economic liberalism, while the Conservative Party under Cameron shifted in the direction of social liberalism. So, by the 2000s as was described in Chapter 2 a kind of liberalism had become hegemonic, as both parties converged on it. This sounds like a golden age for liberals but that view should be qualified. Neither party ever ended up completely inside what we may call the 'pure liberal' quadrant and the kind of liberalism that they both did espouse to some degree was a technocratic one, based on expertise rather than values. What we certainly have at present, in Britain and elsewhere, is the appearance of a politics that is certainly post-liberal and, in some cases, (such as Hungary and Poland for example) explicitly and vocally anti-liberal. What liberals may hope for in that scenario is that the rival pole of politics in the new alignment will not be a different kind of post-liberal politics but a more self-aware assertion of liberalism. In that case we would have a politics rather like that of the nineteenth century, with an opposition between liberalism and a form of non-liberal politics (of a nationalist kind). What will determine whether that happens or not is the outcome of the competition between liberalism and what we may call progressivism or radical leftism for the dominant position in the cosmopolitan pole of the new politics.

Finally, we are almost certainly entering a period of politics in which the salience of economics will decline and that of cultural questions will increase. This will take some getting used to for those on both sides of the old divide for whom economics was the big issue that everything else revolved around. It is this decline in the salience of economics that will, more than anything else, make for some surprising alliances as people who disagree about economics but agree about everything else suddenly find themselves on the same side of the new aisle. This is actually going to be bad news for both radical free marketeers and socialists, as they will find that there is a broad consensus on economics that neither of them particularly like, with a predominantly capitalist and free market economy but one that has a central role for a very active state and is organised, for a while at least, at the national level with a retreat from the levels of economic integration we have seen recently. The new politics will initially have an intransigent and bitter quality, as questions of culture and identity are less susceptible to compromise than ones of economics. It is the task of politicians however to argue and debate and to discover where common ground or at least acceptance may be found.

CONCLUSION

We are now living in a new era of British politics, the tenth such since the English invented modern party politics in 1671. How politics will work out and develop in this new era is uncertain and will depend on chance, the skill and judgement of political leaders, and the outcomes of debates and arguments as much as any structural factors. How this came about and how viewing the politics of recent years in this way, as a story of realignment, helps us to make sense of the otherwise confusing story of Brexit, is the subject of this book. The story told here, and the argument that informs it, mean that we should not think of Brexit as an act of inexplicable national self-harm, a moment of collective madness, or as something that makes no sense, "a tale told by an idiot, full of sound and fury, signifying nothing." Rather it was the outcome of a change in the way politics was structured, of a kind that had happened before and the fact that the key event in that change was Britain's voting to leave the EU and ultimately doing so, was a reflection of the way that particular topic had come to stand for and represent a whole series of other divisions – the ones that will now shape and determine British politics going forward.

In the United Kingdom, politics from the 1920s onwards has been structured around a division over the best way to organise the economic life of the community. This has been the main aligning issue, the one that other divisions have tended to follow and align with for that near hundred-year period. That division had become more important after the 1880s but it was not until the 1920s that it became the aligning question, the one that sorted people into the two great tribes of left and right or Labour and Conservative (before then it had been a different set of questions, which had sorted people into Liberals and Conservatives). It came from the reality that this disagreement was born out of conflicts of interest and experience in British society, between Labour and Capital, management and employee, middle class and working class. Now it is slowly passing from the scene. In the 1970s and early 1980s a secondary divide appeared over the question of social conservatism and social liberalism, and the role of the state in upholding social norms. The combination of that with the primary economic divide produced the politics that anyone of a certain age is familiar with, with the two poles of argument being a position that combined an active economic role for government with social liberalism and another that put together support for free markets with social conservatism. By the decade of the 2000s that alignment was exhausted: one pole had moved towards economic liberalism while the other had moved to social liberalism. A kind of technocratic liberalism had come to dominate public discourse.

At that point a new division began to appear, that reflected and derived from a new clash of interests and experiences in British society. This was a division over identity and in particular the connection and relation between the local, specific, and traditional and the global, universal, and novel. Geographically it was a divide between globally connected metropolitan areas, above all London, and the rural and small-town regions of England and Wales. In terms of attitudes and sensibility it was a divide between what one author has called 'somewheres' and 'anywheres' (Goodhart, 2017). The economic aspect of this was a clash of interests between those who worked or were invested in parts of the economy that were local, often not traded internationally, and not integrated into global networks and those who were part of an international networked economy, built around city regions rather than nations. What connected that economic tension with the conflict over attitudes and sentiments and sense of identity was the critical role of the meritocratic labour market, with formal academic attainment both giving access to the networked and global economy and through experience imparting a series of outlooks and beliefs that were not shared by those who had not passed through that academic sieve. This means that a very visible facet of the new division is that between the more and less formally educated. Another is that of age (although this may well be derivative, from the educational and work divisions). One way of summarising this emerging division that applies to many countries and not just the UK is the concept of a clash between the core and the periphery. In that model the periphery means not the literal physical periphery only but those geographical areas that are not part of the global but specifically located core zone of every country and which are also peripheral in the sense of having their concerns, anxieties, and beliefs slighted or ignored by those with both economic and cultural power.

This new division initially had little political effect – other than large numbers of people giving up on politics. With time it started to produce a popular movement of resistance to and protest against the established and officially approved way of doing things and the people associated with that. This began to find political expression in terms of votes at the very end of the 2000s, even if not in seats in Parliament (because of the electoral system). The new division came to focus in the British case on the question of the UK's membership of the EU. This was partly because of the longstanding reality that the English and Welsh public was much less European-minded than most other European publics. The main reason though was that the EU and its rules and actions had come for many (rightly or wrongly) to embody and symbolise many of the policies, attitudes, and ways of living that they disliked and resented. For others exactly the opposite was true: the EU still represented the same things but these people liked and supported them. One of the most important ways in which the EU came to embody a practice that some resented to the point of hatred while others liked and admired it, was the principle that abstract laws and regulations should be more important than and override political decisions and the wishes of popular majorities. This question, which became important as a popular complaint in the runup to 2016, is likely to become one of the defining political issues of the next few years.

By the middle of the 2010s the new emergent kind of politics, growing out of the new division, had become significant enough that it produced a situation where it was politically necessary (not just expedient) to promise and then call a referendum on Britain's continued membership of the EU, the question that had come to be a stand-in or signifier for the whole range of questions in the emerging new division. In that referendum one part of the side arguing for Leave showed that as well as being more effective and competent they had a better understanding of the new dividing issue and of how to put together a majority based on that divide than either the side advocating Remain or some of their supposed allies. As a result, they won the vote, in the face of a united front from the Establishment and the great and good.

After the result some of the flabbergasted Establishment tried to put it into effect, albeit in a constrained way and without fully understanding what lay behind it but a large and vocal part had refused to accept its validity and had sought to obstruct and reverse it. In addition, the vote itself and the campaign of obstruction had together made the part of the population who did not share the worries or beliefs of the victors more aware of their own beliefs, interests, and positions and so the other side of the new alignment came into clearer definition and became more self-conscious. This made a continuing argument over Brexit inevitable – there was no way it could be settled easily because it symbolised the profound and ongoing division in British society, which politics was now rapidly aligning around.

Eventually the Conservative Party identified itself clearly and explicitly with one side of the new divide. By doing so it became the party of the 'somewheres,' the rural areas, coastal areas and smaller towns, against the metropolitan centres and the 'anywheres.' As a consequence, the nature of its electoral base changed and it became a much more plebeian and provincial party than it had been for a very long time. The Labour Party is halfway through a transformation of the opposite kind, into a party of the urban, educated, professional classes and the metropolitan areas. It is now much more middle-class than it has ever been. Neither of these transformational outcomes is inevitable. If the Conservative Party had not made a deathbed conversion it would likely have been severely damaged or even replaced by a more aggressively populist party of the kind that is making progress across Europe. This may still happen if it loses sight of why it succeeded in 2019. On the other side it is not certain that the Labour Party will be confirmed as the party of the other pole of the new alignment. If it does not face the demographic and political realities of its situation it will be replaced or severely damaged by a liberal cosmopolitan force. The odds are against that, for various reasons, but not by much.

The result of the 2019 election, when we look at the geographical distribution and social composition of the votes, shows that the new aligning division had finally found expression in votes at a high enough level to be reflected in seats. One side of the new divide had effectively come together in the shape of the transformed Tory Party with the Brexit Party consigned, for now at any rate, to the role of fringe support and warm-up act. This means that in the UK one side of the new divide is going to be more moderate and less ideologically coherent than if it had come together around or been led by a more overtly anti-systemic party, as has been the case so far in France and Germany for example. That in turn means that it will be more electorally successful because of having a wider appeal and because of the way the UK's electoral system of FPTP works.

By contrast the other side of the new divide is split and not yet coherent in the same way. In particular there is a clear and deep division around the whole question of radical cultural politics and the 'woke' agenda of radical identity politics but also, although to a lesser extent, over economics. In the 2019 election the combined vote of the Tories plus the Brexit Party and the DUP was about 47% while the other side had a combined total of 53%. The 53% was much more divided than the 47%. This is actually only approximate, because a significant number of socially conservative and nationalist voters either did not vote or stuck with Labour because of distrust of the Tories on economic grounds while a significant part of the Tory vote was composed of people who on the new alignment are on the liberal cosmopolitan side but were not prepared to switch this time because of the Labour Party's leadership and economic position. What we can see though is the outlines of how UK politics will work in the new alignment: the next five years will be crucial in determining what form the cosmopolitan pole takes in opposition to the nationalist one, and whether it can come together as an effective type of politics.

The realignment in Britain (or actually the two or three realignments in Britain, as we have different ones in England and Wales, Scotland, and Northern Ireland) is only the specific British example of a much wider phenomenon. Political developments that have the same features and derive from the same underlying social conflicts and clashes of interest can be seen in the United States, in Canada, and in almost every country in Europe. The only European democracies where it is not happening so far are Portugal and the Irish Republic and, until very recently, Spain. Everywhere the kind of politics that led to Brexit in the UK case and has been bridled by the Conservative Party, is on the rise. Outside the UK it is not going to take the form of demands to leave the EU, for historical reasons, although it may well take the form of demands for sweeping reforms of the EU's rules and structures. We should not be certain that those demands will be for a reassertion of the traditional nation state and a diminution of the closer union that has been both goal and practice since Maastricht. That is certainly where we are at the moment but there is a very real possibility of a move towards actually supporting greater European integration but on the basis of a forceful reassertion of a historic Christian and white European identity. This is still uncertain. What many predict, some in hope and anticipation, others with trepidation and despondency, is that we are now in a post-liberal era of politics, that the realignment in Britain and elsewhere is bringing about the close of a liberal era and the rise of a new post-liberal politics on both poles of the new alignment but particularly the right. What actually seems more probable, both in the UK and elsewhere, is the eventual emergence of a no-longer hegemonic but more clear and self-conscious liberalism as one of the two poles.

Certainly, the politics of the UK and other parts of the world shall not lack for excitement or debate.

BIBLIOGRAPHY

Ashcroft, Lord 2016 'How the United Kingdom voted on Thursday… and why.' 24/06/2016 https://lordashcroftpolls.com/2016/06/how-the-united-kingdom-voted-and-why/

Ashcroft, Lord 2019 'How Britain voted and why: My 2019 general election post-vote poll.' https://lordashcroftpolls.com/2019/12/how-britain-voted-and-why-my-2019-general-election-post-vote-poll/

Barnett, Anthony 2017 *The Lure of Greatness: England's Brexit and America's Trump*. Unbound.

Bickerton, Chris 2019 'Arrogant Remainers want a second vote: That would be a bad day for democracy.' *The Guardian* 16/01/2019. https://www.theguardian.com/global/commentisfree/2019/jan/16/second-brexit-referendum-mps-democracy-peoples-vote

Cable, Sir Vince 2019 'We can't wish away first past the post: centre-left parties have to find common ground.' The Guardian 17/12/2019 https://www.theguardian.com/commentisfree/2019/dec/17/first-past-post-common-ground

Carl, Noah 2018 'Leavers have a better understanding of Remainers motivations than vice versa.' LSE Blogs 04/05/2018 https://blogs.lse.ac.uk/brexit/2018/05/04/leavers-have-a-better-understanding-of-remainers-motivations-than-vice-versa/

Clarke, Harold D., Goodwin, Matthew, and Whiteley, Paul 2017 *Brexit: Why Britain Voted to Leave the European Union*. Cambridge University Press.

Cohen, Daniel 2019 'Loud, obsessive, and tribal: The radicalisation of Remain.' The Guardian 13/08/2019 https://www.theguardian.com/politics/2019/aug/13/brexit-remain-radicalisation-fbpe-peoples-vote

Curtice, Sir John 2020 'Sir John Curtice on the Lib Dem General Election performance.' *Liberal Democrat Voice* 17/01/2020 https://www.libdemvoice.org/sir-john-curtice-on-the-lib-dem-performance-in-the-december-general-election-63137.html

Datapraxis 2019 Tory Landslide, Progressives Split: A Datapraxis Analysis of the UK General Election. https://www.dataprax.is/tory-landslide-progressives-split

Dennison, James and Carl, Noah 'The ultimate causes of Brexit: history, culture, and geography.' LSE Blogs 24/07/2016 https://blogs.lse.ac.uk/europpblog/2016/07/24/ultimate-causes-of-brexit/

Economist Magazine 2016 'Explaining the Brexit vote.' 14/07/2016 https://www.economist.com/britain/2016/07/14/explaining-the-brexit-vote

Eatwell, Roger and Goodwin, Matthew 2018 *National Populism: The Revolt Against Liberal Democracy*. Pelican.

Edgerton, David 2018 *The Rise and Fall of the British Nation: A Twentieth Century History*. Penguin

Electoral Calculus 2020 'Voter Migration by Party 2017 - 2019' 16/01/2020 https://www.electoralcalculus.co.uk/pseph_transition2019.html

Electoral Calculus 2020 'Voter Migration by Group 2017 – 2019' 21/01/2020 https://www.electoralcalculus.co.uk/pseph_group_migration_2019.html

Electoral calculus 2019 'Three-D Politics and the Seven tribes.' 20/04/2019. https://www.electoralcalculus.co.uk/pol3d_main.html

Elliot, Gregory 1993 *Labourism and the English Genius: The Strange Death of Labour England?* Verso.

Evans, Geoffrey & Menon, Anand 2017 *Brexit and British Politics*. Polity Press.

Evans, Geoffrey and Schaffner, Florian 'Brexit identities: How Leave versus Remain replaced Conservative versus Labour affiliations of British voters.' *The Conversation* 22/01/2019 https://theconversation.com/brexit-identities-how-leave-versus-remain-replaced-conservative-versus-labour-affiliations-of-british-voters-110311

Ferguson, Thomas 1995 *Golden Rule: The Investment Theory of Party Competition and the Logic of Money-Driven Political Systems*. University of Chicago Press.

Ford, Robert 2016 "Older, 'left-behind' voters turned against a political class with values opposed to theirs." *The Guardian* 25/06/2016 https://www.theguardian.com/politics/2016/jun/25/left-behind-eu-referendum-vote-ukip-revolt-brexit

Ford, Robert and Goodwin, Matthew 2014 *Revolt on the Right: Explaining Support for the Radical Right in Britain*. Routledge.

Geary, Ian and Pabst, Adrian (eds) 2015 *Blue Labour: Forging a New Politics*. IB Tauris.

Goodhart, David 2017 *The Road to Somewhere: The New Tribes Shaping British Politics*. Penguin.

Goodwin, Matthew J. and Heath, Oliver (2016) 'The 2016 Referendum, Brexit and the Left Behind: An Aggregate-level Analysis of the Result.' *The Political Quarterly*, 87 (3). pp. 323-332.

Gray, John 2019a 'Brexit has left the British political class trapped by its own history.' *New Statesman* 13/03/2019 https://www.newstatesman.com/politics/uk/2019/03/brexit-has-left-british-political-class-trapped-its-own-history

Gray, John 2019b 'The closing of the Conservative mind: Politics and the art of war.' *New Statesman* 23/10/2019 https://www.newstatesman.com/politics/uk/2019/10/closing-conservative-mind-politics-and-art-war

Gray, John 2020 'Why the left keeps losing.' *New Statesman* 15/01/2020 https://www.newstatesman.com/politics/uk/2020/01/why-left-keeps-losing

Haidt, Jonathan 2013 *The Righteous Mind: Why Good People are Divided by Religion and Politics*. Penguin.

Henderson, Ailsa, Jeffery, Charlie, Jones, Richard Wyn and Wincott, Dan "How Brexit Was Made in England." *The British Journal of Politics and International Relations*, 19, no. 4 (November 2017): 631–646.

James, Emily 2016 'The top ten brands favoured by Remainers and Brexiteers.' Campaign 01/08/2016. https://www.campaignlive.co.uk/article/top-10-brands-favoured-remainers-brexiters/1403991

Jennings, Will and Stoker, Gerry 2017 'Tilting towards the cosmopolitan axis? Political change in England and the 2017 election.' *Political Quarterly* 88 (2017) 359 - 369.

Kanagasooriam, James 2019 'Why Remainers were shocked by the result but Leavers less so.' Spectator Blogs 19/03/2019 https://blogs.spectator.co.uk/2019/03/the-brexit-paradox-that-spells-doom-for-the-independent-group/

Kaufman, Eric 2018 *Whiteshift: Populism, Immigration and the Future of White Majorities*. Allen Lane.

Kaufman, Eric 2016 'It's NOT the economy, stupid: Brexit as a story of personal values.' LSE Blogs 07/07/2016 https://blogs.lse.ac.uk/politicsandpolicy/personal-values-brexit-vote/

Kaufman, Eric 2020 'Why the left is losing.' *Law and Liberty* 13/02/2020 https://www.lawliberty.org/2020/02/13/why-the-left-is-losing/

Luttwak, Edward 1994 'Why fascism is the wave of the future.' London Review of Books 07/04/1994 https://www.lrb.co.uk/the-paper/v16/n07/edward-luttwak/why-fascism-is-the-wave-of-the-future

Menon, Anand (ed) 2018 *Brexit and Public Opinion*. The UK in a Changing Europe. https://ukandeu.ac.uk/wp-content/uploads/2018/01/Public-Opinion.pdf

Oborne, Peter 2008 *The Triumph of the Political Class* Pocket Books.

Opinium 2016 *Dead Centre: Redefining the Centre of British Politics*. Opinium and Social Market Foundation 14/09/2016 https://www.opinium.co.uk/wp-content/uploads/2016/09/Dead-Centre-British-politics4_lr.pdf

Ramsden, John 1998 *An Appetite for Power: A New History of the Conservative Party.* Harper Collins

Richards, Lindsey and Heath, Anthony 2019 'Brexit and public opinion: national identity and Brexit preferences.' The UK in a Changing Europe 31/01/2019
https://ukandeu.ac.uk/brexit-and-public-opinion-national-identity-and-brexit-preferences/

Rovny, John 2019 'The Brahmin left versus the merchant right: A comment on Thomas Piketty's new book.' LSE Blogs 16/09/2019 https://blogs.lse.ac.uk/europpblog/2019/09/16/the-brahmin-left-vs-the-merchant-right-a-comment-on-thomas-pikettys-new-book/

Rutherford, Jonathan 'From Woodstock to Brexit: the tragedy of the liberal middle class.' New Statesman 18/12/2019 https://www.newstatesman.com/politics/brexit/2019/12/woodstock-brexit

Seaton, Jean (2016). "Brexit and the Media." *The Political Quarterly*. 87 (3): 333–337.

Scruton, Sir Roger 2016 'Who are we?' *Prospect* 14/07/2016 https://www.prospectmagazine.co.uk/magazine/who-are-we

Shipman, Tim 2018 *Fall Out: A Year of Political Mayhem*. Collins.

Shipman, Tim 2017 *All Out War: The Full Story of Brexit*. Collins.

Stocker, Paul 2017 *English Uprising: Brexit and the Mainstreaming of the Radical Right*. Melville House.

Thomas, Owen 2019 'The Importance of Remainer and Leaver identities.' *Populus.co.uk* May 2019 https://www.populus.co.uk/insights/2019/05/the-importance-of-remainer-and-leaver-identities/

Wheatcroft, Geoffrey 2005 *The Strange Death of Tory England.* Penguin Reprint.

Wikipedia. 2017 United Kingdom general election. https://en.wikipedia.org/wiki/2017_United_Kingdom_general_election

Wikipedia. 2019 United Kingdom general election. https://en.wikipedia.org/wiki/2019_United_Kingdom_general_election

Young, Michael 1961 *The Rise of the Meritocracy 1870 – 2033: An Essay on Education and Equality*. Pelican.

APPENDIX

Table 1. British Political Eras and Realignments

PERIOD OF ALIGNMENT	REALIGNMENT EPISODE
1671 - 1715	1715 - 1725
1725 - 1756	1756 - 1763
1763 – 1783 (Period of Faction Politics)	1783 - 1792
1792 - 1832	1832 - 1846
1846 - 1886	1886 - 1893
1893 - 1922	1922 - 1931
1931 - 1975	1975 - 1983
1983 - 2015	2015 - ?

Table 2. The Alignment of Politics 1970s to 2010s

SOCIAL DEMOCRATS	LIBERTARIANS
Economics – interventionist Welfare – redistributionist Social Politics – liberal Cultural politics – individualist	Economics – free market Welfare – welfare sceptics Social politics – liberal Cultural politics – individualist
TRADITIONAL COLLECTIVISTS	**FREE MARKET CONSERVATIVES**
Economics – collectivist Welfare – egalitarian & contributory Social politics – conservative Cultural politics – traditionalist	Economics – free market Welfare – moderately sceptical Social politics – conservative Cultural politics – traditionalist

Table 3. The Emergent New Alignment

RADICAL COSMOPOLITANS	COSMOPOLITAN LIBERALS
Economics – green socialism Welfare – strongly egalitarian Identity – cosmopolitan Culture – radical subjectivism	Economics – free market Welfare – egalitarian redistribution Identity – cosmopolitan Culture – individualist
NATIONAL COLLECTIVISTS	**NATIONAL LIBERALS**
Economics – interventionist Welfare – national contributory Identity – nationalist Culture – traditionalism	Economics – moderately free market Welfare – national based Identity – nationalist Culture – Traditionalism

Table 4. The New Scottish Alignment

LEFT NATIONALISTS	RIGHT NATIONALISTS
(Most) SNP Green Party (Some) Labour	(Some) SNP
LEFT UNIONISTS	**RIGHT UNIONISTS**
(Most) Labour Lib	Scottish Conservatives Dems

Table 5. The Social Divisions of the Referendum

RADICAL REMAINIA (C 16%)	LIBERAL REMAINIA (C 32%)
Younger, metropolitan and Scottish or Irish, educated. London, Scotland, university towns, Bristol, Liverpool, central Leeds and Manchester.	Younger but slightly older than RR, more affluent, metropolitan and suburban, SE England. Educated but slightly less than RR. Middle-class Unionists in NI and Scotland.
LEAVERSTAN (C 22%)	**BREXITSHIRE (C 30%)**
Older, mainly working-class, living in small towns, older industrial areas apart from Scotland. Working-class Unionists in NI. Less educated.	Older, less educated, slightly more affluent, middle class, living in rural areas, coastal areas and suburbs.

Table 6. The Condorcet Paradox in Parliament

GROUP OF MPS	FIRST CHOICE	SECOND CHOICE	THIRD CHOICE
Strong Leave	Hard Brexit/No Deal	Leave With a Deal	Stay in
Strong Remain	Stay In	Hard Brexit/ No Deal	Leave With a Deal
Reluctant Leave	Leave With a Deal	Stay In	Hard Brexit/ No Deal

Table 7. First Round of Indicative Votes

MOTION	AYES	NOES	ABS.	MAJORITY
NO DEAL	160	400	74	-240
COMMON MARKET 2.0	189	283	162	-94
EFTA MEMBERSHIP	64	377	193	-313
CUSTOMS UNION	265	271	98	-6
LABOUR EXIT	237	307	90	-70
REVOKE A 50	184	293	157	-109
REFERENDUM ON DEAL	268	295	71	-27
MANAGED NO DEAL	139	422	73	-283

Table 8. Second Round of Indicative Votes

MOTION	AYES	NOES	ABS.	MAJORITY
CUSTOMS UNION	273	276	85	-3
COMMON MARKET 2.0	261	282	91	-21
REFERENDUM ON DEAL	280	292	62	-12
REVOCATION	191	292	151	-101

Table 9. Distribution of Voter Tribes in the New Alignment (From Electoral Calculus)

LEFT COSMOPOLITAN	LIBERAL COSMOPOLITAN
Progressive (11%) Strong Left (4%)	Kind Young Capitalist (24%)
NATIONAL COLLECTIVIST	**NATIONAL LIBERAL**
Traditional Labour (10%) Centr Somewheres (12%)	ists (24%) Strong Right (15%)

ABOUT THE AUTHOR

Stephen Davies, a Senior Fellow at AIER, is the Head of Education at the Institute for Economic Affairs in London.

ABOUT AIER

The American Institute for Economic Research in Great Barrington, Massachusetts, was founded in 1933 as the first independent voice for sound economics in the United States. Today it publishes ongoing research, hosts educational programs, publishes books, sponsors interns and scholars, and is home to the world-renowned Bastiat Society and the highly respected Sound Money Project. The American Institute for Economic Research is a 501c3 public charity.

INDEX

Made in the USA
Coppell, TX
07 August 2021

60107860R00173